Psychosophy

Psychosophy

Psycho-philosophical Research on the Nature of Human Kind

Julio Ozán Lavoisier

MLBD PUBLICATIONS

Motilal Banarsidass Publications

MOTILAL BANARSIDASS
PUBLICATIONS
4741/23, Ansari Road, Daryaganj, New Delhi - 110002 (India)
Email: mlbd@mlbd.com | sales@mlbd.com
exports@mlbd.com | publications@mlbd.com
Website: www.mlbd.com

Psychosophy
by
Julio Ozán Lavoisier

First Edition Published in 2025

Published in India by Motilal Banarsidass Publications

ISBN : 978-81-97917-76-9 (PB)

Printed and bound in India

I dedicate this book to Constance Wells Goddard,
with whom I shared these ideas, these realities, for fifteen years.

I would like to express my gratitude to my brother Pepe without whose cooperation this book would have remained in my archives. So too to Professor Mme. Marguerite Buffard, from Aix-en-Provence, who has voluntarily translated this work into French.

Contents

Part Two: Psychosophy and Psychology

Prologue

Reader, the book that you have in your hands is an original work, rich in ideas and suggestions that deserve to be taken seriously for the good of each and every one of us, and for humanity in general. It is not easy to say to which genre it belongs as it transcends the habitual boundaries of scientific, literary, philosophical and religious classifications. If we had to enrol it in a school or philosophical tradition we would do so within the framework of eternal philosophies as its source of inspiration is common to these schools and essentially coincides with them. Besides this, the work has all the elements that constitute a true philosophy. Ozán Lavoisier has a vision of a mystical philosopher.

The author refers to this work as an essay and gives it the name Psychosophy, which would be a new science and art –in the sense of a technique– related to contemporary psychology, but broader than this due to its transcendent dimension, and much more profound than psychoanalysis because it throws light on planes and levels of understanding ignored by the latter.

In these preliminary pages I will try to briefly examine this "essay", indicating the main themes and pointing out some difficulties that may mislead the unwary reader.

The circumstances that have given rise to the work of Julio Ozán Lavoisier are characterised on the one hand by the decline of religious, aesthetic and moral values in contemporary industrial societies, with a consequent depreciation of human life, and on the other by his spiritual experience that moves him to criticise the idea of man as terminally ill in keeping with the insanity of present day society. If the reader does not perceive the disorder of contemporary life, or if he thinks it can be resolved with economic and psychological palliatives, psychosophy is probably not for him. Man's maladjustment is not only between his conscious and unconscious. The most serious problems of contemporary civilisation are related to the loss of contact with nature and with the Universal Spirit.

It is essential to be aware of the unnecessary fears and desires that occupy and preoccupy the human being, according to Julio, who avers that the path to transcendence begins after this awareness. This requires the reader to not only go through the printed material but also to practice the necessary spiritual exercises. Naturally everything depends on whether the reader wants to participate in the experience for himself. For this reason, the author says that if we truly want to know the Sacred, which is Peace, we have to experience it in ourselves. Having psychosophy as the basis a personal experience is not to be dogmatic. As in Buddhism, the only authority resides with the one who has the experience.

The spiritual technique advocated by psychosophy has some similarities with Buddhism, as can be observed when Ozán Lavoisier says that when the aspirant is fully established in the unitive conscience, primitive manifestations are already in evidence for him, as he is waiting to take the final leap to the transcendent, and he will have to take this ultimate leap into the Void, that is, without the help of a personal god. This knowledge is irreducible to scientific methodology as the categories of space and time cannot be applied. For this reason, Ozán L. does not ask that his vision of reality be believed but that it be verified. "I am not speaking for those who want to continue living in a reality of abstractions but for those who want to better understand the Reality in which the human being lives". Every attempt to say something about Pure Consciousness would be in vain, as it is the Absolute itself that no words can describe. Of course, in order to be able to adjust the spirit to these levels a secluded life is indispensable, but also the guidance of a clear teacher, preferably a Zen Buddhist, is required. It is not in the interest of psychosophy to recount the marvels that result from real knowledge but rather the drive to experience it. One of the ways is the control of dreams; but this requires permanent vigilance and, again, a secluded life in order to avoid external stimuli, like those that are engendered in modern cities that become "*dangerous* for he who is *distracted for being vigilant*". The modern jungle does not lend itself to these kinds of spiritual exercises.

In order to submerge ourselves in our inner world we must stop swimming on the surface of our external representations. The spirit can descend naturally and effortlessly to the plane of direct perception. Of course, Ozán L. concludes, "this operation is not as easy as I have just summed it up to be".

He dedicates a few beautiful pages to Plato that the reader should find for himself. Of Mircea Eliade, whom he cites approvingly at various times, he says: "One of the few in our time who has applied himself to the study of religions with the sincere desire of discovering truths, not novelties, and, moreover, with the respect that they deserve". Regarding Eliade, who I knew personally, I believe that there are some scholars of religions and mythologies who do not seem to have achieved a mystical experience, yet nevertheless have illuminated religious modes of life for the benefit of a large number of readers. Perhaps the reader is among them. This is not the case for those who, with no respect for mystical traditions, and the consequent ignorance of the spiritual reality of the human being, have still risked opinions about religious reality.

For this reason, Julio writes: "The only incontrovertible proof of the existence of the Essence (or if one prefers, a God present and at one with me and with everything), is un-transmissible. It is not only impersonal, but more than personal, as it cannot be transmitted even to the discernment of the individual himself who experiences it. One only tests and proves God from His own perspective".

In order to facilitate the understanding of the mental planes in play, the author has drawn them in various schemas, recognising that it is not a question of geometric planes but of states of mind. Here we encounter the difficulty that Bergson referred to when he counterbalanced the fluidity of moods and the rigidity of spatial representations. Julio first draws the path from the individual conscience to the unified conscience passing through altruist conscience or latent unitive conscience. Other schema illustrate the path of the spirit towards its unification from other angles. In its path it has to overcome the unitive conscience, the seat of aesthetic, moral and religious consciences, each one of these faculties enables a path of knowledge. Julio has no illusions with respect to these diagrams. "Modern man, ensconced in his egocentric perspective, and preoccupied with the external world, barely has time to attend to his conscience".

In the Second Part the author establishes the relationship between psychosophy and psychology. For this he comments on three notable psychologists who have made forays into the field of religion. The spiritual experience laid out in the First Part allows for a critique that, to my knowledge, has no precedents. The Second Part marks a milestone in the critical history of psychoanalysis, and for this reason will surely become a classic text, not in the sense of a scholarly text, but in that of a masterpiece.

The author insists on the need for moral purification in order to achieve true knowledge. For the subject-object duality to disappear, the elimination of the former is a condition, which implies having followed a rigorous path of purification and having reached a transcendental reality that is already in the domain of the Sacred. That is, to reach God it is necessary to have had a religious experience. And this cannot be inferred; no personal experience can be inferred. By making religious experience synonymous with religion, Julio seems to forget at times that religion can be understood as something that affects the social plane, even if we admit the irreducibility of what is religious to other planes; but the omission is only circumstantial, as soon as the occasion presents itself, the link between both realities is restored.

This or any other possible omissions in the present work do not in any case detract from the essential message of psychosophy, which with open arms, like this prologue, offers itself to the reader as a new way of seeing the world.

Juan Adolfo Vázquez, Pittsburgh, 1999.

Author’s Note

Juan Adolfo Vázquez is Professor Emeritus at the University of Pittsburgh, Pennsylvania, U.S.A.

His works include the essays “Metaphysics and Culture”, “What is Ontology”; “The Profile of the Adventure” and “Metaphysical Essays”. A professor of metaphysics during the early years of his career, his interest turned to the study of comparative religions in which he has worked for more than forty years. On these subjects the following works can be consulted: *Outline of Myth analysis* and *The Reconstruction of the Myth of Inkarri.* He has been the editor of the journal “Naos” in Pittsburgh, a collection of notes and material on the sacred. He is presently engaged in an extensive work on South American myths, of which the first part has been published.

Professor Vázquez, who was 82 years old when he wrote this *Prologue*, was a promoter of modern anthropological humanism, whose task would be “reformulating and expanding the old Eurocentric humanism, through the inclusion of other spiritual traditions”. His profuse work and erudition have led him to translate works from English, German, French and even Maya. *Estudios Humanistas* and *The Sacred and other essays,* have been edited recently.

Clarification on the Use of Some Terms

As in almost all philosophical texts, the reader will find words that are new or which have a specific meaning, like *unitive, transcendental, Sacred, God,* etc., which he should try to understand in the way they are presented here. Particularly the concept of *psychosophy* should be interpreted in the context of this system of thought, independently of other views or schools that have adopted this concept.

There are some concepts that will become clear as one progresses through the book, the use of which I have not been able to avoid from the beginning, like *Reality or Universus,* that try to express the All that includes material and spiritual reality. The words *Mind, Essence or Universal Spirit* refer to *That* that comprehends (that includes and understands) this totality. This context is sufficiently broad that any reduction to a simple definition could seem artificial.

Translator's Note:

In the original Spanish the concept *vivencia unitiva* implies the simultaneous perception of the different planes of understanding, in particular the intellect and the sentiments that converge in the *vital plane.* As a result, it has been translated as a *unitive vital experience*; readers must remember this every time they find the concept *experience* in spiritual matters. The concept *Divinity,* according with the will of the author, has been translated, most of the time, as *the Sacred.*

Preface to the English Edition

I believe that the English edition of this book has been too long in coming. In fact, it has been 20 years since it was published in Spanish; busy with the production of other books, this one had been left behind, having been out of print for years. That is why I have not wasted this opportunity to publish it with a publishing house as serious and prestigious as this one, which can make it available to the educated public of the East and the West to whom it is addressed.

Indeed, it could be said that the understanding of all my work becomes clear only in the light of my *Psychosophy*, for it is the tool I have used to explain the philosophical- psychological roots of our mind, indispensable for all further development. The concept of *Psychosophy* had already been defined in my first work: *"Psychosophy is a knowledge of the first causes which aims at the plenitude of human beings and their integration into the world by means of the unification of the mind."* A basic principle of this discipline is that *"Psychic and moral equilibrium are correlative."* However, it does not deal with personal or subjective problems because it can only germinate in mature spirits, from a certain level of consciousness. That is why *"Psychosophy begins where psychology ends"*, *"it starts from an essential perspective, not from the manifested but from the manifesting."* (*The Return to the Sources*, Ed. Rueda, Madrid, Spain, 1993, Ebook 2022).

Since then, other *"Psychosophies"* have appeared, which are announced as novelties, or works have been rescued and compiled under the same title, but which have nothing to do with my proposal, which the attentive reader will be able to distinguish. The fundamental difference is that none of this *Psychosophies* have a philosophical origin nor dimension (see, for example, *Origen and Destiny of Man*, Ed. Dunken, Buenos Aires, 2008, in Spanish, and Delhi, 2015, Har-Anand Publications, in English). I would like to make it clear that my discipline does not seek novelties, but *"perennial truths found in ancient traditions"*, and is at the antipode of all psychologism, and particularly - in the words of Mircea Eliade - of "that odious spiritual hybridism inaugurated by Mme. Blavatsky with the Theosophical Society, continued and aggravated by the innumerable contemporary pseudo-morphoses", in which we can include all obscurantism or esotericism, as it has come to be called, whose intrusion into the field of comparative religions, and even of psychology, has generated a confusion as undesirable as it has been inopportune. My *Psychosophy* is essentially *"a philosophy which makes use of a transcendental psychology which underlies a theory of knowledge, a metaphysics, an ethics, an aesthetics and a philosophy of history, that is, a philosophical system."* This system has been developed in subsequent works.

Preface

A veil has fallen over the face of humanity and this impedes it from seeing what underlies things and what transcends them. A whole mysterious world brimming with beauty and poetry has been covered, leaving only the most obvious aspects of reality visible. What we perceive with our senses does not pass now through the deepest filters of intelligence, we do not weigh our resolve in our consciousness, we do not feel other beings with our heart. Of our neighbour we only know what he possesses, we only observe his gestures; we do not see anything behind his eyes, they are transparent orbs that tell us nothing and that he uses to see us in the same way. Such is our lack of communication that we talk of nothing but things and facts. Preoccupied with the tangible and evident, our psychic apparatus has become so sluggish that it does not perceive the spiritual; a shadow has been cast on all that is beautiful, what is elevated has been put out of reach and creativity is now hidden, and whatever is vital for our happiness slips through our fingers like water. And as we alienate ourselves from these *life sources*, we are left alone and isolated, while fear and selfishness grow in our guts. In this way the veil thickens and looms over man. There are few at present, too few, who lift up their heads from the human anthill to gaze at the stars, and even fewer who can appreciate the Order of the Universe. Alienated from it, we try to impose *our* animal "order" on the rest of creation! And then we are surprised by the ecological disequilibrium, the wars and the brutality of our species!

One needs to look back only briefly to realise that there is something strange in the fact that the human being, who has been able to get to know the world around him in such detail, cannot come to terms with the knowledge of himself. As we know, the rule is that each one thinks, or rather believes, that he knows himself quite well, that he conforms to and accepts the family and society that has been his lot, with the kind of mind that he has. Nevertheless, it symptomatic that those who know themselves better discover greater galleries full of surprises in the mind's labyrinth. Is man thus destined to live resigned to his ignorance and a stranger to himself? Psychosophy's answer is a categorical No! The labyrinth has an exit. But... one has to penetrate the labyrinth, to plunge into the dark depths of the mind until one touches the very bottom, and this implies a *sacrifice* that very few are willing to make.

In the course of this book the main galleries that should be explored will be discovered, as well as those that it is advisable to avoid. Naturally, the author cannot discover the minor galleries to which the circumstances of life have led each one to, and neither those that each has constructed; as one tends to believe that it is the external circumstances that determine our lives and forget that each of us is creating our own reality. Many times, in fact, we go down slopes simply because they are easy to descend without thinking about whether we will have to ascend them again later. But, in order to reassure and encourage the reader who is well disposed to these trials, the author must confess that it would not have occurred to him to begin to expose these paths of knowledge if he was not certain that they were real. These paths are not paved with reasons that are attractive or even, perhaps, convincing to the intellect. The author, it is true, has used reasons to express this reality, but these are not sufficient, the reader who wants to tread firm ground must see beyond them. The reasons are like a map, they are not reality. Although this is obvious it is not sufficient for the intellect, because as we will see, if man could leave the map that he has made of reality, he would also leave the dark labyrinth of his individual mind.

Although it does not appeal only to reason, this book inclines, like all philosophical essays, towards clarity. This means that it avoids all obscurantism or "esotericism". If the reader is searching for immediate or "magical", solutions he need not take the trouble to read these pages.

This work is one more call to spiritual life. By this I understand an artistic, ethical, contemplative, creative and harmonious life. In order to understand psychosophy it is indispensable to have an open and receptive spirit that is open to appreciating nuances. All fundamentalisms, religious and irreligious, including every fixed creed, will constitute an impediment to its understanding. This discipline is part of the direct knowledge of the essence of particular religions, and it maintains that the misuse and errors of the latter are a consequence of the lack of this knowledge. It is to avoid the deviations to which ignorance of this essence has led, that psychosophy induces wisdom.

Part One

PSYCHOSOPHY

CHAPTER ONE

General Outline

In the XIXth century some decisive changes occurred that have become so engrained as to transform both the human being and the planet on which he lives. This historic transformation has not only been due to external circumstances, but also, and primarily, to a change in man, in his way of thinking, believing and, as a consequence, seeing and seeing himself in the world. The external circumstances, which can be summed up in what has been denominated the Industrial Revolution are sufficiently well known for us not to need linger on them. On the contrary, the internal ones that can relatively be called "circumstances" as they do not surround man but condition him like external circumstances are, due to their obscure origins, generally ignored.

The internal change has not necessarily meant an improvement. However, since the Industrial Revolution, man has had the permanent and growing feeling that he is evolving. But this is not what is happening in reality; he is just modifying his surroundings, and as these change at a progressively accelerated rate, with an imposing urgency, contemporary man does not have the time to reflect on himself and to delve into the innermost recesses of his being. Because he lives like this, conditioned by these circumstances and ignorant of himself, the illusion that he is evolving alongside technology becomes a reality. But the *reality* is that since he has not improved, he has lagged behind and he is no longer in control of his circumstances. In contemporary man therefore there is a gap between two realities, a lack of concordance between an external reality, which according to current beliefs is composed only of objects or matter, and an internal or spiritual reality. It now turns out that the very same sciences that have wrought change in our external circumstances tell us nothing of this other reality that is internal or spiritual. Rather, occupied in "changing the world", they contribute to alienating us from it and in increasing the *décalage*.

The internal change becomes manifest in the mid-XIXth century in the work of L. Feuerbach (*The Essence of Christianity* was published in 1841 and his principal texts appear during this decade). According to this philosopher "Divine essence is nothing more than the essence of man". If this were a sentence from Plato, we would interpret it as saying that man participates in the divine Essence, but for Feuerbach divinity is nothing more than a *projection* that man makes of *his* essence onto a fictitious transcendent being. When man becomes aware of this, in the opinion of this thinker, he discovers that his only reality is nature and henceforth he will only depend on it. The World is thus stripped of its essence, but not so man, whose essence is reduced to "the faculties of thinking, exercising the will and manifesting the heart". God would, then, have been born from these faculties. The human being would depend no longer on God, he would have transferred this dependence to the spatial-temporal reality, which is the only reality. When the world loses its divine Essence man is left without religion. Feuerbach is aware of this and for this reason he proposes "a transformation of theology into anthropology".

I would like to make the claim that if psychology had existed as an independent science in Feuerbach's time, in all probability it would have appealed to him instead of anthropology, since for him the change in man was decidedly psychological. We can recall that in his opinion the human being discovers himself when he "becomes aware" that God is his own *projection*, and that religion, which sustains this misunderstanding, is, for the same reason, an alienation. For Feuerbach anthropology would henceforward be the new religion. Although when he talks about politics he avers that this would be the religion of tomorrow; this is not surprising after hearing him say that the State "is the *providence* of man". A little later Karl Marx, with the same logic, will believe that the realisation of philosophy, also paradoxically, takes place when it has been subsumed by the updating of his socio-economic theories.

In conclusion, the two disciplines that until then had been occupied with the spirit, religion and philosophy, were declared obsolete and apparently superseded by types of knowledge whose vision did not *transcend* the material world. We must not forget that this new vision is the result of a *new belief* that sustains the non-existence of a universal Essence. The same argument, so commonly used against believers, that their beliefs depend on a faith, can be used against these *new religions* or doctrines of faith.

In this work I am not interested in the superstructures of these doctrines, but in the fundamentals of their premises, that is, the causes that generated this new faith, and also those that maintained the traditional faith, which will inevitably lead us to the initial causes. This does interest us, because the new faith, atheism, is not only found in the basis of historical materialism but it also underlies all sciences in general and the thinking of the greater part of the contemporary *intelligentsia*, even when the latter does not identify with any of the materialist doctrines. It is all too easy to suppose that Feuerbach's thinking is the consequence of a reaction to idealism, and that my ideas in turn are a reaction against materialism; but this vision would not explain the real driving force of these changes. Feuerbach's vision is in line with a change of perspective and although he might have experienced it as a *sudden awareness*, it is, in fact, only a consequence of his alienation, of which he was, I suspect, completely unaware.

It is not my purpose in this essay to place my theories in opposition to those of the materialists, but to clear the panorama of the spirit so that man can better see his mind and thus from a firm base comprehend his true position in the World.

If we observe the human spirit in its development, we will see that it has been realising a three fold process, parallel and interrelated with individuation, exteriorisation and alienation[(1)]. This triple process has been slow but constant and it has resulted in the spiritual crisis of contemporary man. The end of this long process, in which man has been progressively affirming himself in his individuality and thus losing awareness of the *presence* of a universal Spirit, is precisely the Feuerbachian inversion. This marks the culminating moment of the crisis of the spirit, the breaking point, the alienation from All, that I have called *essential alienation.*

However, when the said crisis becomes evident, two manifestations of the spirit opportunely emerge that tend to remedy it. From the very heart of our culture psychology was born, as a direct response and a specific therapy for the unease that takes on pathological dimensions. This science has not taken long to discover a rich quantity of religious material lodged in the unconscious and has been able to interpret some aspects of its complex symbolism, in which it has found a useful instrument to understand the discontent of its patients. However, for the vast majority of our psychologists, religion is nothing more than that same instrument and a product of the contents of our unconscious. And this is so because this new discipline is also a typical heir to the ideas and beliefs of the XIXth century. Thus, we can suppose as probable, for example, that if these psychologists attend to a patient who vehemently believes in the objective existence of a Divinity, they will ask themselves the same question that Nietzsche's Zarathustra asked: "How does this man not yet know that God is dead?" It is true that our psychologists do not ignore that this reality lives on in some way in the soul of man; they accept it then as a psychological reality, a vague explanation that cannot satisfy the patient. While he believes that man is a creation of God, our psychologists *believe*, like Feuerbach, that God is an objectification of man.

It is worth asking ourselves then: if the cause of the spiritual crisis that afflicts our culture was the lack of religion, I mean, of the spirituality that it knew in some way how to keep alive, can our new confessors, the psychologists, cure it? Can this science, inheriting beliefs that were born in opposition to the doctrines in charge of keeping the spirit alive, revive it or will it end up killing it? Can individual spirits live without a universal Spirit, or do they need it like animate bodies need the atmosphere? Can a civilisation continue without a morality sustained by an absolute principle, that is, absolutely objective and impartial? Can the human species live in order outside of a universal Order, or would the lack of this lead to destruction and chaos? I leave the reader alone with his conscience to answer these questions. I remind him of the fact that man has produced with incredible alacrity and in incontrovertible excess all the means for his fatal destruction, while pollution, desertification and overpopulation (which directly affects the former), increase progressively day by day and seem to be out of control and inevitable.

Thus, our species is clearly threatening to destroy itself, be it rapidly or gradually.[(2)]

The symptoms are serious, and although the modern soul healers, the psychologists, might know it, what is evident is their ineffectiveness in detaining or changing this trend. It should be clear that I am not suggesting that they are in any way *guilty* of this situation. I simply want to point out their impotence in the face of it, since I believe this is a reality that we cannot ignore when diagnosing the general state of contemporary man.

The other opportune manifestation of the spirit was the irruption of Far Eastern religions into our culture. Opportune, because when the Western spirit seemed to be emptied of religion, the great knowledge accumulated over millennia in the Orient filled the lacunae; and it is precisely in the middle of the XIXth century that *The Sacred Books of the Orient* began to be translated. These texts in my opinion contain all the necessary remedies to cure the ills that afflict our civilisation. But the cures are so many and so varied that the Westerner finds himself lost before them, like a layman inside a pharmacy full of medicines not knowing which he should take. This leads him to try a little of each, one after another, and he becomes enthusiastic about a guru or impassioned by a new esoteric "science". His very alienation has plunged the Westerner into a vicious circle of ignorance that has him trapped. As he has lost contact with the spirit, he does not know where to look for it and often does not even recognise it. Proof of this is that the conjurers who make objects appear have a much greater audience in India than the masters who impart true knowledge.

There are, indeed, only a few who know what they want. And of these, those who for better or worse look for a spiritual outlet are very few. The vast majority do not admit their unease, they try suffocating it by increasing their consumption or their comforts. This majority is the engine of the apparently "blind" technological cogwheel that drags down our culture and threatens the entire world. We need only to look at China, which has imported a socio-economic doctrine, product of the very consolidation of the European spiritual crisis, and at Japan that has been totally transformed by a kind of technological pragmatism, a trend apparently at odds with the previous one but born of the same process. As if this were not enough, this thawing in the higher peaks of the spirit begins to be observed on the other side of the Himalayas, in India, the last stronghold, perhaps, of the *eternal* snows.

Could it be then that religions are all a thing of the past, as proclaimed by A. Comte (who judged without knowledge of religions other than those that had then affected Europe), forerunner of the two aforementioned streams of thought, materialism and pragmatism, which inundate the contemporary world? Are all religions alienations, or is it man who has alienated himself from the Spirit and therefore does not understand their message?

In any case it is a fact that religions, like psychology, are impotent when faced with the frenetic dynamics generated by industrialised society. Strictly speaking, all those of us, ecologists, activists and thinkers, who are trying to slow its pace are dragged along by it. I believe, however, that if this resistance were coordinated and sustained by a coherent philosophy founded on a common awareness, it could become an efficient force. It is the aspiration of psychosophy to lead to this *awareness.*

In any case, these disciplines, philosophy, religion and psychology are the only ones that specifically deal with the spirit. They are, at least from a theoretical point of view, the only hope. Unfortunately, at present there is too much disagreement among them so that their forces, instead of uniting to produce an effective current, neutralise themselves by opposing each other. In the present work I will try to clarify these differences with the purpose of making their tasks convergent.

Notes

(1) For the historic development of this process I refer the reader to my work on the *philosophy of history: The Spirit in History.*

(2) Some facts that the reader should take into account: There is sufficient nuclear weaponry stored to destroy all life on earth, not once but a hundred times over! More than twenty hectares of forests are cut down every minute. It is estimated that before the Industrial Revolution one species disappeared per thousand years, in 1980, one per day, in 1990 one per hour... In 1800 the world population was 906 million; in 1900 it was 1,610 million; in 1950 it became 2,100 million; in 1970 it increased to 4,000 million; in 1987 it went up to 5,000; in 1999 6.000 million... (data from F. J. Ayala, Antony Huxley and other authors).

CHAPTER TWO

Western Sources

Here I would like to write about certain personal circumstances directly related to the origin of psychosophy which will help the reader to better understand it, especially if these circumstances are familiar. This will not be surprising. I have known of many who were brought up in the Christian religion and turned their backs on it, and later when they did not find satisfaction in the pleasures of secular life, developed a new interest in spiritual affairs. This has been a defining characteristic of our generation that grew in the post war years, skeptical of material progress, and who would react in their youth against the absurd optimism of a consumer society.

Of course, I am referring to the responsible, critical and conscious sections of our generation. The others, who make up the majority, never returned to the spiritual fold and continue to wear themselves out in the turbulent world, oblivious to these problems.

Our generation, particularly at the beginning of this process, directly or indirectly, consciously or unconsciously, has been influenced by existentialist thought.

I do not know to what extent philosophical trends are learnt but I can observe to what extent they are forgotten. Today existentialism is considered to have been "surpassed", but it would be more correct to say that it has been forgotten, because to have *surpassed* a philosophy, one has first to squeeze it like a fruit in order to extract its nutritive elements; otherwise, it will be wasted. This is unfortunately what has been done with this doctrine which contained various key messages for understanding the sickness of contemporary man. The existentialist thinkers were perhaps the last ones to seriously tackle the situation, the last ones who appealed for responsibility and *commitment* to oneself.

We all possess the latent or conscious urge to seek our freedom. This problem of freedom has constantly preoccupied philosophers, but the existentialists knew how to take it to a more intimate or personal level, thus sowing in our generation the desire to seek and the need to experience this ideal. I think this is what fundamentally led to the generational shift and made so many intellectuals of this period turn in their youth to being active existentialists or "angry young men", as they were known. It was the age of "the rebels", the *Beatnik Generation* of the United States, amongst whom the ideals of the countercultural movement of the 1960's would take root.

However, in my personal search I did not find the answers I was looking for in existentialism nor in other doctrines. Even many years later, after having covered the long and at times painful trajectory of Western philosophy, I was subject to its schemes and a victim of its negativity, and without having found my freedom, was filled with anguish at this failure. The absurdity of life made me feel like Albert Camus' *The Foreigner*, with whom I deeply identified. I had lost faith early on, as soon as I began to develop a critical sense. A faith as an inexplicable paradox, as a simple contradiction in the style of Kierkegaard, was intolerable for me, like any dogmatic posture, but without faith I had nothing to sustain me other than mere nothingness; I was never satisfied with this (as neither, I think, were any of the existentialists). If my unease did not lead me to the extreme of suicide, a philosophical problem that every "absurd man" should pose to himself, as Camus unequivocally declared, it was because I accepted this life as the opportunity to get to know Reality.

The mysterious attraction that nature exercised on my spirit allowed me to open myself to the world and emerge from this dead end. I had been closeted within myself; suicide can only be contemplated within that confinement. When we feel the weight of anguish in our hearts we begin to ponder the inner abyss. Kierkegaard, who had passed through these states of mind, defined anguish as the "vertigo of freedom". When we come face to face with the absurdity of our lives, we are ready for a radical change.

All the existentialist philosophers contributed in their own way to my subsequent vision. I should mention each specifically in order to clarify their weight, but as this would be excessive for this essay, I will leave those comments for another time. Nevertheless, I would not like to overlook one of them, the only one who really searched for other avenues of knowledge that would later be used by psychosophy, and to whom, for the same reason, I must express my gratitude: Karl Jaspers. He is, in my opinion, the most interesting and consistent thinker, not only in his reasoning but also in his experience and objectives, which is something of greater importance (although in our Western philosophy, unfortunately for this discipline, these values are generally reversed). Originally a psychiatrist and psychologist, he became increasingly interested in the eternal problems of philosophy, until he devoted himself entirely to them and became a fully-fledged philosopher.

Jaspers chooses the concept of *Transcendence* to refer to Divinity, thus implying in its very definition that it exceeds reason. This is not new in our thinking; it was established with Kant. What is original in Jaspers is *the way* that he proposes to approach this objective. Transcendence, for him, manifests itself to man in nature, in the concrete world, not directly but through it. He clarifies, in effect, that what is manifested is intermediate, between the Transcendence and things, and is thus, like the former, unintelligible. Jaspers calls it *the cipher.* That is to say, although it cannot be reasoned, it can be *deciphered* in some way, while Transcendence is the absolute *Other*. Transcendence thus unveils itself, in some way, through the aesthetic experience, although it also takes into account certain actions of men, implying a moral aspect; though he does not emphasise this point. For psychosophy, the aesthetic experience will be considered as an avenue of knowledge towards the Transcendental, but it will no longer depend on isolated and circumstantial events. It will propose aesthetic contemplation in a systematic manner; indeed, it will consider a primarily *contemplative* life to be necessary. As regards the moral aspect, as will be seen, it will be the very path of this discipline.

It is strange that Jaspers, being a psychologist as well, does not infer that if transcendence is presented to him as *other*, it is because man is *alienated* from it, which should have made him reflect on how to alleviate his alienation. This will be one of the basic principles of psychosophy. But for Jaspers the human being is immersed in phenomenal reality, he has to live within the coordinates of time and space. This is his reality; his being is limited by it. He has, however, an outlet, not as *being*, but as *being able to be*. As far as being is concerned, man is not free, whereas when he *chooses his being* as a possibility, he exercises his freedom. This is his *existence.* This existence is also unintelligible; no reason can be given for it, but it can be *experienced* as an indubitable reality. When we choose the path of existence we overcome the circumstances of the concrete world, and through this we become *existent*, real human beings. If we remain prey to the conditions imposed by the phenomenal world we are no different from animals and plants. Like them, we adopt a passive attitude, we apply our instincts, emotions and even our reason to a conditioned and conditioning world. But by including *all* reason as part of the phenomenal, by recognising it as useless on the path to freedom, in my opinion, Jaspers closes a huge door to knowledge.

This, albeit in a very different manner, had already been undertaken by Kant, but Jaspers is our contemporary, which is to say that on closing this door he shuts in science and technology. The great illusions of our century![(1)] However, I believe that both philosophers went too far here by not leaving the door ajar, not in order to let science and technology pass through, which would do very well to remain confined to this world, but rather *transcendental intuition,* which has been to this day the most effective tool of our philosophy. We will see further on how psychosophy will leave the door ajar to reason as well as to feelings.

The introduction of *experience,* on the other hand, as an element in the knowledge of Transcendence, not now the objective experience on which the sciences are based, but the personal and intimate experience, seems to me to be the fundamental contribution of Jaspers to our philosophy. For oriental philosophy, however, this is nothing new. Psychosophy, which makes use of both contributions would be no more than a collection of hypotheses without this element.

Freedom is *experienced* for Jaspers, not as one who is not free believes, by capriciously exercising it (the immense majority), but when one manifests what one truly is, when one expresses *oneself.* It is easy to agree with this; but when we realise that the self is that of each one, we understand that Jaspers is trying to make of the subjective an objective value. This subjective vision, this individualism, so dear to existentialism in general is, as far as I understand, the main crack through which the content of this philosophy would fall. Indeed, it is difficult to maintain general truths when each individual has his personal truth. This is a contradiction, and in good measure, a negation of philosophy. Jaspers, in particular, maintains an extreme individualism even in the moral order. It is not surprising that our philosopher keeps himself within the horizon of what I have called *individual perspective* and he ultimately admits man's *failure* in his search for unconditional freedom on finding the limits of the phenomenal reality that he cannot transcend.

Even so, man continues to aspire to unconditional freedom; a restlessness in which Jaspers finds the failing of the human being. Psychosophy, far from finding fault in this aspiration, sees a revelatory sign, a *cipher* if you like, that reveals the transcendent nature of man. But Jaspers stays within the limits of phenomenal reality. He and all men, he thinks, run into this reality. And not only our species but everything, because everything is destined to die, to disintegrate, to fail; everything is devoured by time: the *failure* is cosmic. However, in this recognition of failure a feeling is awakened in Jaspers, with a certain mystical nuance, of impotence, acceptance, surrender; it is thus that *failure,* by showing the unreality of the world, becomes the universal key *cipher* that reveals Transcendence.

To what extent this is revealed to him we can but deduce. But as he does not directly extract any message from it, it does not provoke any "divine inspiration", to use a Socratic expression, it does not make him change his vision of the World, we can suppose that the light that the *cipher* gives is too faint and Transcendence continues to be what it was before: transcendent. In effect, when Jaspers announces to us that the *Absolute* signifies participation in the eternal, in Being,[(2)] it seems that we are overflying the Platonic world of Realities, but as soon as he clarifies this affirmation, we are brought down to our habitual perspective: "In psychological language, the absolute is not a spontaneous state of consciousness in the human being". (*Op. cit*) And when he speaks to us of the ontological nature of the absolute, he uses the old resource of faith, empty from a philosophical point of view: "The absolute is not real but for the faith that allows it to live and the faith that allows it to see it "..."it is not of natural origin, it exists because of decision". (*Op.cit.*) This indicates that for him, the absolute is not in our own nature, that such participation is uncertain and indirect and it has a certain ontological distance from man. To bridge this gap Jaspers does not resort to knowledge but uses the same resource: "The absolute, as a premise of action, is not a question of knowledge but an object of faith." (*Op. cit.*) That is to say that the absolute as a moral premise is nothing more than a vague inspiration. "As I explore the motives and objectives of my actions, I cling to the finite and the relative." (*Op. cit.*) Finally, generalising dogmatically about his own experience, without considering that of numerous mystics, he exclaims: "There is no direct knowledge of God nor that of existence. Here there is nothing but faith."(3). We realise that he has finally brought us down to earth; that we are, fundamentally, the same as before.

We cannot deny that Jaspers has had a certain *experience* of Transcendence; but certainly, the poor sample that he extracts from it cannot be equated with a vivid religious experience. It was necessary to get closer to the Transcendent, have a more enduring contact with it in order to know it better. Psychosophy will no longer see man *confronting* the world, but will seek the psychological aspect of this relationship, and will discover in this way that failure is not due to the resistance that opposes tangible reality, but the *identification of man with the psychic faculties that generate an interdependent relation with the concrete world.*

Notes

(1) It can be recalled that Jaspers, after the famous and sinister tragedy wrote *The atomic bomb and the future of man.*

(2) *Introduction to philosophy, L'exigence absolue.*

(3) *Introduction to philosophy, Le Monde*

CHAPTER THREE

Eastern Sources

I mentioned that the mysterious attraction that nature exercised on my spirit (surely similar to that felt by Jaspers) allowed me to open myself to the World and escape from the impasse that, if truth be told, was self-created, as I had been closeted within myself, or rather, within the ideas that I had about the world.

Once I understood this confinement, that is, the *egocentric perspective* with which I viewed my circumstances, I sought a natural and secluded life and at the same time began to be interested in the doctrines of the Far East and especially in Buddhism. I had observed then that this doctrine with its acute transcendental psychology negates the existence of the ego, making my confinement illusory. The *anguish* in the face of the undeniable reality of death was a kind of suffering. So was the thought of *failure* at the limitations of our freedom. This is what the Buddha declares: life is suffering as long as we are subject to our ignorance; for this reason, Nirvana provides the means to escape this suffering and attain unconditional freedom. Psychosophy puts it like this: life implies suffering and contains, potentially, freedom: the knowledge of the former implication is a condition of the latter, freedom.

How is it that our contemporary philosophers could not find a solution like the Buddha had done 2,500 years ago? The answer is this: Western thinkers in general have been incapable of finding other avenues of knowledge apart from reason and faith. Our existentialists, as we saw in the case of Jaspers, were no exception, they chose one or the other. It is true that they all looked beyond reason to find a way out in order to transcend this reality, but they continued to use reason as a tool. And as they continued a long tradition as regards this point, we can presume that our philosophy was in the grip of a vicious circle. This is what I have indicated as the *vicious circle of reason*. Trapped in it, man does not know how to leave even when he tries, because he trusts only in reason to grasp reality, including the reality of feelings. In this way his whole reality is enveloped by reason, beyond it he only encounters *nothingness*. From this perspective Jaspers could not see that the failing, the obstacle faced by the spirit towards freedom, was not in the *material obstacle* but in the said vicious circle.

Jaspers had the wisdom and audacity to recognise the insufficiency of reason and to use more intimate and subtle means, but he did not see the need to draw up a psychology to discover their internal mechanisms, and thus use all their potential. For this reason, as we have seen, he was ultimately forced to appeal to faith.

My desire then was to find a way to access these mechanisms and make them evident. But once here I realised that traditional psychology was inapplicable for my purposes, since psychology relies on the experience it draws from its patients and I wanted to tread, like the existential philosophers, in the terrain of personal experience. Thus, I was compelled to develop a new science of the psyche, which I have called *psychosophy,* an *integral discipline of the spirit* that makes use of philosophy and religion to lead man to his unconditional freedom.

Philosophy and religion, I said earlier, had been wavering between reason and faith for 2,000 years without ever having reached a satisfactory agreement; because faith and reason had different exigencies. There was even talk of the God of the philosophers and the God of the theologians, an absurd arrangement through which the Absolute was attempted to be adapted to the relative vision of man. I am not trying to deny the virtues of faith or reason, but there was a third position, in my opinion the most efficient and secure, and the only one that could reconcile both disciplines: *personal spiritual experience* — which is the stronghold of the Eastern tradition.

Since the objective of Eastern philosophy depends on personal experience, for the Eastern philosopher, a *theory* of knowledge that is not accompanied by a *practice* is decidedly insufficient. Besides, he conceives perfectly well of a practical way without theory, as in the case of Zen, but we would look in vain for the opposite example. For the Eastern philosopher this is unacceptable because he himself has followed a practice and has made his own personal experience. His philosophy has this experience as its basis and *praxis* as its means. It has been received and transmitted in this way; it is part of his tradition.

And here we reach a fundamental point that I have tried to impress on the Western thinker, not only because the understanding of Eastern thought depends on its assimilation but, and above all, on *the understanding of the first principles and causes*, which is the objective of philosophy in our tradition (*Metaphysics*. Book I, chap. I). The legacy of the ancient Aristotle is right there and is as valid today as it ever was, even if we have cast it aside. *The understanding of the first principles* (this should be understood once and for all), *does not depend on ability or intellectual effort, nor on the logical structure that is achieved with them, but on the level of consciousness*. Intellect is obviously indispensable, as are the organs of sight in order to see, but if one wants to see what is on the other side of the hill, one will first have to climb it. This ascent is achieved by changing the levels of consciousness. Later, vision will help us to see the panorama clearly, but if we do not make the ascent we will see only what is in front of our eyes: the ground, the concrete reality of the everyday. The Westerner has applied himself feverishly to this scenario, yet instead of climbing the mountain has begun to dig into it. He has developed so much science and technique in this work that he has ended up transforming the planet. And although he has piled up a lot of rubble, he still has not found the real treasure, nor will he find it no matter how much he perfects his instruments, because the treasure is *on the other side* of his reality.

The subtle spirit of the East has understood that what is decisive is not the accumulation of knowledge, but on the contrary, the lightening of the load in order to elevate oneself and contemplate Reality *as it is,* from the heights, not *as it is thought to be.*

For the simple reason that the man from the East has not alienated himself from Nature, that he does not suffer the innumerable sorrows that are implied from its wrenching loss, he has not, up until now, had the need for a psychology in the Western sense. For this reason, there is no lack of psychologists to remind us that the East does not possess a *science* of the psyche. If Western psychology is a science, it is a subject which we will deal with later. If what is actually implied is that the Orient for this reason does not *know* the human psyche and has not developed a *knowledge* about it, it is because a specific function of decisive importance has been ignored in thinking of the Far East. This function is, precisely, that of maintaining man in contact with his own Nature, for which it has developed a profound transcendental psychology. I am referring to, and will refer to from now on, the most elevated and finely elaborated doctrines of the East: Buddhism and the most precious fruit of Hinduism, Vedanta.

If we define *psychosophy* as a *knowledge of the first causes, transcendental, through self-knowledge, whose objective is the wisdom and plenitude of the human being and his integration into the universal Order through the unification of the Mind,* we cannot deny the kinship with the doctrines mentioned. This link becomes even closer with Mahayana Buddhism, especially with the school that would be the fundamental premise of Zen.[(1)]

Having admitted the kinship, I would like to highlight a decisive point. In the West it is taken as natural and evident that all kinds of relations be unified and explained by discernment and this kind of kinship is inevitably attributed to cultural influences. Without negating them or their importance, this kind of interpretation ignores what is most essential: *the source of common inspiration*, a non-temporal and non-spatial absolute principle, which subordinates cultural influences to a (non-accumulative) prior knowledge. Thus, for example, for those who have a field ready and prepared, it will be highly useful to study the different forms of irrigation, but if these studies are unable to generate water, they will be no more than sterile information.

Buddhism and Vedanta have active and ready representatives who are more than sufficient to explain its *dharma* (doctrine), but I believe that psychosophy makes the psychological panorama of these doctrines much clearer in the eyes of the Western scholar, as well as that of religions in general.

I also believe, and this has been the experience of many Westerners, although they might not admit it for sectarian reasons, that the religion in which we were brought up, Christianity, can be seen with new eyes and its sense can be recovered when the gaze of the Far East alights on it. I am not trying to establish the superiority of these doctrines over Christianity. My interest lies in our culture recovering its spirit and it is irrelevant if for this purpose it uses various doctrines or does so in the name of one religion or another.

It can be argued that the religions of the East also show signs of crisis. But if this argument is objectively valid the same "objective" posture inverts reality, because *in reality the one who is in crisis is man.* In order to be correct, we have to start by objectively judging our subjective reality. Religions depend entirely on the spirit. If the spirit sleeps, rituals become mechanical; if it languishes, institutions are mummified. In any case it cannot be denied that the spiritual influence of the East has shaken many who earlier thought that religion was not their cup of tea. This is due to the fact that it has opened up a wide spectrum of possibilities for the spirit that were not contemplated earlier. This does not mean that the Westerner now has more gods, but rather more access routes to the same end. All the shades of the spectrum lead to the same eternal centre. I also believe that our circumstances are sufficiently pressing to open ourselves up to other ways of seeing reality. Of course, if the Westerner lacks criteria to judge his own culture, we can suppose that he will also lack the means to judge that of others. However, many times what we need to understand our own situation is a change of perspective, and the spirit of the East, which has developed in various circumstances and in different ways, can help us in this change.

If, as we have been seeing, the objective of philosophy and religion depended on the level of the consciousness, a means was needed, a knowledge equipped with a specific method that, together with a praxis, could elevate the spirit to other levels. I think that psychosophy can achieve this goal.

Notes

(1) The said link is explained in the *The Evolution of the Spirit* (Har-Anand Publishers, Delhi).

CHAPTER FOUR

The Ill Termed "Conscious"

I said at the beginning that the human being has followed a slow but constant *process of individualisation, exteriorisation and alienation*. This process surely goes back to the time when he became conscious of his individuality, when he started becoming what anthropologists have called (not without optimism) *homo sapiens*. Psychologists such as Fromm and Jung indicate that this moment is one of rupture with the original state of spiritual undifferentiation, which was maintained by the predominance of the unconscious in man. Fromm explains that the myth of the loss of earthly Paradise is in keeping with this theory: Man would have lost Paradise at precisely the moment when he becomes conscious of his self, that is, of himself as an individual differentiated from his circumstances. This seems a reasonable hypothesis. In effect our species was not transformed only then, it has continued to assert itself with ups and downs and numerous variations(1) in its individuality, ultimately identifying itself almost completely with an individual or egocentric perspective.

Thus, we see that the human being, *in his origins, became objectified from the World and, recently, in the XIXth century, from the universal Spirit,* becoming isolated in this way from matter and spirit and enclosed in his individuality. The advantages that have accrued to him from this, as our scientists do not fail to remind us, are there for all to see; succinctly put: man has taken charge of the planet on which he lives. But, apart from the fact that serious internal, psychic and external harm starts manifesting itself, there is a whole reality that has escaped his gaze: the spiritual. The vision that his perspective gives to him, far from covering the totality of the psyche, leaves extensive sectors, as well as important centres of it, distant from his perception.

Since these sectors and centres become clear in the light of psychosophy, I will try through it to present to the reader *a total panorama of the mind.* But for him to see it clearly my description will not be sufficient, he has to *gain* a perspective that allows him to see *his* mind, otherwise my description will be like that of a foreign country that he has not had the opportunity to visit. Psychosophy is not only a theory; it does not expound on an ideal utopian reality, but on Reality, and its specific function is to provide the means to make it conscious. To this end, if psychosophy views this Reality from another angle, I think it is wise to start from the angle that the reader is familiar with, the recognition of his habitual landscape.

The normal human being imagines that his senses put him in direct contact with external reality. In this way his mind acts like a clear mirror or retina in which the world is reflected. This makes him believe that he observes an objective reality on which he reflects objectively. But this is more than just an *idea* that man has made of his way of knowing and of what he knows. Man has effectively objectified the world, and on doing so has installed his self, his centre of operations, his conscience, in a perspective that allows him to see what surrounds him from the outside. This centre is *discernment.* It should be noted that, paradoxically, this has not been an entirely *objective and conscious* decision, a resolution taken after weighing his internal and external circumstances, but the result of a long internal process, more or less latent, semi-conscious or unconscious. When we refer to *all that surrounds him*, we should also include his inner reality, that is, his senses and other levels of understanding. This means that his perception is not, in the first place, direct, his self is not in the gaze of the psyche, in its centre, but on an angle from which he perceives what is seen, heard and felt.(2)

Man has the same relationship, from his angle and perspective, with the other levels of understanding which he does not *see* directly, but rather as *represented* on a screen that the same discernment configures. This means that there is no supposed direct relationship between subject and object, but rather an *intermediate reality* is interposed between them; the screen on which *discernment configures what will be reality* for the self. We have here a distinction which is not the usual one of subject and object, but that of *direct and indirect perception*. The reader will do well to remember this as it is of great importance in the theory of knowledge that psychosophy proposes and, as a result, for his own knowledge. From the moment, then, that the human spirit is objectified from reality, external or concrete, internal or spiritual, it does not look at it directly but at the screen on which it is reflected. This screen, for its part, is far from being limpid and is always ready to take in the objects of the senses, because it constantly reflects images, ideas, words and memories. These come from other centres or planes of the psyche, such as the unconscious and what I have called the *animated plane, or seat of sentiments*, a plane that generally remains semi-conscious. The manifestations of these planes are not represented as clear images on the screen of discernment so are only partially intelligible. These manifestations affect reason, memory and imagination, creating a complex interplay of representations that take place while the self contemplates external or internal reality. It is in the midst of all these influences and interferences, which are not fully comprehensible, that discernment tries to *sift through* reality.

As discernment is by nature an external faculty, it can, despite such interferences, adequately distinguish and sift through the concrete world whose *forms* are clear to its understanding. But when this faculty is used by man for his own knowledge, the situation is very different, as besides the representations of the internal planes that are unclear, a good part of the interior world, and not the least important part, lacks form. This formless content is poorly digested by discernment, which by not assimilating it does not incorporate it (consciously) into *its* reality. But this does not mean that this non assimilated material is left outside the psyche. It remains in some dark corner of consciousness, in some sector of the memory, which it is difficult to access for the very reason that it has not been classified. Discernment does not only *repress* what it considers *taboo* in the unconscious or what it cannot consciously accept (these repressions, studied by Freud and his successors, generate traumas or *complexes*), it also accumulates in it everything that, even when it is important for the spirit, it does not know, simply, how to discern. In these cases, even when neurosis is not directly produced, gaps are created in man's reality, sectors of *ignorance*, and their accumulation increases his insensibility. This generates a vicious circle that will leave the spirit poorly prepared emotionally and sentimentally, that is, *progressively exposed to imbalances*.

The reality of contemporary man is, thus, *empty of all reality exempt of form* because it has been identified with an external, limited faculty of relative vision: discernment. It is this identification that has made the spirit, the self, the man *externalised* and thus alienated from his spiritual reality. It is this alienation that has led him to believe in the non-existence of a spiritual reality. His beliefs as well as his elaborate materialist philosophy and his general vision of the world are consequences of the same. This identification, which, I repeat has not been conscious or deliberate, is what has generated what we now call the *conscious*. This, the discernment and the self, constitute a Trinitarian unity that man finally accepts as a natural inheritance without noting the *process of alienation* that it has been subject to. Psychosophy has ample grounds, as will be seen, to question and reject the unity of said trinity. For this reason, it does not call *conscious* what is today understood as such but the *external conscience or discernment or external plane.*

When man observes an object with discernment, he sees it from the outside. As soon as he discerns it, he experiences himself as different from the discerned. Now, since the point of view of the self is that of discernment, we understand why man is separated from everything, except from his own discernment, which he cannot observe because it is in him. As discernment has to be outside in order to know, it cannot be objective with itself. Therefore, we can conclude that man can hardly know what he considers to be "conscious", and since from this he cannot have more than a vague idea of what happens on the internal planes, it is not surprising that the human being does not know himself. He is also convinced, besides, that his consciousness (his discernment of himself) depends entirely on his will, but he forgets the *dependence* that it maintains on the very mechanisms of discernment. The reality of present day man is made up of reasons that he believes are always used in his favour, but, due to his erroneous perspective, he cannot see the most fundamental, that which underlies all reasons, the very mechanism of reason. Identified with his discernment, which is a faculty to attend particularly to his survival, he applies himself to this with fervour. In other words, the obsession that contemporary man has with the utilitarian aspect of life comes, of course, from his interest, from the will of his consciousness, but this is determined by the instrument or faculty that he uses: discernment. This *mechanism is decisive for man in his way of being* without him being aware of it. Psychosophy invites him to change his perspective and his consciousness so as to be able to, among other things, appreciate this fact; but it warns him of a reality implicit in what is mentioned: discernment *pushes* him to maintain his individuality, that is to say, in order to leave it he has to fight against (what he understands by) himself.

The self or ego, therefore, is not only identified with discernment, but is formed and structured by it. The fact that we can discern *about* our self makes us believe in its existence. But *what* we discern we neither see nor perceive, we only do it when we think about it, we construct it when we discern it; in this way we grant it its attributes and its being. The self, in reality, is a group of adherents around an entity without its own existence, but which gives unity to the group; this group of adherents *forms* the image that we have of ourselves. It is this self-as-image with which the majority of human beings identify, and when they want to know themselves (those few who try) they apply themselves in the useless task of constructing and restoring their own image. Whoever wants to know themselves should look beyond their own image, identifications and representations, and seek something more stable and real. From the *image* that man has of himself to the Reality of the human being there is a good stretch of road to be covered; it is this stretch that psychosophy would like to cover.

I think that what has been said is understandable and that the reader will, in principle, be in agreement. The argument of the non-existence of a personal self, moreover, perhaps does not represent a novelty for him, since it had been expressed by the Buddha 2,500 years ago, albeit in a different manner. But it would be very surprising if the fact of *being in agreement* with what has been said would make him radically change his attitude with respect to his identity and the World. Nevertheless, this lack of vital reaction in the face of a rational understanding can lead him to reflect on a more intimate and decisive level. Well, this is precisely what the author intends with all these arguments.

Notes

(1) I will elaborate on this in *Origin and Destiny of Man*. Har-Anand Publishers, Delhi.

(2) People who can directly perceive with their senses are exceptional. This virtue is the legacy of a few artists. We can, for example, recognise in Leonardo da Vinci, in Rembrandt and in Monet the faculty of seeing without interferences; incidentally, for this reason Cézanne very appropriately said that "Monet is only an eye - but my God, what an eye!"

CHAPTER FIVE

A Mutable Spirit for a Mutable Reality

Man, in his present state, can only perceive the impermanence of concrete reality when it becomes clear to his senses, even with the help of precision instruments. This makes him live out of step with reality, which flows permanently, while he perceives it only when the object changes its position, form, colour or some other feature. He observes that it was here, now there; that it was one way and then another. However, between these two moments of comparison the process is not interrupted; there is a reality that cannot be denied, even though the intellect does not detect it. His manner of apprehending mutable phenomenal reality is through concepts that by definition are immutable. Nevertheless, as these applied concepts correspond relatively to the object and he can, thanks to this, act effectively on sensible reality, he has come to the belief that he is progressively approaching Reality. But this is not the case. Reality is always separated from concepts and from man. They are two parallel worlds that never meet. It is true that the correspondence between subject and object has been increasing in a qualitative and quantitative manner but what has not increased is the identity between the two. The fact is that man *is progressively alienated from his reality*, and instead of engaging and integrating with it he keeps separating from it. When he wants to understand it, he, the "self", which is also a set of concepts, an abstract but supposedly fixed entity, makes use of concepts.

The bridge that man constructs between himself and flowing reality rests on two fixed and abstract extremes, that is to say, they are not supported by reality. As man lives on this bridge that constitutes *his* reality, we can say that he *lives in a world of abstractions*. To the extent that he identifies with discernment he takes its representations as the truth, and thus when he applies this faculty to his own knowledge of himself, he also constitutes a set of them. Naturally, he does not *become* a set of representations. This would be ontologically absurd; however, logic is insufficient to surmount this obstacle. For this reason, man thinks that he *is* the succession of ideas which he makes of himself.

How then can man leave this world of abstractions and enter reality? Is he destined to look at the river of life from the bank or can he navigate it and flow like it in the present?

In order to overcome the distance that separates him from reality it is necessary that he transcends an entire Universe, the whole world that he has constructed with abstractions and that has converged in his ego. As all this Universe conforms to his *individual perspective*, he does not need to travel in space and time in order to transcend it (*the lack*, as has been observed, is not in space-time limitations), but to transcend its perspective. Psychosophy has the means to make this aspiration effective.

In our daily tasks we can observe that our *centre of attention* is as much in a place or an object as in a thought, in a memory, in a desire, or in some place that constitutes our reality of the moment; the centre is not fixed. In these shifts we habitually keep a general centre of reference with which we identify ourselves; this we call the "self" or the ego. This is situated around a more or less stable zone. But if we follow the movement of our centre of attention, and the best way of doing so is by *identifying with the moveable spirit*, we will see that it is not, as we latently believe, something fixed, but that it also changes, as if we were dealing at times with different individuals. Thus, we can say that if the centre of reference or the "self" of a subject gravitates around the area of sentiments, it is of a sentimental nature, if towards the intellect, it is intellectual, and so on. But although our spirit may have a zone or preferred abode that reveals a psychological type, it shifts, and on doing so it drags our "self" to other centres. Thus, there are days when we feel (and we *are* at that moment in time) more emotional, more intelligent, less perceptive, less audacious, etc.; when faced with the same situation we react differently in tune with the position of the spirit. For example, we attend the funeral of a dear friend and we do not shed a single tear because we are resolving the situation in a rational manner, but later, perhaps due to a memory, that displaces our spirit to other centres, we start to cry; at that moment we *are* sentimental, we are identified with *that* being. In a similar manner although we might not be aggressive, at times *we are overtaken by* anger. Who are we then? We can answer: we are all of these things, the one who is at times sentimental, at others contemplative or rational, with certain marked preferences, etc. But *are* we this, the result of a statistic that can vary with time or are we something more essential and permanent? *What we really are is a spirit that is shifting*. This reference is a door for anyone who wants to come out of their "self", that supposed unchangeable entity that apparently sees the world objectively, as well as a means of surpassing the egocentric perspective; for anyone who becomes aware that all reality has converged in such a narrow enclosure.

From the point of view of his "self" man is not aware of the shifts in his spirit. At most he can confirm them when they have already taken place, the same as when he contemplated external reality. This is so because his external consciousness, from which he observes, is not made in order to live or appreciate the present and perceive the natural flow of things, but instead the past and future, while the present escapes him moment by moment.

The solution can now be glimpsed and it will eventually become clearer through the correct and systematic observation of inner reality. In effect, whoever contemplates himself without prejudice will be able to confirm that his habitual reference, his ego, is an illusory entity. Once this is accepted, not only by reason but on a vital level, he will be ready to accept his true identity: the spirit that underlies all his experiences. But this spirit, he will observe, has a very different nature from that of the ego. Not only can it be experienced at a vital level but, in contrast to the ego, which is an abstract static entity, it is as mutable as the reality it experiences, and this allows it to accompany it in its flow.

At first the aspirant will find this more than unstable, he will find it vertiginous as he will not now have a mediate relationship with reality, a spatial distance that allows him to observe it objectively. Likewise, he will no longer have the time to be able to discern it, and he will thus soon find himself *in a memory* (and this will not be a memory that comes to his "self"), *in* a sensitive experience, or *in* a motivation to try and generate a thought, that wants to activate the imagination. The only way to overcome this vertigo is to be extremely attentive; practice will gradually diminish the sensation. This constant experience will make him aware of his true identity, which can be enunciated thus: "*I am that vital experience of the spirit that moves through the Mind*".

But this is not man's entire reality, only his mutable aspect, which will serve as a vehicle to reach his other aspect, and thus to the totality of his being.

We can say that the "self" is not man's first reality but, rather, his first unreality. If we accept this, we cannot then agree with the well-known statement by Ortega y Gasset: "I am me and my circumstances" (*O. C. VI, p. 347*). This sentence tends to make us think about the opening of the 'self' to its circumstances and the incorporation of these into the 'self', which seems all well and good, but does not at any point question the point of departure, the 'self' that leads us to adopt an equivocal position. The 'self' is an erroneous principle to bring us closer to reality; it inevitably affirms us in our individuality and makes us see the world and our fellow men as a store cupboard full of utilities. Proof of this is found in Ortega himself who ultimately reduces reality (circumstances), which the 'self', man, confronts, to "obstacles or facilities". This vision, undoubtedly inherited from Descartism [(1)], has had dire consequences for the environment which is the permanent *circumstance* of man. In conclusion, *the first reality of man is the experience of his spirit,* which underlies all his circumstances, his 'self', his external consciousness, as well as other levels of understanding and the concrete reality that surrounds him. This is the first reality of man as an individual. It is this correct reference that can allow him to overcome his individuality; it is this awareness that will open doors to other higher levels of awareness.

Psychosophy thus proposes another way to know ourselves and another way of knowing in general. Another way of knowing ourselves does not mean *having other ideas* about ourselves, but *realising the experience of what we are*, in each circumstance and in each present situation. Not to continue enriching our ego but our spirit through real and direct experiences. Another way of knowing does not mean acquiring other knowledge that we must accumulate in the usual manner but the use of a *different method of knowledge*. It follows from the above is that the knowledge to which we are accustomed, the *accumulative-objective knowledge* is inapplicable when there is no fixed point of reference in which to accumulate the concepts or ideas that we make of concrete or spiritual reality. This other knowledge is not, then, accumulative nor objective, as there is no subject or 'self' that observes the object; nor is it for this reason subjective, as it tries precisely to free us from the ego with all its identifications and emotional ties; it is not solely internal or external but it tries to unify these two realities. I have called this unifying, spontaneous, direct, successive and dynamic knowledge *unitive*. Although this knowledge is neither objective nor subjective, its purpose is to progressively unify the subject and the object through the different knowledge paths that it proposes. These paths, which will be developed as we progress, constitute the *unitive method*.

I would like to draw the attention of the scholar of philosophy and religion to this distinction between accumulative and unitive knowledge as it seems to me to be a double contribution of decisive importance in the theory of knowledge of these disciplines. A double contribution because it draws us out of the *latent belief* (2) that knowledge *is* simply accumulative, and also because it introduces us to a new type of knowledge: unitive. This is presented, as corresponds to psychosophy, in its philosophical and psychological aspect as well as in its theoretical and practical aspects.

Obviously this does not mean that whoever wants to make use of this knowledge has to discard all his accumulated knowledge as if it were useless. He does not have to get rid of it, but he should bear in mind that the more he accumulates the more difficult it will be for him to move around freely. He will do well, then, to leave what has been accumulated in parenthesis until he can find a stable place for his spirit in which he no longer feels unsatisfied and anxious, but at peace, as if he were in his natural abode; there he can opportunely take all his books, all his memories and all his classifications.

Does such a place exist? Yes, and it is precisely from there that man in his ambition, like the prodigal son, has wandered away, and to such an extent that he no longer knows how to return; and hence his alienation. In fact, he is not totally alienated (at least I hope not) because if he were to be he would be in moral chaos and in this condition he would not survive for long.

All of us have an internal moral reference, a conscience at an instinctive level, I would say, that tells us what is right and what is wrong. We know that this reference is solid and correct but modern man, ensconced in his egocentric perspective, and preoccupied with the external world, barely has time to attend to his conscience. The notorious immorality of contemporary society should not surprise us.

Religions have always tried to maintain an intimate and permanent contact with our conscience. Psychosophy proposes nothing new in this sense, but it does not conform to this intimate deal. It seeks, through a growing knowledge of the mind, to detach the spirit from the 'self' so that once liberated from such a heavy burden it can attain its true consciousness. Ultimately, it aspires to the *identification of the conscious with moral conscience.* The path used by psychosophy, although it might try to cover it in its entirety, is one that religions have always used: the moral path. Lamentably it is here where man almost inevitably slips, even if he wears religious habits, and doctrine can do little to avoid this because this path must be travelled alone, alone with one's conscience. All that psychosophy can do is to attempt to trace the path as accurately as possible.

Notes

(1) I have already referred to this in the Chapter *I think, then...* on *The Return to the Sources.*

(2) That being so, as I have explained in *The Return,* it is accepted as something certain and known, and it is passed on from one to generation to the next without being questioned.

CHAPTER SIX

A Schema of the Psyche

Instead of configuring a plan of the psyche for the reader, as we have been discovering the different places to which the spirit moves, I have decided now to advance this illustration to clarify the panorama and thus avoid getting lost on the way.[(1)]

This schema (which is effectively just one, designated by the letter "C", that comprises the other schemas 'A' and 'B'), tries to encompass the entirety of the Mind as seen by psychosophy.

Nothing could be further from this vision than to interpret the schema as corresponding to a brain in which there are various fixed centres, as if the psyche were a mechanism in which an object moves, be it a neuron, electric energy, a chemical substance or anything else that the sciences can detect. Because for psychosophy the Mind is of an essentially *spiritual nature* that transcends at any given moment not only the physiological but also the psychological aspects of it.

As can be seen, in effect, in this schema, what psychology understands as the psyche is reduced to the external and internal planes (conscious and unconscious) encompassed there by the circle of individual consciences, while much beyond this horizon other consciences extend themselves, whose importance the reader will progressively discover. This schema should not be viewed with a geometrical logic as this would lead to logical contradictions when in *reality* they do not exist. Like all my psychosophy and my philosophy in general, the schema tries to adjust to reality and not to a logical order; this, at all times, will obey the demands of the former.

My objective is not to *fill* my vision of reality with convincing reasons, as I well know that in this way, although I might achieve a greater number of adherents, I would not be able to entirely satisfy their spirits. Complete satisfaction can only be had by attaining knowledge that is is too subtle to be held in the rigid grip of logic. Thus, for example, when I refer to the *central plane*, I will say that from it the spirit is in direct contact with the content of the neighbouring planes. If then we see the diagram in which we find the schema, we will say that the central plane is separated from the other planes, but being in this plane does not mean being in a geometrical position, but being *centred*. In other words, *the central plane is a spiritual state, not a place*.

Placing memory in a fixed place would have also been to adapt reality to the schema and not vice versa. As we all know there are some memories that are on the surface and at hand, there are others that are a little deeper which are difficult to recover, and others that have been submerged with time and are now not memories as we have forgotten them, but which a dream or extraordinary event bring to mind again. This makes us think that in order to keep them on the surface one has to activate or update them otherwise they will sink until they have settled on the *internal plane*; but this still does not indicate to us a stable centre of reference. Besides, as memory is a passive faculty, motivated by causes external to it, without an understanding that would allow us to discern it, its placement would inevitably be somewhat hypothetical.

We have already seen the peculiar ontological situation of the ego. On assigning it a place in the schema I do not want to say that it exists, but that it is approximately in that sector where the majority of people have their base of reference and their usual perspective.

The schema "B" illustrates that the plane of the senses is outside the plane of understanding and it only has direct contact with the central or vital plane. In it, like in "C", the different consciences as well the different planes of understanding are highlighted. These are: 1) The *external plane of representations or discernment*; 2) the *intellectual plane or that of intuition*; 3) the *central or vital plane*, that due to its way of knowing we could also call *unitive*; 4) the *animated plane or that of sentiments and emotions*; 5) the plane of *internal representations*, which would correspond in general with what has been called the "unconscious".

I am aware that discernment, intellect, reason and understanding are usually taken as synonyms. This lack of precision has caused a lot of confusion, not only while translating texts from distant cultures but also, as has been observed in the case of "reason", with Greek and Latin texts. Even Aldous Huxley in *The Perennial Philosophy*, uses these terms indiscriminately, to the detriment of this magnificent work. Shankara's *Viveka-cudamani* has been translated as: *The Crest Jewel of Discrimination*) where the same author does not cease to warn us that thought occupies itself with the relative and not with the Absolute, this and not that being the objective of real knowledge. Cases like these abound; those cited as examples suffice.

To put an end to this confusion and make the language of psychosophy more precise, I have decided to separate the said terms that correspond to different faculties. We already saw the role of discernment when we spoke of the (ill termed) conscious; we will then see each one of the other planes. They are all part of *understanding* and all these faculties contribute, each in turn, to knowledge. In line with this terminology Shankara's book, for example, would be better translated as: *The Crest Jewel of Understanding*; and this understanding would be unitive.

The internal plane would be the habitation of dreamlike life, but it is not all "unconscious", if we take as a reference the psyche of the common man. For him, who seldom leaves his individual conscience, the entire content of the *unitive conscience is unconscious*. The morally healthy man, educated in the arts and other humanities, has access to altruistic conscience and in this way, as illustrated in the schema, to aesthetic, moral and religious consciences, manifested in him on a decreasing scale, between semi–conscious and unconscious. With these consciences he has an *indirect relation;* he accesses them through isolated intuitions. The fact that religious conscience transcends the habitual horizons explains why psychologists observe it as an unconscious manifestation; a subject I will develop in the second part of this essay.

Needless to say, that this whole order depends on the personal attributes of each individual: there are those who have an intimate relationship with their dream-life, or a natural inclination towards the aesthetic and moral life, etc. In a similar manner fortunate intuitions can alter this order, but the rule is that in order to generate these intuitions or shifts of the spirit, the subject must *prepare themselves to generate the right conditions.* Psychosophy tries to help in this task.

In schema "C" we observe how the planes of external and internal representations diminish in proportion to the increase in the central plane. This is so because as the spirit becomes unified these fades until they disappear from psychic reality. It also means that, inversely, the control of the activities of discernment, such as dreams, contributes to this process.

The intellectual and animated planes, as can be appreciated, have a greater reach than those others, they do not diminish in the process, but their moral, aesthetic and epistemological functions rise with the different levels of consciousness.

In the same schema "C" we see two directions in which the spirit moves, that of the planes of *understanding*, drawn horizontally, and another from left to right, which is effectively the ascendant direction in which we find successive *levels of consciousness*, indicated by the circles that encompass *unitive and unified conscience*. The different levels of consciousness give a particular vision of reality, so this should be expressed according to the change of perspective that they generate, but, for the better understanding of the reader, I have adapted the language, as far as possible, to its habitual perspective, maintaining the subject-object duality.

The process that the spirit must follow towards its unification is illustrated in schema "A", as well as the process of return or *unitive individuation*. It can be seen in the same that as the spirit elevates its level other consciousnesses appear that escape the vision of the *individual conscience*, and this in time ends up being outside the horizon of the *unified conscience*.

Although the aesthetic, moral, philosophical and religious consciences are clearly distinguishable they all obey a similar perspective that gives them common characteristics. For this reason and in order to avoid naming them each time I refer to them, I have grouped them within one conscience that I have called *unitive*.

Even if in my earlier essay, I identified the origin and objective of religion and philosophy in the schema that I then laid out I referred only to religious conscience. This is so because Western philosophy is so linked to intellect and analysis that while speaking of a philosophical conscience, I feared that one would think of those faculties that are, correctly speaking, just complementary to philosophical conscience and which operate on another plane of understanding. But speaking only of religious conscience lent itself, in turn, to thinking about the usual resorts of the same, sentiment and faith, which again leads to an erroneous interpretation. For this reason, I believe that in clarifying the true nature and function of this conscience, it would be more correct to denominate it religious–philosophical. In the first place it should be understood that in this conscience as well as in this plane of understanding in general, neither philosophical nor religious speculations have any place. The content of this conscience would be the specifically creative aspect of philosophy, but it would not be reduced to intuition but accompanied instead by an elevated sense of a moral and religious order, that is no less inspiring. The same could be said of religious conscience, the content of which would not only be religious sentiment but also religious intuition. The feeling on this level and plane is already pristine and very pure and thus far from the planes of representations, where it is too impregnated with fears and desires and in this confused interaction there is generated what is commonly understood as "religious conscience"; very different from that which is located in *unitive conscience*. In effect there is only this one, which is reflected in the different planes in which this pseudo religious conscience is configured according to the variable influence of each one of them. This accounts for the different forms that religion takes, including its aberrations. In conclusion, philosophical intuition and religious sentiment become one in religious–philosophical conscience. Unfortunately, said confluence or experience seldom occurs in one spirit. In general the philosopher is nurtured by intuitions and the religious person by sentiments so they do not drink from the same fount but from its divided waters, hence the usual misunderstanding between them.

In keeping with my own experience, I have not hesitated in fully identifying philosophical and religious consciences, but taking into account the aforesaid, in particular the predominance of the intellect in Western philosophies, I think that it would be more in tune with an objective vision to enlarge the philosophical conscience in this schema towards the intellectual plane, and the religious conscience towards the plane of sentiments; without breaking the *original unity* between both consciences. Since this religious–philosophical conscience contemplates the transcendent or metaphysical aspect of both disciplines, it would also be appropriate to call it transcendental or metaphysical.

The unitive conscience from an individual perspective is not entirely clear, for this reason it is *latent*. The *mediate unitive conscience,* which overlaps the altruistic conscience, is an extension of the *unitive conscience* that reaches and incorporates the internal and external planes.

Knowing that the letter can kill the spirit, I am not unaware of the dangers that a schema of the psyche can entail. But my objective is not to *capture* the spirit but exactly the opposite, to find an exit for it from the labyrinth of the mind, to *liberate* it. I know that with this schema I have challenged to some extent the purity of the spirit, placing myself on the edge of the profane, but bearing in mind the present turmoil in relation to these subjects and the evils that accrue, I think it wiser to sin explicitly instead of leaving implicit what is not there, as this can generate new confusion.

Notes

(1) This schema, and also that which refers to the different planes of understanding and levels of consciousness, have been dealt with, albeit with other explanations, in *The Return to the Sources*.

Schema "A"

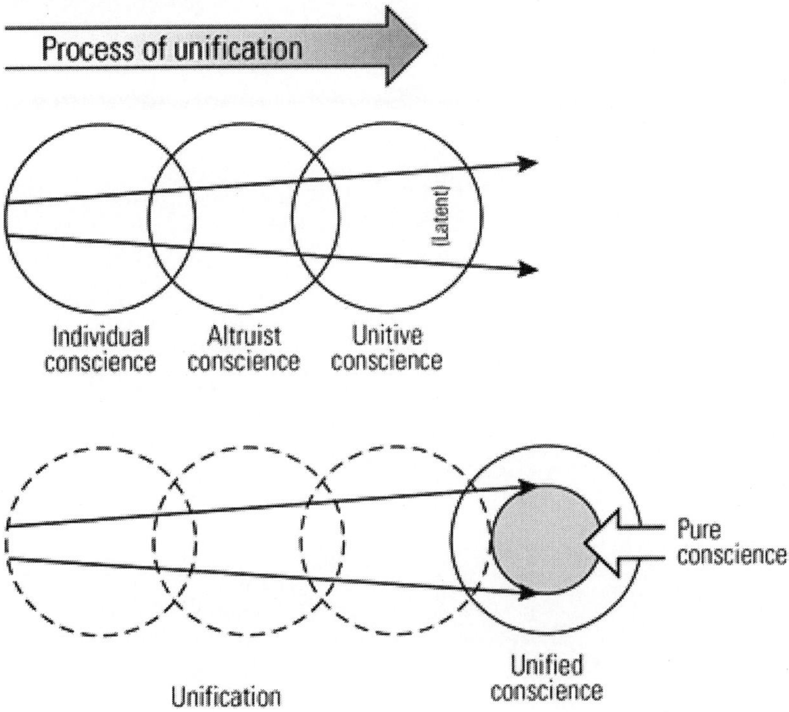
Process of unification
(Latent)
Individual conscience
Altruist conscience
Unitive conscience
Pure conscience
Unification
Unified conscience

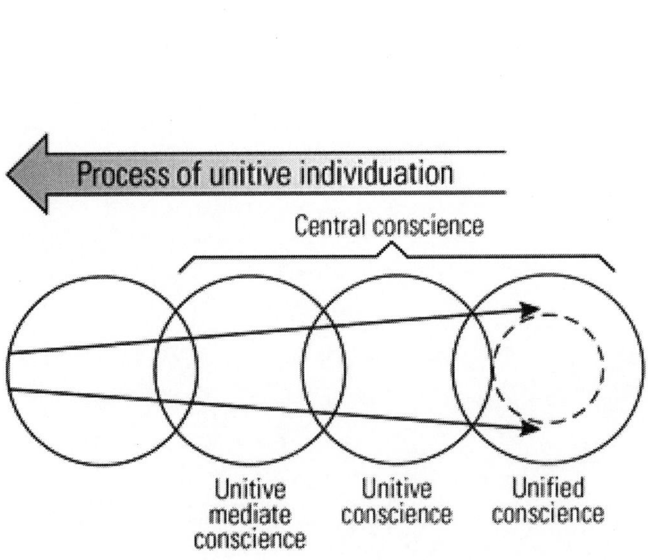
Process of unitive individuation
Central conscience
Unitive mediate conscience
Unitive conscience
Unified conscience

Schema "B"

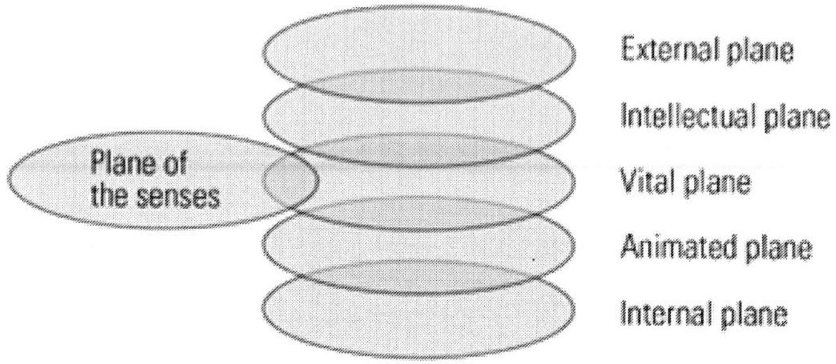

Schema "C"

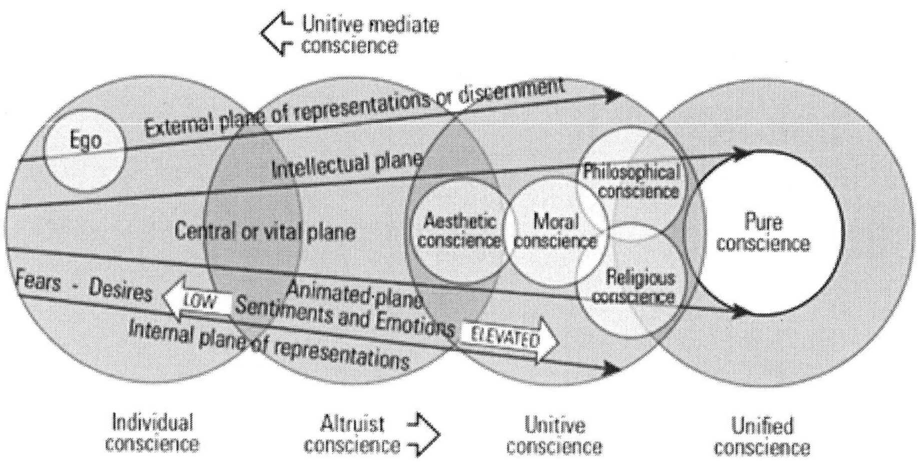

CHAPTER SEVEN

The Conscious and the Unconscious: A Vicious Circle

Psychosophy, then, distinguishes five planes of understanding that are the principal areas where the spirit usually resides or visits. Since for this the spirit itself has the power of knowing, in one way or another, to a greater or lesser extent, all the sectors that it visits on its journeys, all the planes of the psyche, even the one that has been called the *unconscious,* are objects of *direct* knowledge. Other planes can be added but they do not call for understanding because there is no consciousness in them, that is, that of the senses and that of memory, although they are, as we know, indispensable to the knowledge of the sensible.

The spirit normally resides or settles itself on two planes, the *external* (discernment) and the *internal* (unconscious), as the other three, being of a dynamic nature, do not offer a comfortable shelter for the spirit within the individual sphere. It is not surprising that the spirit has sought shelter on the external or internal planes as these are closed spaces, like rooms, that have doors through which they communicate with the other planes.

Although these are the usual shelters of the spirit it does not rest in them, on the contrary, it is here that it is most agitated. When the spirit remains closeted in these spaces this agitation degenerates into a vicious circle and becomes obsessive; this is a common characteristic of contemporary man. Permanent and mostly unnecessary anxieties as well as the great deal of speculation generated by fears and desires make this agitation constant. If to this we add the ceaseless activity of modern life, we will understand why the spirit does not find rest in these abodes.

The internal and external planes are *interdependent*, what happens in one is reflected in the other; there is a permanent traffic or exchange between them. This makes the agitation in one disturb the other thus generating vicious circles between both planes; this affects the whole individual area, and makes the knowledge of other planes difficult. The more the spirit establishes itself on the external plane the more unconscious the other planes of understanding become, especially the internal one, making the unconscious content steadily accumulate in it. This unhealthy relationship between these two planes has created the vicious circle which keeps modern man in relative mental instability.

I could dwell at length on the relationship between these two planes but I think there is sufficient written on this, as psychologists and psychiatrists have been expounding on this theme for a century, although they too might be victims of the vicious circle. Psychosophy does not particularly engage itself with this relationship because it has concluded that it is fruitless. It is also aware that the content of these planes, as we saw earlier, is not real in the strict sense, and psychosophy is interested in realities. In order to bring the spirit closer to these realities, the first thing proposed is to retrieve it from these aforementioned vicious circles and bring it closer to other planes of understanding; that is, what is most interesting in the so called "conscious" and "unconscious" is the way to overcome them. From the beginning, as can be seen, it separates from psychology in search of other destinations for the spirit.

The other central planes are not closed, on the contrary, their limits are on the peripheries of the psyche, and the central one lacks limits. It is true that there has been a psychologist (C. G. Jung, who we will come to in the second part), according to whom the *unconscious* has no limits, but this statement is easier to express than to demonstrate, and does not prove in the least that he knows what lies beyond the horizon. He can only aver that there are some realities that transcend his knowledge; hence his hyperbolic affirmation.

Psychosophy makes use of these central planes to retrieve the spirit from its egocentric perspective and from the vicious circles that it creates because they are *access routes to other levels of consciousness*, or if expressed from a epistemological point of view, they are *paths of transcendental knowledge*. These planes are the specific field of psychosophy as the internal and external planes are of psychology.

The central planes are dynamic, as the spirit does not stagnate there as it does on the planes of representations where, like a fish in a pond, it goes round and round without finding a way out, but moves freely on open ground and it is in these movements that it thrives on creativity. They are creative, not accumulative as on the external and internal planes and therefore generators of their representations. This does not mean that they do not generate anything; rather they create the representations which they have the capacity to order in a certain way. The *external plane* is used for its faculty of *sifting* or separating and of relating or uniting, depending on the intuitions of the intellectual plane, as we will soon see. When this operation is carried out in a systematic and meticulous way, discernment turns to logic; which is not a different faculty but a rigorous use of its potentialities. Discernment can be considered *creative* if logic is accepted as such. In my understanding without intuition it is not so. The internal plane orders in its own way, symbolically, and creates images for it that do not lack imagination, but inspiration, as we will see, is provided by the other planes. We will deal with this plane at a later stage because in order to see it clearly it is first necessary to overcome the vicious circle to which we have referred, and to know the content and functions of the central planes. Meanwhile the reader will do well to put aside any *ideas* that he might have about the "unconscious".

Surpassing the external and internal planes does not mean eliminating them. Psychosophy does not propose a negative path that implies the sacrifice of reason or the knowledge acquired by it, but rather a consistently positive path to reveal and develop other faculties more apt for self-knowledge and the understanding of spiritual reality in general than those that man uses today. We will see in the next chapter that far from eliminating the intellect it tries to extract the most possibilities from it, to the point of establishing its limits.

The alienation and ravings of the human being should not be attributed to these faculties nor to any others, but rather to their incorrect use, due largely to the lack of knowledge of the *unitive faculties,* which do not only open the horizon to other realities but also allow him to better see and understand his habitual faculties.

Incorrect use does not mean opposition to the ethics that psychosophy has adopted. For this discipline correct actions derive from knowledge. Greater knowledge corresponds, inexorably, to a more solid morality, and inversely, dishonesty is proportional to ignorance. But it must be understood that this knowledge is unitive, as no cumulative knowledge is sufficient to drag morality along with it. Besides, *unitive knowledge* is far from being merely theoretical. Moral practice, more than a complement, is an inseparable part of it.

Given that psychosophy insists on the necessity of an active moral practice, it obviously cannot, at least when transmitted by means of a text, provide it. It can only provide theoretical knowledge, so the aspirant himself must remedy this lack otherwise he will not be able to understand the theory. Such is the nature of the unitive knowledge.

All material possessions create dependency. Since religions incline towards liberation it is only logical that they warn us on this matter. This being understandable for anyone who thinks about it, I will not insist on this point, although it is obvious that the majority of people do not even bother to consider it. Psychosophy is particularly interested in pointing out the dependencies created by *spiritual possessions*, as these form an intrinsic part of man and therefore it is more difficult to notice them.

It should not surprise us that discernment, which is one of the greatest assets of our species, in all probability, is our most deeply rooted dependence, to the point that the "self" has come to identify with it; and this is one more proof of the faith that Western man has in reason. I would like to add that this faculty is not just an instrument of man but that man is in turn instrumentalised by this faculty, which, in forcing him to *think* in a certain way leads him to see, believe and *be* in keeping with it, hence the necessity to control it, meditation being the most effective classical remedy. This is another practice that the aspirant should procure for himself to complement this reading.

There are many who believe that by practicing some spiritual technique and by briefly learning about some spiritual *current* they are already on the "path" and can dispense with morals and religion, when one has a good *technique* (one of the "divinities" of our contemporary culture). All spiritual techniques, all *yoga*, is sustained by moral conduct and has a moral and religious purpose; if one believes otherwise one would be wasting time by practicing it.

Nothing is easier than carrying along our ego on every path, to every place, in every situation; we are accustomed to this. It seems to us inconceivable to go anywhere without it, it is for this reason that so many of those who choose the spiritual path apply themselves "with dedication" to constructing an image of their "spiritual" self. They think that they will accumulate spirituality as if it were part of a *curriculum*. The result of this attitude is invariably negative, because instead of acquiring knowledge they acquire obstacles. These create an image which might be an illusion but the more it is built on the more difficult and wearisome it becomes to find and remove its foundations. The *spiritual image* is thus a trap on the pathway of the spirit, into which fall all those who ignore the subtle forms of dependence.

It is a strange paradox that man today, who believes that he is living only on realities has as his first reference an illusory entity and in it he makes the entire Universe converge. This image is not necessarily the product of his egoism but is born of the necessity of his discernment, of *creating ideas* of reality in order to apprehend it. This need, however, has to disappear now that we are entering the field of spiritual realities, otherwise the panorama that appears ahead will not be understood.

CHAPTER EIGHT

The Path of Intuitions

What is commonly understood by reason I have separated into two planes: that of discernment and of intellect. The reasons that have led me to separate the speculative faculties are multiple, and the most important are linked to the theory of knowledge, which is so valuable to psychosophy that I will try to summarise it below.

If there is one concept that has given rise to misunderstandings and polemics in our history of thought it is *reason*, and this is due to the simple fact that it has been designated for all cognitive capacities. Thus, those who have gone further with their intuition have been attributed with a reach that those with less intuition cannot share, and they have been opposed with a logic, which is at times rigorous and convincing, with which they "demonstrated" that what they had intuited was illusory. This means that as each one speaks from his own experience, there has been no agreement nor objective definition of this concept.

If the concept of *reason* changes in keeping with the perception of individuals, it is natural that it might have acquired a different sense in different cultures.(1) Suffice it to recall here that the Greek philosophers had a much broader *idea* of the concept than we have today. The *logos* and the *nous,* which are terms that can be translated as reason and mind, had a meaning and a scope that modern man, even science, cannot understand because they do not perceive them in the same way. The *Logos* was for the Greeks the formative principle of the universe, the Soul of the World. The mind was then bound to this principle. By reasoning man *participated* in this formative principle. The soul was *part* of the universal Soul. It is evident that at present we are referring to *another* reason. For centuries we have had another idea about it. It is time to clarify this matter.

Psychosophy tries to re-establish the cosmic dimension that the Greeks had of the soul. For this discipline if contemporary man does not perceive this dimension, it is not because he knows more or better than the ancient Greek (which he tends to believe as he possesses more knowledge about things and a superior technology) but because he has followed a gradual process of spiritual obstruction, due to which he has been shut up in his discernment, dividing his mind and, as a consequence, alienating himself from the Soul of the World. In clarifying such an important concept as reason and highlighting its different functions and limits, psychosophy hopes to contribute not only to a better awareness of the human psyche but also to a more suitable understanding of the history of thought.

For this reason I have considered it indispensable to distinguish between a faculty in which we exercise our will (with the conditions already laid out), *discernment*, and another that is relatively distant from us and does not depend on our will: intuition. In this *difference of nature* one can find the key to the understanding of these faculties as we will see in the next pages.

Just as the meaning of the concept of *reason* has been changing as man accentuates his egocentric perspective, our position with respect to some concepts produced by reason, such as that of *universals,* that is, generic concepts or ideas, has also altered. We say that a particular species of animal or plant exist when, actually, they do not; only concrete beings exist: this cat, that lettuce. Particular individuals exist, Peter and John, but not *man.* This is a *universal* concept.

Contemporary man, who is conditioned, without his being aware of it, by the perspective he has adopted, does not posit this problem of universals. They do not constitute a *problem* for him. He already has his answer: "The universals do not exist in tangible reality but they exist in my mind; man has the faculty to create them". But if one thinks deeply, one will see that this is based on a simple baseless *belief.* As we will see, some basic principles of psychology are based on the same belief, that the *psyche* spontaneously "creates" certain images. These answers, however, need proofs. If it were demonstrated, for example, that when particular neurons are electrically stimulated, they *generate* these ideas or these images, then something would have been proven. But this demonstration has not been done; and even if it were possible, one would have to explain why *these* ideas or images and not others are created.

The explanation of the *universals* is indispensable to the understanding of the origin of categories. E. Kant notes (in his *Critique of Pure Reason*), that for the knowledge of sensible objects, reflection that follows experience, empirical deduction, is not enough. In order to *establish necessary and universal laws*, he correctly thinks, concepts that are not in one's experience are necessary, which are given preference before it (*a priori*), and for this reason they are called *pure concepts of understanding*, and these are the categories of quantity, quality, relation and modality. Kant makes another observation of capital importance: it is not only the concept that transcends sensible reality, but for this to happen a *pure or transcendental perception is necessary, i.e., that there be a subject, a unit of transcendental consciousness*. Psychosophy will revisit this idea, which it will explain through the displacements of the spirit.

Let us now see in the light of psychosophy the functions of the different levels of understanding and their interrelation in the task of knowing reality in general.

The *intellectual plane* has three fundamental functions. One is the capacity of intuiting super-sensible or metaphysical reality; another, that of providing *a priori* forms of time and space; and another, that of performing a synthesis of the multiple by means of *a priori* concepts or categories that facilitate the knowledge of sensible reality. As can be seen, in these last two functions, psychosophy has adopted the Kantian theory of knowledge, but adapted to a different vision of the psyche.

For Kant there would only be two planes of knowledge: that of sensibility, that would provide the pure intuitions of space and time, and that of understanding with its capacity to generate categories. These, for Kant, are not intuitions but just syntheses of the multiple. However, in my understanding, for the conception of these syntheses, intuitions that are nourished by the perception of Unity are necessary. As these are both intuitions, they are faculties of the intellectual plane. Whether the categories are produced on one plane or another, as far as the knowledge of the sensible is concerned, is irrelevant. What is fundamental is what is established by Kant, that these *a priori* syntheses are those that make the knowledge of this reality possible; and this has been exhaustively demonstrated. But from the point of view of the knowledge of the psyche and its mechanisms for understanding, which do not seem to have been of special interest for Kant, it is important to establish the difference, as for psychosophy the understanding of these mechanisms is an *indispensable condition for knowledge of the transcendent.*

As we have seen, discernment has an interdependent relationship with external reality, its representations have a correspondence with it but they do not transcend it. *The horizon of discernment is determined by sensible reality*. What Kant calls *transcendent* is, then, what transcends discernment and it is only a mechanism of reason. The forms of time and space as well as the categories occur in a place *distant* from discernment and before reaching it and for this reason they are *a priori*. This place is the *intellectual plane*, that is, the said forms are transcendent to discernment but not to this plane. The intellectual plane *provides the forms* that make this synthesis possible and thus the union of the multiple on the neighbouring plane of discernment. Thanks to the intellectual plane man intuits the forms that are not in sensible reality: the geometric forms, the universal forms and categories in general.

Intellect responds in this way to the needs of discernment. The latter posits the question and the former provides the answers, the forms that have to be used in the concrete world; their function is in this case predetermined by discernment.

But the intellect does not extract (or intuit) the answers from the sensible, but from the *supra-sensible,* from the *Unity* that is the *Form that enables the forms* to be applied to the multiple in order to understand it or, which is the same, to unify it (synthesis). The intellect *learns* in Unity to unite; discernment learns in the multiplicity of sensible reality how to separate; this is what makes up reason. By depending, then, on discernment the intellect has an interdependent relationship with the sensible world; it has a *practical sense,* a sensible concrete objective.

The consequences of this are literally colossal; greater, in truth, than modern man can imagine. We can summarise them in this way: Man is progressively anxious in acquiring more and more goods, obsessively preoccupied with the utilitarian aspect of life, a terrible vicious circle that the mechanism of discernment has imposed on him, he has been shutting himself up within this faculty until he obstructs his *unifying faculties*, thus restricting his intuitions, a transcendent capacity by nature, within the limits of his *individual perspective.* I am not only talking, as can be noted, of a theory of knowledge that may interest a minority of specialist intellectuals, but also about a psychological situation with ontological consequences. I am saying that man is alienated from the World in which he lives, and not just from the World there, but from the Soul of the World here, in him and in each one of us.

It may seem excessive that in order to establish a simple category a transcendental intuition that reaches Unity is necessary, but if one thinks like this it is because one is *discerning* reality instead of *perceiving* it. Unity, like all transcendental reality is *represented* to discernment as something *outside* this World, as *another* World. However, Unity is in the multiple, it is everywhere, in front of us. We *are in it* in the same way that we are in the multiple. It is not Unity that is *outside,* but man who has *exited it* (in his mind). Thus, if we think that Unity is an abstraction that unites the multiple, we can think that the multiple is an abstraction that disunites Unity.

We see then that the intellectual plane, far from being exhausted in sensible reality, extends to supra-sensible reality. This means that besides facilitating the knowledge of the former, it is a *path of knowledge towards the transcendent*. It is not now a transcendental knowledge that is applied to the sensible in the Kantian sense, but a knowledge that is applied to the *transcendent itself,* and for this reason it goes in only one direction, towards Unity itself.

From Unity the spirit by means of pure *a priori* intuitions extracts the forms of time and space. These precede all categories; they are a condition of them. We could also say that Unity is a *condition of our present unity of conscience*, of our consciousness; the latter is actually unimaginable without the ideas of time and space. This means that *because there is a Unity of transcendental consciousness, there is a unity of individual consciousness,* and the relationship depends on these pure intuitions. In other words, the unity of transcendental consciousness is Unity itself.

Kant had correctly inferred that for there to be pure transcendental intuitions there had to be a unity of transcendental consciousness but he had not perceived the latter. That is why he did not know its *nature* and did not relate it to the transcendent itself. He was only one step away from it but he felt very sure in his discernment which he did not want to abandon (neither did he know that he could or should do so) and he kept within its limits.

But what has made it possible for the spirit to achieve Unity? How does one know that this corresponds to the unity of transcendental consciousness? For this the spirit has had to transcend the individual perspective and reach another level of consciousness, which I have called *unitive conscience*, and it is there that it can have *transcendental unitive intuitions*, thanks to which it can have the perception of Unity itself.

The level of this unifying conscience allows then the access to another unit of higher conscience, thanks to which *unitive intuitions* are possible. These intuitions are possible because they have a *unidirectional sense* i.e. they do not enclose or hide a utilitarian sense or, which is the same, there is no beneficiary in them nor a "self" that wants *for itself*.

The establishment of the spirit in the *unitive conscience* is hardly achievable by working only on the intellectual plane. This must be complemented by other paths of understanding. If I have overreached in speaking of this conscience, it has been so in order to explain in this chapter all the possibilities of the intellect, but, I repeat, all the possibilities of this do not depend only on it.

For the simple reason that he lacked them, Kant denied man in general the possibility of having (unitive) intellectual intuitions, thanks to which the spirit could achieve *noumenon* itself (*the transcendent itself*), which for him was a divine attribute. For psychosophy the *unitive faculties* are a divine attribute that man possesses. *Unitive intuitions* are not only possible but are, very importantly, part of his reality. These intuitions have as a platform a level of consciousness *that does not depend on speculative faculties*.

Kant, like many Western philosophers, was left speculating with discernment, developing this faculty to the maximum and extracting from it everything that he could, but he moved within the vicious circle of reason.

It will now be understood why I have left in Kant's hands the theory of knowledge of sensible reality. This has already been exhaustively explained and it corresponds marvellously with my vision; I have only needed to modify the theory marginally to establish continuity.

The objective of psychosophy is not the knowledge of sensible reality. This only interests it as a *means* of achieving the supra-sensible. And as soon as the spirit perceives *something*, any glimpse of the supra-sensible (any *cipher* of Transcendence) is no longer (as Jaspers had warned) within discernment, as our discipline barely uses this faculty. It uses it to express Reality, not to achieve it. For psychosophy it is not necessary to develop the muscles of discernment, but to grow the wings of intuition, which it secures not with the wax of reason but with the iron of morality. It all depends on what interests us. If we want to know the trees in the forest we need to accumulate and organise a lot of particular knowledge, but if were are concerned about how to find our way out of the forest, we only need some general knowledge.

It has been said that *Unity* is the pure Form that enables forms in general. This is not Essence or Spirit in itself, it is a manifestation of it, its first manifestation as form. It is a *primary manifestation* of the Spirit that is perceived by the intellect when it reaches a high level of consciousness. But it is not the only primary manifestation. There are others that even if they are part of one indivisible reality are perceived by the different human unitive faculties according to their functions.

The other *primary manifestation* that is perceived by transcendental intuition is *Order*. Although man does not normally perceive this primary manifestation, Order *in itself* is sufficiently intuitive to nourish and apply itself in the sensible world. Without it scientific and technological improvement would not be possible. Every cognoscenti *a priori* intuits (presupposes) that there is an order that precedes and underlies the object of his understanding; otherwise, he would not even try to extract laws that explain it. But the human being normally perceives only the *secondary manifestations* or derivatives of the same. He appreciates only its consequences. Order and Unity are the same; for there to be an absolute Order there has to be Unity. The spirit extracts the perfect ideas or their prototypes from this Order (we will return to this theme later on when we touch upon the theory of reminiscence), as well as the ideals of perfection;

because the knowledge that Order generates does not only permit the knowledge of ordering but also inspires *the desire to order.*

But the spirit only gets to this point on this path of knowledge, because even if the intellect can reach the transcendent, sustained by other faculties, and only through intuitions, it can merely perceive its forms. This means that even if it can overcome sensible reality, *it cannot transcend the reality of forms*. It cannot then have an experience of the Spirit or of the Essence itself; it can only infer it through its *formal primary manifestations*. How does the spirit know then that these manifestations are those of the Essence? Has it been only through inference? No, it is part of the method of psychosophy to avoid the inferences in the path towards the knowledge of the first principles. For this reason, the spirit has used other paths of knowledge as we will soon see.

The lack of knowledge of these other paths, as well as the excessive confidence in the speculative faculties by our philosophers, is what has led them almost invariably, with the sole exception perhaps of Plato, to seek a good part of their premises by means of *inferences*, in such a way that the premises result in being a *product* of them. For this reason, their systems do not hold up, and not for lack of speculation. As Kant had well observed, the premises of all knowledge, as universal and necessary laws, should be found in a pure *a priori* form. This lesson was not learnt by the German idealists. For this reason, their huge castles collapsed, while Kant's secure fortress still stands. The premises of philosophy have to be already *as they are*, thus one has to find them and not infer them. Psychosophy is directed towards this *encounter*.

We have seen the reach and the limitations of the path of intuition. Just as the knowledge of sensible reality depends on the pure forms, including dependence on the *pure primary forms*; and just as discernment depends on the intellect, the path of intuition depends on a *higher Unity of conscience*. Since of this the intellect can only perceive the forms that are useful to discernment, it should be no surprise that it has resulted in a dependant relationship with it, thus forgetting its unitive faculties. This is a constant danger, a constant temptation for the spirit to remain on the speculative planes.

The intellectual plane is dynamic by nature and does not offer stability to the spirit, which tends to fall time and again (and even viciously) within the limited individual perspective. In order to overcome this definitively, intuitions are not enough; the spirit comes and goes in them, finding itself, eventually, at the same place. However fantastic intuitions may be, *they will not provoke a change of reference, an intrinsic change*. After them we are fundamentally the same. In order to provoke a radical change in man intuition needs a sentiment that supports it, an elevated feeling that *maintains* it at that level, a *transcendental unitive feeling*.

Let us, then, look at the unifying faculties of other planes of understanding.

Notes

(1) For a more detailed exploration of this topic I refer the reader to my philosophy of history: *The Spirit in History* (*Ebook*).

CHAPTER NINE

The Path of Sentiments

This path is represented in the schema under the name of the *animated plane*, which I have so denominated because there is no a motor in the psyche that alters the spirit more and that produces more motivations. As we have seen, these are interpreted by the external and internal conscience, each in their own way, yet both by means of representations. But while the internal conscience has a close relationship with the animated plane, for which it ceaselessly registers what occurs there, the relatively alienated external one often ignores the same stimuli. However, as these consciences have an *interdependent relationship*, they constitute a *sole conscience,* although it is completely divided in the ordinary man, so that when a stimulus affects the spirit in a *vital* manner, the lack of attention of one conscience will be compensated by the other, in a manner that what is not registered by one is registered by the other.

As the external conscience functions on the basis of representations, it depends on the forms of sensible reality supplied by the senses and, as we have just seen, on the pure forms that the intellect provides. But when it has to resolve a *reality without forms* like the stimuli that it receives from the animated plane, which lacks them, it loses much of the *real content* of this plane in the resolution or translation that it carries out, it always *distorts it* in some way. As far as man identifies with the external conscience, he will feel like a stranger to his emotions. This is what happens progressively to contemporary man who goes from indifference to emotional outbursts, childishly obeying motivations he cannot control. However, notwithstanding this, he seems to progressively affirm the belief that the more adult he is, the more he should attend to the utilitarian aspect of life and neglect his emotions; when it is precisely this attitude that impedes him from growing. This attitude is not only due to the lack of comprehension of daily emotions, but also, and above all, of his superior sentiments, because if he knew the potentialities that this animated plane contains, he would *ipso facto* change the *ideas* he has of his sentiments.

It would not be possible, naturally, to describe all the motivations that affect man, but there are two concepts that seem to encompass all of them: *fear and desire*. Of the many motivations that control man like a puppet, these are the two main strings. Any attempt at self-knowledge will be inevitably frustrated if the aspirant does not control these strings instead of being controlled by them. Like in a paraglide (for those who know of this formidable airborne vehicle) all the strings on which the control of the craft depends converge in two. These are the ones one should learn how to control.

As desire is in the body and mind and on all the planes and levels of the mind, it is possibly arbitrary to place it on a single plane, but I have placed it on the animated plane for various reasons. In the first place, because I am interested in highlighting that emotional aspect of desire, that although the most decisive for knowledge, is the one to which least attention is given. Another reason is that fear (undoubtedly an emotion) and desire are like two magnetic poles that use the same energy in opposite directions; they attract or push the spirit away, distancing it from the feared object or bringing it closer to the desired object. Besides, both are permanently linked to the sentiments or emotions and their energies are not easily separable. They also underlie the other planes in a similar way, all of them being semi-conscious to the external conscience.

As fear and desire are two powerful energies capable of creating all kinds of "reasons", the so called "conscious" ends up believing them to be "real". Whoever wants to know oneself can only leave the external plane and approach the animated plane to see closely what really happens with one's own eyes (those of the spirit, it is understood) and no longer settle for a reality transformed by external mechanisms. In other words, one should desist from indirect, objective and analytical knowledge and limit oneself to *observation,* not from the point of view of a "self", but from a spirit independent of it *without a role* in the game.

Fear and desire apparently have their origin outside the psyche. This is what we *think*, but it is not so. They are *permanent energies* that lie in the psyche, where they rest as if waiting for a stimulus in order to show their strength. What is outside the psyche is the stimulus and not the origin of fear and desire. For this reason, psychosophy advises one to stay where the true cause and effect takes place, without paying too much attention to the stimulus, the secondary cause, because this externalises the spirit and makes it establish a dual relationship between the feared or desired object and the subject, who the more he thinks the more patent he makes the stimulus, thus adding more fuel to the fire. Whoever does not observe the energies where they are produced ignores the number of times the stimulus is multiplied. He then believes that the attraction or repulsion is real and great, when in *reality* it can be treated as, and generally is, a small incentive augmented by other motives that are also ignored. Among these the most common are the permanent dissatisfaction of man and his innate insecurity. These two basic motivations underlie, stimulate and condition transitory motivations.

For this reason, we can suppose, without fear of being wrong, that he who has chosen a simple life has done so because he knows himself well, and on the contrary, he who (believes) he needs to increase the number of external stimuli is governed by forces that he ignores; although he may believe that he *chooses* the quantity of things with which he surrounds and protects himself: his *private* properties, his multiple *insurances,* his bank *accounts,* his general material comfort.

Fear and desire are the two great pincers that hold man in his individual perspective. Without a complete, direct and permanent knowledge that allows one to neutralise these forces at their origin, naturally and spontaneously, each time they are generated, it is impossible even to talk of any transcendental project.

In the neglected garden of selfishness anger and hatred grow, weeds very difficult to eradicate because the egoist never sees his own faults, but looks for them in others, such that when he finds them he discharges his anger and projects his hatred and thus his conscience is clear and he is again ready to satisfy his selfish desire. This creates a vicious circle from which it is almost impossible to escape; that person is condemned in life to attack the other and wear down his own heart incessantly. This martyrdom is a product of ignorance. For this reason, he who is a prisoner of anger or of hate should without delay, before falling into the vicious circle, revise his own schemas in their entirety.

Although it might not be us projecting hatred, we can be receiving it as third parties, so it is very useful in any case to know this evil, because if we do not recognise the cause that motivates it, we cannot forgive, and if we do not forgive, we *fill ourselves* with hatred in some way. Hatred, even in its subtle forms, like those tangential comments laced with a hidden dose of perversity, manifests itself as violence, and given that all violence is contagious because it triggers a natural defence mechanism, as soon as we obey it we respond to the *desire* of the offender, which is to make us share his hatred. Thus envy, another weed of the same garden, does not project itself only on other objects but, and above all, on the spiritual possessions of others. Few things generate so much envy as virtue. This proves, paradoxically, that an innate wisdom underlies ignorance. In effect, he who has rejected virtue and has chosen the path of selfishness *knows* (although he might not discern it) that he has yielded to his base inclinations. Hence, he latently envies his virtuous neighbour, but instead of imitating him, meaning he would cease to be himself, which is the last thing the egoist wants to do, he wants his neighbour to be like him; so, he *sows* hatred in him, dropping a few seeds whenever he has the chance. If the neighbour receives this hatred, it is because he still has an ego that can harvest it, and above all he fertilises it with reasons, and thus evil has been transplanted. Whoever knows himself does not have an *image* that he needs to keep clean, he observes aggravations falling into a void, and that soon disappear.

I have not placed these weeds, anger, hatred and envy in the schema (chapter VI), because fortunately they are not permanent energies in the human psyche. Fortunately, too, only one extreme of the *animated plane* is dark. As the spirit moves farther from it, it finds a clearer landscape and a broader horizon, such that it can displace itself from the basest emotions to the most elevated sentiments. If the energies of this plane are correctly used, the spirit can access the luminous extreme, but for this one must be attentive because the same energies can attract or push it to the opposite extreme. In effect, the fear that shuts us up in our individuality is in the opposite direction from the fear of remaining in ignorance; just like the desire to possess material goods tends towards one extreme, the desire for freedom tends towards the other. How then can we use these forces correctly? By knowing if the spirit is attracted by *selfish or unitive energies*. These two energies decide the direction of all the individual energies that constitute the content of this plane. The perception of these forces and the direct and spontaneous knowledge of the direction that the spirit is taking in each action, and before this, in each *intention,* are indispensable to know whether one advances or retreats on the road to self-knowledge.

The reader would be mistaken if he thought that these *unifying energies* are a hypothesis with which I try to explain only a psychic reality or a concept that responds to a mere ideal, since I am referring to a tremendous reality that has always been there, long before man had ideals. The reader would also err in believing that I am speaking of physical energies alien to the human being that determine his action, when we are dealing with energies that are of a purely spiritual nature, that are an intrinsic part of him; and that are, strictly speaking, the very spiritual nature of him. He will correctly infer if he concludes that he himself will not be alien to the experience of them.

The unifying energy par excellence is, in effect, *Love,* a sentiment that every healthy individual has had the pleasure of experiencing. Loving another being, giving of oneself, submitting to someone or to something guides the spirit in an ascendant direction. This noble sentiment has, therefore, since ancient times been an efficient resource used by all religions to counter selfish forces and elevate the spirit to the highest levels.

It is very important, however, to clarify what this powerful energy is and how it functions, because to love, simply, is not enough. Vulgar love, that of the majority, is possessive, it wants *for itself;* it points towards the ego and has a descendent direction that tends to affirm the spirit in this narrow individual territory. Only within this can jealousy grow, an aberrant feeling of the same family as envy, which in the name of love tries to justify selfishness. Whoever wants *for himself* does not love, he only desires.

One of the obstacles that hinder us from loving others is the usual projection that we put on the loved subject of our subjective vision, due to which we put what *should be* before what really *is*. This makes us see them with reservations, in a conditioned and fragmented manner, when true love asks for everything that is the opposite: that it be direct, unconditional and open to the entirety, so that the effect is one of sympathy and a union of souls. This does not happen when we put personal interests before pure sentiments and utilitarian faculties before unitive ones; only by inverting this "order" can we see others as *they are* and love them unconditionally.

Love is noble and lifts us up to the extent that it is a pure *giving of oneself*. It implies an attitude of submission that tends to eliminate the ego, condition *sine qua non* for transcendence. The animated plane is thus another path of access which the human spirit has towards the *transcendent*. But since love may not be enough to eliminate the ego, we are going to turn to our moral conscience to see what it tells us.

CHAPTER TEN

The Path of Vital Experiences

On the plane of intuitions, we have looked at the limits of reason in its upward direction (in the schema "C" from left to right), but it is also important to establish the limits with respect to the field of sentiments (in the schema shown below) whose borders are not well defined.

There are certain understandings that are not clear, whether they are part of intuitions or of sentiments, and it is even suggested that they may belong to the field of the senses. I am referring to the intuition of the hunter; or what has been called the female sixth sense; the *sensation* of danger; in short, the ability to sense or glimpse an underlying reality. Psychosophy has found a place for this *sixth sense* between the plane of intuitions and that of sentiments, which it has called the *vital plane* precisely in order to highlight this spontaneous and *natural intelligence*, this vivacity of the spirit, this *instinct* of foresight without calculation. It designates as *vital experience* that amalgam of intuition-sentiment-sensation, which the mind's eye (to use an unerring expression by Plato) perceives and *experiences directly*. For this reason, it also calls this the *plane of perception or of direct understanding*. As can be seen in schema "B" this plane is found precisely between the planes of the senses, the intellectual and the animated. Such an important centre of confluences of all these faculties needs greater attention. This plane, like the other two central planes, has two functions; one transcendental, the other practical, as it also forms part of the normal process of knowing sensible reality.

I believe we are now in a position to sum up this process, since we know the functions of the other planes that contribute to understanding.

As soon as the sensory object is registered by the senses on the plane that bears its name, it is perceived *directly* on the *central or vital plane*.

As this *reception*, I would say, occurs before it does in discernment, there is no distinction between subject and object; the "object" of the senses is perceived as a totality or partial unity, undifferentiated from its circumstances. A first *impression*, a first *intelligence* takes place on this plane that will be transmitted without delay, but already mediately, to the other levels of understanding; the animate one will interpret it on an emotional level, and the speculative plane will interpret it rationally, complementing each other as we saw. The *internal plane* will also receive the impressions, although it is particularly affected by what occurs on an emotional level on the *animated plane*, with which being a neighbour it has a very close relationship. What happens on an emotional level will affect all the planes including the representations of the external plane, that is, the final result of the process will be conditioned by it. The process in principle has an order and direction, but simultaneously a complex interaction takes place that can only be observed by a very centred and attentive spirit. Since the knowledge of this central plane is decisive for achieving this state, we will return to it and explain in more detail the functioning of its faculties.

It seems obvious that if the act of knowing begins on this plane, I should have started with it, but man begins and ends this process in the centre where he has established his *unity of conscience*. For this reason I have started with the external plane, which is not, as has been said, the correct centre, but rather an angle (sufficiently obtuse) that man has adopted to act more efficiently on external reality. But what contemporary man generally does not realise, as his consciousness is reduced to that centre, is that in this way he is condemned to be in a *permanent and dependent* relation with external concrete reality, which has so alienated him from *spiritual reality* that he eventually believes that it is non-existent. We will try to install ourselves on the central plane so that the spirit familiarises itself with its new abode and from there it can extend its knowledge to more elevated planes and thus begin to be more interested in realities than in utilities.

We have to begin with the area of individual conscience that this plane covers. Unfortunately, it cannot be seen with clarity from this extreme but, precisely, from the opposite; and for this reason in the schema, it appears very narrow in the individual area and wide at the other end. This means that as soon as this plane is perceived, the spirit has in some measure transcended the individual conscience and has come nearer to *the unitive conscience.* This implies a reduction of speculative activities and the interferences of the internal plane in a parallel manner; for this reason, in the schema, these planes decrease in proportion to the increase of the central plane. As the speculative activities are the usual ones in man, it would be appropriate to express it the other way around: as the activity of discernment decreases and the spirit remains centred on the central plane, the level of consciousness will increase.

This relationship between the descent of speculative faculties and the ascent of the spiritual has not been ignored by religion, although it is only in the Far East that its implications have been fully understood. It is not surprising therefore that all kinds of sophisticated spiritual techniques have been developed there in order to detain the permanent mental agitation that usually occupies man's entire psychic reality. Anyone who has seriously practiced meditation will have observed, particularly immediately after several consecutive days devoted solely to this objective, that he is in a surprising state of alertness, more sensitive to subtleties, as if his senses had been sharpened or his aesthetic faculties developed. It will also be noted that he is more perceptive with respect to small actions and revelatory details, not only in his neighbour but also in himself, as if his ethical faculties had been revived. It is also feasible that he has verified something that goes completely unnoticed by ordinary mortals, and even by himself in his daily life: that when he discerns, he is distracted from this state. The same also happens if he plans something for later as if he were thinking about something that he left off doing. And the same takes place if he remembers or desires or fears something, or is perturbed by some situation; for example, how would he return home or what would they say to him there. His spirit *observes* that all this *takes him out of* his meditative state, that it *alienates* him. If he observes his comings and goings and above all the *motivations* that underlie the same, the fear or the desire that *make him* remember or project, and he manages to maintain himself in or return to the initial stage of *spectator* of the transitions of his spirit, it is because he is looking from the vital plane, because he is *centred.*

Centred on this plane, he will notice that the sixth sense of which we spoke, that capacity of spontaneously *noticing*, of having the foresight of the hunter, of intuiting circumstances before reasoning them, without analysing or comparing them, sharpens and falls in his domain and, as the spirit progressively establishes itself on this plane, stops being fortuitous and becomes *natural*. Of course, as happens with all human faculties, it will also depend on the innate capacities of each individual, but these will increase in all cases. But this does not complete the picture and is not even a fraction of it. The attentive spirit will notice that these *experiences* are not only useful when applied to external reality, they are an incomparable instrument for its own knowledge and they are the keys to keep opening the doors towards the transcendent. Within the area of individual conscience, the functions of this plane are relatively reduced. They are limited to a kind of instinct, very useful for he who lives in nature and depends on it for his survival; this instinct, thus, is more developed in primitive man. Civilised man has completely forgotten these faculties, while he has developed the speculative ones with which he has established a rational relationship with nature, which is apparently more beneficial. I do not think like this, but I will not labour on this entertaining subject(1), because what I am interested in highlighting is only that the human being does not seem to have noticed the potentialities that he entails on a vital level.

As can be seen, this abode of the spirit is neither external nor internal as these *take him out of* or *alienate* him from his state of *direct perception*. Evidently man cannot deprive himself of thinking, nor should he do so, nor should he stop remembering or desiring, nor attending to all the physical needs and the faculties of the other planes that respond to the same. But psychosophy does not propose the sacrifice of any faculty, but rather a change of the centre of permanent reference, that is, of the *conscious* one; a proposal founded on the absolute conviction that this change is entirely positive for the development of our species. We will now see the advantages that emanate from this *new consciousness*.

It is only logical that man's *consciousness* is *established in the present* and this is the first distinctive feature of this new centre. The current centre of his spirit, the external consciousness, allows him to foresee and act efficiently on tangible reality but it impedes him from *seeing things as they are in the present*. Reality is present, the future and the past are abstractions, whether they correspond to reality or not. But the present is not the point or the line that divides the past from the future. This is another abstraction; the present is a reality and for this reason depends on an experience. We will try then to settle ourselves gradually in the present. This without fear of losing any of the other faculties, as once these are acquired, they are so forever. Now we are in the process of acquiring new faculties.

I should clarify here that if I have said that this *vital plane is dynamic*, it is not like the neighbouring planes, the intellectual and the animated. In these the spirit cannot find repose, while the central is the only plane on which it can truthfully be found being, precisely, in the present. As it cannot remain here constantly it must move around in order to attend to the different human needs, but it will be *conscious* of these transitions; in effect, being centred on this plane and being *conscious* of these shifts are synonymous. But it is also dynamic because this *consciousness* is not static, it varies in accordance with the level on which it is placed.

This is a very important and at the same time delicate point, because we are accustomed to seeing reality from one single consciousness, that is, we believe reality in keeping with our state of perception and according to the place where our spirit finds itself. So, as I said, when it descends to the plane of sentiments, *we are* more sentimental, when it rises to the intellectual plane, we are more intuitive, etc.

Since there are different levels of consciousness within the central plane, the spirit will perceive reality differently in accordance with them. For the peace of mind of the aspirant, psychosophy advances the different levels of consciousness and explains how he will see reality in each of them. But what he has to accustom himself to from now onwards, is to know permanently (to be aware) that his spirit is not in a fixed but a dynamic consciousness and that it has unlimited possibilities. This is of decisive importance, because the *identification* with a determinate consciousness causes the spirit to be circumscribed to its limits, thus restricting its possibilities.

As it is on the central plane that the reception of what is registered by the senses takes place, as well as of all the internal motivations, in order to establish ourselves in it we will remain in the first stage of the process of knowing, in its very reception. In this there is no complex or elaborate knowledge to which we are accustomed, with relationships, synthesis, results, etc., but rather a spontaneous, instinctive, direct understanding of a totality or partial unity undifferentiated from circumstances, limited only by the senses or by the area of the concentration of the spirit. It perceives situations globally, dwelling more on the atmosphere of the whole than on the particularities that form it, although it will not stop paying attention to the particularities when they aid a particular situation. In this way even if the spirit does not extract a conceptual synthesis, it perceives the essential, the significance of each situation, albeit not infallibly.

This *understanding,* which is *at one* with the senses, that is, does not have their *objective* as such, *participates in the intelligence of the intellectual plane and the sentiment of the animated plane*, but in a pristine state, prior to all intellectual synthesis and all elaborated sentiment. It is this kind of understanding that participates or uses both faculties that I understand as *vital experience.* This is the tool that we have to use on this plane.

This *stage* of knowledge is not normally conscious because the habitual *reception* is not direct as takes place on the *external plane*. But when it occurs on the vital plane the immediate reception becomes entirely conscious. A little concentration and practice (and not reflection), are sufficient for this. If there is no *objective* of our senses or of our consciousness, we feel we are in *direct contact* with both external and internal reality; only the *experience* of the spirit (not mine but that of the spirit) underlies every situation.

When we leave our "self", a supposedly fixed entity, and remain with our mutable spirit, we observe that all psychic reality underlies the experience of our spirit. So then, perceiving directly, guarding only the experience of our spirit (not as a separate entity) in each circumstance, is the way we configure the *central plane*, the way we establish ourselves in our *true consciousness*.

The advantages this has for our inner knowledge are multiple, because the spirit does not now have to maintain an image, that is, it is totally impartial to its circumstances, both external and psychic, it finds itself in a direct relationship with the content of each plane. This, however, without adhering to them, as if submerged in them yet remaining impermeable; that allows one to have intimate contact with the contents of consciousness without adhering to them. There is no longer a "self" here that *is carried away* by anger, that is *dragged* along by desires, that is *hostage* to fear. There is only a *spectator* who observes impassively, perceptive, attentive and vigilant, not the representations or the elaborate, but the *motivations* that generate the representations. The spectator observes the fear and the desire as they germinate, before they appear on the surface covered by excuses, reasons that follow interests, before they take on these *forms*; he observes the root of these excuses and interests, and these *false realities never materialise*.

I do admit that centring the spirit in this way is no simple task, but once it has been achieved the aspirant is on the path of self-knowledge. Once this centre is known, since one can observe the movements of the spirit, one can perceive when one is distracted and will know how to return and the more one practices this game, the more one will know it and *know oneself* until it is definitively established on one's *vital plane*. Once established on it, one will be incomparably better positioned to note the external as well as internal stimuli, so it will be very rare to *repress* something on the internal plane without having previously noted, digested and dissolved it.

By *preventing* these repressions, one will consequently avoid the eventual interferences from the internal plane which will give one more opportunities and time to remain *centred*; and so on progressively.

Notes

(1) Developed in *Origen and Destiny of Man.* Har-Anand Publishers, New Delhi, India.

CHAPTER ELEVEN

The Aesthetic Path

Before analysing the transcendent side of the vital plane, I would like to assure myself that the reader will also be able to accompany me on this journey. If it has seemed to the reader that by dwelling on the transcendent aspects of the neighbouring planes, I am using a language for the initiated and thus incomprehensible to him, I would be inclined to believe that it is because he has not paid sufficient attention to some of the necessary *complements* that I had earlier recommended. These were: a mainly contemplative life; a moral *praxis*; and the exercise of some spiritual techniques. Up until now, the said *complements* were a condition to settle the spirit on this vital plane, but once installed on it, the knowledge and practice of contemplation, meditation and moral vigilance should help us to move on this plane towards other levels of consciousness and establish ourselves there. It would be a pity if the reader is unable to follow me when my intention is precisely to *initiate* him in this knowledge, I will try to clarify what these *complements* mean for psychosophy.

Man is faced with two realities: one is the total reality in which he lives, and the other is the particular human reality. These are not opposed to each other but definitely occupy our attention in different ways. While the former invites us to contemplation, the latter urges us to discern and to act. There are naturally human activities that lead us towards contemplation like religion and philosophy but these are precisely the disciplines that we have ignored.([1])

Most human beings are fully absorbed by the artificial domestic reality created by and for them, and modern industry has done nothing but increase this absorption, so that even in their leisure moments they are occupied in the same labours. This *active* or political life does not occupy only a part of man's tasks, but almost all his reality, furthermore, imposing the use of certain faculties. When he starts using these, they alienate him from total reality and the contemplative, or more precisely, *unitive faculties*. As the levels of consciousness depend on these faculties, the need for a contemplative life will be understood, and for the same reason the awakening of these faculties which are today lying dormant in man. This is one of the main objectives of psychosophy.

It is simply not possible to have a correct idea of the Whole in a modern city. Saturated with man-made things, by *utilities*, by consumer objects, numbers and names everywhere (and in all *forms*), the *utilitarian faculties* are permanently attracted and activated. Cities are like a human *Whole* that tend to occupy our entire mind, that is, they have become a totality that tends to fix our attention on a small portion of our mind. In natural life, on the contrary, everything invites us to contemplation: the infinite scene peopled by stars that twinkle as if incessantly inviting us to transcend ourselves; the indescribable transformation of nature with the change of seasons; the birds of the night that wake us up to make us dream; the very trees that have been contemplating for centuries; the mystery of the forests; the moonlight playing in the puddles; the flower that makes us marvel one day and the next only leaves a question mark. All this makes us *experience* our life in a different way. Without experiencing our life within its true context, which is infinity, we can only have *ideas* about Reality.

In nature we do not find utilities, but *objects of aesthetic contemplation,* a whole Universe where we can contemplate its becoming, an infinite whole to marvel at. Those who get bored with it are decidedly alienated from their contemplative faculties and ignorant of the potential that it contains: *the aesthetic transcendental functions*. But there is an important point on which psychosophy lays emphasis, by not contemplating reality with its *unitive faculties*, man not only ceases to know *the transcendent*, but also nature itself. He thus destroys it, because without being entirely conscious of it he prioritises his utilitarian faculties that make him see nature as an object for himself. This reason alone: the *unconsciousness* of destroying the very environment in which he lives and on which he depends, should be sufficient to make him doubt what he currently calls the *conscious*.

Aesthetic contemplation is a support and a sensual relaxation for he who has chosen a spiritual life. The senses all call out for satisfaction, and he who has that life cannot, to a great extent, accede to these requirements. Nevertheless, he who desires aesthetic pleasure can rejoice in it as much as he wants which, instead of being alienated by it, will strengthen his unifying faculties. In this sense the aesthetic conscience offers a much more gratifying panorama than the moral conscience. What happens is that the more the spirit is settled, the more sensitive it is to injustice and to the abuses of men, and the panorama so presented is truly desolate, and *unitive man* is too lonely to not gratify himself in some way! Without the aesthetic in general, it is feasible that the world would be intolerable to him; there is too much moral misery, of which economic misery is mostly a consequence, to bear.

Contemplation and meditation not only have, for psychosophy, the objective of retarding or stopping the incessant mental flow, that is to say, only a negative function, but also that of *displacing* the spirit from the external plane to the central plane, and once it is centred there to allow it to elevate itself to the *unitive conscience*. Or, what comes to the same thing, the control of external faculties is a function that gives rise to the development of the unitive faculties. In order to help the spirit in this second trajectory the *complements,* in particular *moral vigilance*, must be progressively increased and refined. This does not necessarily mean a greater effort because in practice the *unitive faculties* are strengthened thus facilitating the task.

This is a characteristic of unitive knowledge: it keeps *inter-relating* everything in its path, as it does not depend on memory, on concepts or on analysis to establish relations, it works intuitively. It is this intuition, *the faculty itself* that grows along with knowledge; it is not its *objective* that is increasing. For this reason, at the end of the day, self-knowledge will not consist in knowing this defect or that tendency of oneself, but of having discovered unifying consciousness itself. *Knowing oneself is thus the awakening of another faculty*, applicable to all objects of knowledge and to all circumstances.

The unitive conscience can be experienced by the spirit on its ascendant path towards Unity, or from it, on its descending path towards individuality. It is only then, as we will see, on its descending path that the spirit becomes notably clearer. This being the case, and as this constitutes the *base*, I would say, from where the spirit can *launch* its intuitions and vital experiences towards Unity, I will advance some characteristics of this consciousness or some *symptoms* through which the aspirant, who will be on the ascendant path, can recognise this and settle himself on the said *base* until its eventual unification.

There is a relationship between the body and the spirit that is poorly detected by external consciousness, nearer to the former than to the latter, but which becomes evident from our unitive conscience. Of course, in order to reach this, it is necessary to have earlier established a harmonic relationship between the two sides of our being. Since every good book on Hatha Yoga deals with establishing this harmony I will not insist on this point(2) . What does not seem to be clear to many is that in order to walk *with the body* on the spiritual path, it is necessary to *spiritualise* it as well, that is, one has to lighten and purify it at the same time as the soul. Being a carnivore signifies a double ignorance. One is moral, as avoiding the suffering caused to animals is a priority in every harmonious, unitive being. The other reveals a total inexperience of the immediate effects that the flesh produces in our body and indirectly in our spirit. The weight that is produced in the body is transmitted to the mind as a kind of somnolence, a heavy cloud that does not let the spirit dissipate or freely rise; it feels *overwhelmed.* This is what gives rise to the bad temper and impatience that predisposes one to violence. If one does not come out of this state it becomes part of a person's character.

Talking about alcohol, tobacco and toxins in general is also redundant. I will simply say that they produce enough psychic instability that the spirit cannot find repose, without which there is no self-knowledge. Whoever is addicted to them will have to personally free themselves of them, as it would be difficult for a spiritual discipline to help him. But with this we have taken a step backwards to the bosom of individual conscience. Let us return to *unitive conscience*.

When the spirit is *centred in the unitive conscience* all reality becomes spiritual. With this I do not mean to say that a subjective phenomenon is taking place, that a psychic state awakens, making us see what is not there in reality, nor even that it is an objective reality, that is, independent of our personal experience because the *spiritual phenomenon is unitive.* As our perception increases, spiritual reality becomes proportionally more apparent.

It is only natural, therefore, that when the spirit is *centred,* the senses better perceive the *spiritual aspect of reality*. While dealing with a spiritual or unitive reality, describing how the senses perceive is risky and can lead to error, as it is not merely a visual or auditory phenomenon. It should be understood that, before and after the senses, a spiritual event occurs, that things are surrounded and impregnated not only by something perceived by the senses but also, and above all, *significant* for the intellect and for the sentiments. This signification is moral and religious; for this reason, in the schema the aesthetic, moral and religious consciences are encompassed by the unitive conscience. When the spirit is *centred*, there is *not just* an aesthetic experience; if I separate them, it is only for didactic purposes.

Both physical and spiritual activities produce certain respiratory and cardiac rhythms. This may have been observed by anyone who has stopped to observe the relationship between them, but at more subtle levels there are certain energies that manifest as vibrations, related to those rhythms only at the extremes, that are registered with notable precision in the mood of the spirit. The said vibrations are perceived by the senses of the soul.

It makes no sense to talk about the *senses* of the soul from the point of view of anatomy. However from a *unitive conscience*, which is a level of body and soul that our sciences have not bothered exploring much, we face this strange phenomenon in which it is difficult to establish if the perceptions belong to the senses or to the spirit. I believe it would be an error, if only to satisfy the human mania of differentiating everything, to attribute it to either the one or the other, as at the level of the *unitive conscience* the convergence of the body and the spirit, of the tangible and the spiritual, is evident. We could say then that *the senses are spiritualised.* In good time if the sciences find an explanation to this phenomenon, although I fear it a lot, as happens with the "discoveries" that are made in the spiritual domain, it will be perfectly useless.

At this level the sense of sight, like all others, becomes extraordinarily sharp. Colours are enlivened and shapes are defined, but not only to the eyes, I repeat, it is as if they *reveal* another reality parallel to the object, such that it ceases to be a simple thing and expresses something that *transcends* matter; the profane, I could say, *becomes sacred.* Objects become more luminous or show their brilliance better, as if they had their own light, so to say, or as if they had been *charged* with solar or lunar light as happens to flowers when the sun is setting. It is not surprising that the saints are represented with a shining halo. But when consciousness is all that changes, it is not only the sacred objects that shine but everything; all *reality becomes sacred.* However, persons especially gifted with an aesthetic sense can, regardless of any religious appreciation, experience this visual phenomenon; as demonstrated in the paintings of Rembrandt, Monet and Van Gogh, for example.

The ear, by then highly sensitised, or spiritualised, notices all kinds of sounds generated by vibrations that correspond to bodily and spiritual activities. As this auditory perception can be very accurate it can be used, so to speak, as a thermometer to know the level on which the spirit moves. Various *degrees* could be established, but a scientific premise here would be out of place and probably lead to error, as there are endless personal circumstances that cannot be covered that imperceptibly change the said vibrations, and so I will only refer to the most revelatory aspects. When the spirit is very agitated (not necessarily the body; as for example after driving in a car through the city) the internal sound of the ear, because it is definitely not an external sound, is perceived as an uninterrupted musical note *E* almost without cadences; this can be proven by anyone who has time to listen to himself. As calm settles in (if he who is listening makes of this time and silence a meditation), the sound becomes *D* and the cadences are more prolonged. If one manages to keep up one's meditation, the sound will become more melodious and seem like the music of a stream with soft cadences. If one continues thus, one will notice that the stream, like one's spirit, calms down, as if the flow were reducing, until it becomes the sound of a drip of water on glass. I say this because the sound is, in effect, *crystalline,* barely perceptible, but clear and constant, as if it were that of tiny glass bells activated by water that transmits its cadences and its softness; this is the sound that corresponds to the *unitive conscience.*

When this melodious sound is heard, *the spirit is in the present*, the flow of this spring accompanies the becoming, and it is that which corresponds to *natural time*. For psychosophy, *contemplating* does not mean reflecting but *seeing things as they are without any kind of psychic interference.* Things *are* in the *present continuous*, in their *natural flow*. The knowledge of this sound, its experience, can be very useful not only to the aspirant, but also to him who is resolutely installed in the *unitive conscience*, because it will help him to know when he is *distracted,* or gets *alienated from his present* and as a guide to recover this. Although by itself it will not be sufficient; very often an injury, for example, or any type of moral disorder, causes great turbulence in the soul that has to be calmed by other means.

What the aesthetic phenomenon produces is the perception of the object as it is through the *unitive faculties*. This implies a transcendence of individual faculties, and also of the object as such. In this unitive relationship the subject and the object participate in universal Harmony. The aesthetic phenomenon will occur with this participation, to the extent that the object awakens in the subject that magical mysterious feeling, that sensation (or perception) that this order *is fine.*

Perceiving things as they are in their natural flow, directly, without the forms of time and space is the most efficient way of achieving the perception of *Beauty itself.* The beautiful is intimately linked to the harmonious; without conformity, without the consent of the parts, it is not possible to imagine it; the beautiful obeys an order. When the spiritual Order takes over the tangible order, the *Harmony of Unity* is experienced. Just as this absolute Beauty is perceived from the unitive conscience, the plurality of the relative beauties is seen from the individual perspective, in the differentiated particularities. The latter, however, do not have a nature which is different from the former. The particularities are filled with the same Essence and thus with the Beautiful; the spirit of man thus shares the same Essence of all things. He therefore perceives the beauty in them, and tends to establish harmonious or beautiful relationships between the objects of his senses. This, of course, when he is at ease, calm and in a contemplative state, that is, when he is *in order.* The last and highest objective of the aesthetic experience is the perception of Beauty itself, and since it is *in itself,* it is not an idea, but an experience.

Beauty is a *primary manifestation* of the Essence, accessible to the aesthetic conscience but perceptible only from it, that is, from the level of the unitive conscience. Beauty is not, then, in a platonic *world of Ideas* but in the World here and now; it is the Spirit of things, or these are manifesting the Spirit. When the human spirit achieves the aesthetic conscience, *all* that is tangible becomes a *cipher* of Transcendence, not because the spirit sees it here or there but because the Spirit is spread over all things, like dew, and its light makes Reality transparent.

This is what the artist must express so that his work leads to this aesthetic experience; this is the transcendental function of art.

Notes

(1) I should in principle include the arts, but unfortunately there are very few manifestations of contemporary art that induce one to contemplation. For a philosophy of art I will refer to my book *The Roots of Art* (Ebook).

(2) B. K. S. Iyengar's now classic *Light on Yoga* is a good example.

CHAPTER TWELVE

The Ethical Path

In the first stage, as we saw, contemplation and meditation have the function of stopping the incessant march of the spirit on the external plane, so that it can "descend" to the central plane. We can think of the analogy of skating on water, as soon as we stop, we begin to sink. But something curious and revelatory emerges and it is that although in spiritual reality the danger of submergence is much less, the fear that it inspires in us is infinitely greater. This is due fundamentally to a cause that is difficult to acknowledge, in this immersion everything that we believe in is at stake: the "self". We are faced with an ontological-moral problem that enshrines the key to self-knowledge and is the root of all psychological imbalances (I am not saying the sole cause, but the root; trees suffer and also sicken on the surface, and it is here that they are mutilated and truncated). At a very intimate and latent but vital level, where there is no room for excuses, *we know* that the "self" is an image, an illusion. For this reason, the external conscience tries to maintain the "self" on the surface and looks for reasons, entertainment and even occupations for it, thus trying in vain to search for one's identity in alienation, forgetting that the more one affirms oneself in one's individuality, the more alienated one becomes, not only amongst one's peer group and in the world but also within one's own being. Due to this *ontological lack,* the "self" (discernment) is insistently motivated by the *fear of not being and the desire to be*. This moral and existential problem is much more decisive for psychosophy than all the complexes that supposedly rest in the soul. Once this problem is recognised at the vital level, the immense number of unnecessary fears and desires that occupy and preoccupy the human being during his life, fall under the control of the spirit. Only after this realisation does the road to transcendence begin. Of course, for readers who have only followed these words, without any spiritual path or practice, it will not have so much significance for it to be called a *realisation*, but this will now not be attributable to psychosophy; which, as has been stated, cannot carry out this task.

Just as through the contemplation of the natural flow of the objects of the tangible world the spirit can elevate itself to an aesthetic consciousness, contemplating the movement of the spirit can attain its *moral conscience*. Just as meditation calms the mind, morality silences the soul; seen like this, *morality is a spiritual technique.* Besides, other spiritual techniques are only one aspect of the task of tranquillity, of the pacification of the soul; of the multitude of voices that muddle the psyche, it is morality that has to silence the majority. I do not know if I am being understood. The immoral act, and before that the thought, and even before this the immoral motivation, which would include petty selfish desires, cause a disquiet that is proportional to the degree of immorality. He who kills out of selfishness will be at the opposite pole to *tranquillity* and it will be impossible for him to find *peace*. We do not have to be good because it is *written thus*; there are reasons behind the Scriptures. Divinity is Peace, and if we truly want to know and experience it, we have to experience peace in ourselves; in this way *unitive knowledge* functions.

We will have observed that the immoral act agitates the breath and accelerates the heart, not only immediately after the act has been committed but also every time we remember and dream of it. But I do not know if it has been *observed* that it is not the "self" that perturbs the heart, he who *wants* to remember, he who *makes us* dream of the immoral act; it is not our habitual *conscience* which is the generator of these energies. On the contrary, the latter would like to *repress* them. It is the moral *unitive conscience* that *tries to re-establish order*, that *wants* to make the *external conscience* conscious, but this is what the ego does not want, and for thousands of years it has managed to thwart this attempt. But Harmony, which has a whole eternity to establish itself, will remind us through *unitive memory*, through associations of *involuntary* ideas or undesirable dreams, of the act that has perturbed the moral Order. For this reason, because there exists an Order, and not because Divinity is intolerant, one sole immoral act is sufficient to never achieve peace (or Paradise or Nirvana as one likes; unless it is intended that these harbour disquiet like in the Islamic Paradise).

If for any reason the *centred* spirit has *let pass* a single reproachable act, it will still observe, thanks to its practice, not only agitated breathing but also a restless spirit; as it now knows repose, as being in peace is its *normal* state, it will note the *alienating factor*, and it will retrace its steps to see what it has dropped.

Of course, observing the agitation of the heart or the disquiet of the spirit is not all, thanks to it we will know that something agitates us, but we still have to resolve that *something*. Besides the "*technical*" aspect of morality there is the lived and applied aspect. The latter observes the cause itself while the former is an effect. The moral cause is known by a moral experience, that is, by an *intelligence* at a vital level, that we are doing wrong, and a feeling of parallel guilt. The fact, from the unitive conscience is seen directly, while from the *external conscience* (if it arrives there), it is confronted with the interests of the "self"; here in general, morality is *relative.* An *unconditioned* morality is only possible from a *unitive conscience*, as for *correct action man needs to be objective with his "self" and unitive with others*, to be motivated not by individual tendencies but by *unifying energies.*

Only a completely alienated person can maintain that he does not possess a moral conscience. A normal man does not deny its existence; nevertheless, he denies it partially, occasionally, in keeping with his interests at the time. Psychosophy considers that it is due to this *partial alienation* that he never comes to terms with himself nor achieves any stable accord with his peers nor lives in harmony with other living beings. Herein lies the interest of this discipline in *definitively establishing the spirit of man in his moral conscience,* making it his centre of reference. This is not a simple ideal. That this centre is *effectively* the consciousness of man is something that can be proved by anybody who makes of this consciousness his home. Thus, if one is trying to gain an entirely new consciousness, it is natural that learning and even believing in this is not sufficient. The realisation of this aspiration will depend on daily action.

The designation of this plane as *vital* has not been arbitrary. It has the objective of reminding the aspirant that his life is committed to moral action. But action is not everything, as for it to be *moral* the spirit must resort to its consciousness to nourish itself with the *unifying forces*. In this way his knowledge becomes reality; the spirit comes nearer to the *unitive conscience*.

When we referred to the animated plane, we saw that Love was a unitive energy that the spirit perceives through the sentiments, and this plays a decisive role in man's existence. These same unifying forces are manifested on the vital plane. The difference lies in the different modes of perception of these centres, in this the understanding will not be only a sentiment, but also a *spontaneous intelligence* that pushes one to action; it will be a feeling of responsibility, a *moral experience.* These experiences in their pristine state are latent before becoming clear to discernment and forming an ethics.

It is very probable that the reader himself has at some time in his life found himself in a dangerous situation because he has helped a fellow man without personal interest and even without having really reflected due to a spontaneous reaction *motivated* by the urgent circumstances of the *other.* In this case he will have experienced something like *coming out of himself* in order to enter the circumstances of the *other,* entering a reality previously alien to his own but which with his actions has become his own. In this case his spirit will have transcended its individual perspective. These kinds of experiences, precisely due to their vital implication, tend to enrich the soul more than numerous treatises on psychology. If, on the other hand in the same situation, instead of sacrificing the "self" for the *other*, he has allowed himself to be stopped by his own egoism, he will not be able later to avoid remorse. Well then, the motivation for the altruistic act, as well as the remorse for the selfish inaction, will be a consequence of the semi-conscious or unconscious perception of the *unifying forces*. It should be clear that I am not talking about physical energies alien to man that determine his action, but unifying spiritual energies that are an intrinsic part of the human being, which are his very conscience, but not his individual subjective conscience but rather his altruist transcendental conscience. The *unity of conscience* that makes altruistic action possible, the centre where intelligence happens, that precedes action and where duty originates is the *unitive conscience.*

The reader would have noticed the fact that even if for psychosophy it is impossible to achieve a high level of consciousness without an active moral life, it does not formulate any ethics for the aspirant to use it in his ascent. This is due to various reasons. In the first place it is decidedly impractical to try and synthesise in some rules of conduct the unlimited circumstances in which each subject may find himself. All ethical syntheses lead to generalisations that make no sense when faced with a vast diversity, and they can even lead to error.

"Love thy neighbour as thyself", would seem to be a universal principle. However, there are many who secretly hate themselves. Besides, I believe that almost all hatred is an eruption of the fire contained and generated in our own entrails; which is a *projection*. The one who is dissatisfied can only love sporadically and in brief snatches; and this shows that his feelings are more a desire to love rather than true love. And this even though he might love himself because he loves his image in the external conscience, on the surface, while his dissatisfaction is internal, latent, and even though he loves he will not want to admit this defect that darkens his image, he will then unleash his discontent on his neighbour. Today, when personal dissatisfaction seems to be one of the most widespread malaises of the human being, intolerance and quarrels between couples that inevitably make relationships deteriorate and end in divorces are more than frequent. Only ignorance can make love and hate alternate. Thus, the preoccupation of psychosophy is to bring to light both the roots of dissatisfaction and of love.

"Do not do to others what you do not want done to yourself" would also seem to be of general application, but the human being is a heterogeneous being. It is not strange that what we want is desired by others and vice versa. The passionate man wants to be loved passionately while the sensitive lover may be hoping to be loved with sensitivity and delicacy. While the extrovert seeks crowds and an audience, the introvert seeks solitude and silence. The intellectual and the emotional will interpret the same circumstances very differently and will tend to resolve them in keeping with their inclinations(1). These general principles lead us to consider others on equal terms, but as they refer us to our own reference, they do not impel us to change the vision necessary for the "other" to be seen as I.

All ethics ultimately depend on our moral conscience. If it is admitted as such, and only a madman, we said, would deny this, it would be nothing but cynicism to ask for an ethics in order to *know* how to act. Ultimately, at the time of action, the scales will always tip according to the good or bad will of the subject, depending on his sincerity or insincerity, and no discipline can reach this personal and intimate level. It is only in this sense that psychosophy disregards all ethics. This is not to say that it proposes a life without ethics, rather that it wants to signify that it has full confidence in the efficacy of the moral conscience of human beings. For this reason, our discipline concentrates its efforts on providing the necessary indices of orientation in the search for a moral conscience. Its realisation will depend of course, like all ethics, on the good or bad inclination of each individual.

One could maintain that what is good for one is bad for another and vice versa, but for psychosophy this *relative morality* is only possible from an individual conscience, where the good is measured by the benefits it brings to the subject. From this egocentric perspective all doctrine, all ethics, every person and each situation will be judged in keeping with personal interests. From this perspective all reality begins from this narrow angle, first me, then *my* family members and so on, my friends, my country, my race, as far as I can reach; the order extends from me and must accommodate mine perspective. So, evidently, there can only be a relative morality and an uncertain order. Herein lies the need to surpass this perspective. If all reality converges on my "self", I am ultimately alone to judge the world; but if I delve deeper into myself, I will see that the angle on which everything converges opens up to others and even beyond, and that I am not alone when it comes to judging, and that all reality surrounds and commits me.

In referring to the animated plane I indicated that the spirit can descend to the lowest emotions or ascend to the highest feelings. Although we have a certain understanding of what happens on this plane, as we know relatively when our passions are in action, we are often carried away by them because we are not entirely in control of the situation. Even if we can consciously repress our passions, when this flow runs through the external conscience if we stop it on one side it overflows on the other, in some emotional corner of the memory from which it will spring up again as soon as it can associate itself with an occasional idea, or on the internal plane where it will remain latent and also ready to manifest itself when the will is absent. The control of the animated plane, as of all the planes of understanding, can be made effective by keeping the spirit *centred* on the vital plane. This is possible because on this plane there is an immediate intelligence of its contents which it impartially observes, as being in the midst of these *psychic circumstances*, it does not identify with them. Because, as I said earlier while explaining this schema, being *centred* does not mean to be in some place of the same, but in a certain spiritual state. The central plane becomes a reality when the spirit quietens down (and it is only on this plane where it can do so) and remains in a contemplative state, as a *spectator*.

When it is not the "self" but this spectator, who is so because he is free of fears and desires, who uses the faculties of this plane and that sixth sense, the hunter's sense of intuition, which previously had a useful purpose for our survival in the natural world, when applied to inner knowledge it becomes extraordinarily effective, as psychic phenomena are in general vertiginous and one has to "catch them in on the fly ", otherwise they will escape us. We all know the speed of intuitions. It is such that they always surprise us; the latent motivations that make us act, or think or even remember are not slow. However, the *spectator* from the vital plane observes them in a way different from the "self" on the external plane. They appear to the latter suddenly, like bubbles on the surface of a liquid, while *the spectator* sees them take shape and rise, so he is not surprised when they appear in discernment. In other words, those instinctive or primitive faculties, if you like, when they are developed, become an instrument for the *transcendent* and for the knowledge of it in itself, that is, for *wisdom*. It is, actually, thanks to *vital moral experiences* that the spirit can consciously move to more elevated levels of consciousness, because it knows if it ascends or descends morally, if it approaches or distances itself from its moral conscience, if it is attracted by *unifying forces* or by the individual ones.

We are all *relatively* conscious if we morally ascend or retrogress but we are only fully conscious when the facts are evident or when we cannot avoid them or cover them with reasons or distract them with projections. Since moral situations are rarely evident on the external plane, the "self" knows how to find a way of sifting through the nuances until it "gets its own way". The whole game of self-knowledge takes place on a board of nuances, so if we have "vested interests," if we are not fully aware and do not take full *responsibility* in the game, we spend our lives adjusting the pieces according to our whims and we never come to terms with ourselves. The coward may never find himself retreating alone while his companions advance on the field of battle; but he will often find himself lowering his gaze to avoid confrontation, condescending with a smile or simply keeping quiet. Self-knowledge depends on the experience of these small daily acts.

When we covered the other two central planes it was pointed out that the transcendental experiences there were temporary and transitory because the spirit did not find a foothold on them and returned to its initial perspective. This does not happen out of selfishness, as he who has known transcendent reality in some way would do anything to remain in it (the egoist on the other hand does everything to remain in ignorance, or, what is the same thing, the ignorant man does anything to remain egotistical), it occurs due to the very deficiency of these ways of knowledge.

Intuition lacked, as we saw, a feeling to sustain it and sentiments lack the intelligence of the former. The path of integral knowledge is the vital path because *experience* unites these two requirements. This makes experience *sustainable*, and this provokes a *displacement of the centre of reference*, thanks to which the spirit can gradually establish itself in the progressive levels of consciousness.

By avoiding the descents and progressively ascending, the spirit acquires *another perspective* from which this game of self-knowledge gradually lags behind and loses importance. It finally knows him so well that what earlier seemed subtle now seems obvious; the traps of the ego have been discovered; this whole game is represented to him as to the adult the pitfalls of adolescence; *another consciousness* begins to awaken. Disinterest in things, in particular for personal possessions is now *natural,* not only because he is accustomed to living in a detached manner, but because the concrete world in a sense has lost its reality; *his ontological vision of the World is not the same*. The instability and transitory nature of all life, as well as the vanity of man within this temporal context, his useless preoccupations, his unfounded fears, his invented desires become patent now. Only the beautiful is attractive from the world of forms, the virtuous acts from the human world; he is getting closer to the essences. He begins to perceive a reality without form. *The spiritual becomes real.*

This last step is of decisive importance. Firstly, because he realises that he can *understand* at a vital level, and *experience* what is unintelligible (and formless) to the speculative faculties. Secondly, the *unifying forces* appear as an unquestionable fact. It is the permanence of the spirit at a high level of consciousness that allows him to perceive in a constant and insistent manner the subtle manifestations of the Spirit that are the generators of spiritual reality. This independence with respect to speculative faculties, which sustained his ego by the mere habit of being referred to it, as well as the conscious and direct perception of the unifying manifestations, independent of his "self", leads him to become aware of his unitive faculties and a *change of perspective*. When this takes place he is well established in his *unitive conscience.*

It is not only the complete knowledge of oneself that makes this *true consciousness*, but the encounter with moral conscience, and the discovery that this is not limited to our personal sphere, but extends to all that is created; this, *ipso facto* generates a *universal moral responsibility*. The knowledge of oneself, does not end then with the individual, it opens the doors to the transcendent, thanks to which man begins to know himself as a *universal being*. He understands the said universal moral responsibility from the perception of the *moral Order* that is a *primary manifestation of the Essence or universal Spirit.*

This Order is the same that we had intuited from the intellectual plane, except that, perceived by the moral conscience; it is translated into an ethical order. It is the conscious or unconscious perception of this that motivates the human being to act morally. It is the application in his micro-cosmos. Whoever has had this apperception is compelled by the same Order that he contemplates to transmit it to his fellow man, so that *everyone participates in the universal Order.*

Notes

(1) See C.G. Jung's *Psychological Types*

CHAPTER THIRTEEN

The Religious Path

"L'amor che move il sole e l'altre stelle" Dante A.: *Paradiso.*
C. XXXIII

For this journey we have to use the *path of religious conscience*, the precious link that unites the unitive and unified consciences. This does not mean that we have to bring into the picture recognised sacred texts or religious *authorities* in order to *substantiate* this path; nothing of the sort. Psychosophy has personal experience not only as its objective but also as its *foundation*, and is, by definition, *non-dogmatic*, which means that the only *authority* is whoever has the said experience. In order to achieve this, it is indispensable to awaken the religious conscience, there is nothing more precise for this to exhaust all the potential of the unitive faculties. It is natural, then that we return to Love, the strength and unitive faculty *par excellence*.

Only a century ago, life without the element of love was utterly meaningless. Art and letters were inspired by this Muse. This did not happen only amongst the most select. The public in general listened to, read and adored works of art with emotion; forms, tastes, relationships, in short, culture was impregnated with love. One lived in this atmosphere. By the middle of the century, due to the reasons already cited, this atmosphere began to dissipate until it disappeared from the contemporary world. There is now no longer any spiritual weight, not a single mystery remains in the air, life and even death are explained by physical, economic or biological laws. It is as if spiritual reality does not exist, because our faculties to perceive it have atrophied. Only the concrete remains, and love is not concrete.

If we compare what is today described as a *loving relationship* with what it used to be, it hardly has the ingredient of love. It is common these days for relationships to be established under the regime of an *imposition of powers*, like state relations, a game of negotiations according to the means of pressure that each side has at its disposal: wealth, beauty, social position, etc., in short, a trade that adjusts to the laws of supply and demand. These games, it is true, have always existed, but I suspect never were they so *alien* to love as they are today. Love knew how to be the strongest bond on which relationships were established. Today it is no more than an ingredient which progressively tends to be dispensed with. The pragmatic "spirit" has triumphed. What is the objective of the amorous relationship? Mere sexual union and we approach it bluntly...and without feelings. In this way we close ourselves to the most external manifestations of the unitive faculties and we leave the spirit to descend to the most restricted and narrow places of our individuality. Thus we fail in the first opportunities that our spirit offers us to elevate it.

Sexual freedom, like all freedom, is fine in principle. But on exercising it we ought not to confuse the path that leads to *unconditional freedom* with the one that leads to selfishness.

Contemporary man does not seem to realise that when the spiritual, unifying element is taken away from the relationships of love, it is disconnected from the All and its transcendent function is eliminated; in this way it is profaned. Reducing the act of love to an exchange between two people, without any projection beyond them, makes the act a vehicle towards ignorance. On the other hand, if the couple seeks the experience of a freedom that transcends them in the act of love, the act is given a sacred function. It is this transcendent function which gives a religious characteristic to love.

This *transcendent function* has been interpreted and applied in different ways by religions which have seen the need to sanctify the act. The exaggerations and aberrations into which they might have fallen should not let us forget their origins and what they were destined for.

The act of love is a means, not a consummation of love. Obeying the instincts of the moment without being conscious of this unifying force is barbarism and the most radical kind of ignorance. Psychosophy, however, does not propose restrictions; it limits itself to providing knowledge in the conviction that this is the best antidote to avoid barbarism. Prohibiting young people from sexual activity is like stopping children from running. As soon as they are left free they will run until they are tired. The great tide of love should be allowed to flow so that it follows its natural course. After running children find more serene occupations and are more disposed to introspection. Adults will be even more so as they have already learnt the vanity of these games. A disastrous effect is produced in the psychic equilibrium and in the relationships themselves if they are prohibited or punished. There are many who, due to the effect of these prohibitions, have regressed in their spiritual path by not following the natural way. But this does not in any way justify the lack of choice, responsibility and feelings in the act of loving. Ignorance has found "elevated" reasons to justify this *universal irresponsibility,* which psychosophy explains as the *obliteration of the unitive faculties.*

Anyone who, on the contrary, has truly embodied a love will have experienced a kind of spiritual blooming, as if the spirit had left its habitual confines (the body) and had spread not only over the person who is loved but overall reality, covering it with a spiritual *ambience.* In this way what nothing was before becomes *something,* as if the substance of life begins to reveal itself; things are covered with *mystery.* Everything is transformed into a question, what he earlier looked at indifferently now seems to say something to him. The life which was evident to him as a mechanical reality is now revealed to be *a dream.* And here is a fact of the greatest relevance. During this blossoming he will have observed that he has been incapable of acting selfishly, of causing harm to animals or plants; as if his love had spread over all beings. In other words, love has made him see, think and act in a unified way. This has been possible because Love has previously united his spirit with his moral conscience, because it has transported him, and in the most pleasant way possible, to another level of consciousness.

Of course, when our passion is variable and relative, and the object of the same is only a particular subject, love manifests itself as a light mist that occasionally covers some sectors of our reality. It will all depend, as always, on the level that the spirit reaches in its flight. And this does not signify our passion. I would almost say on the contrary, because it tends to place the spirit on the plane of emotions and even direct it downwards. It will depend on other means or supports.

One has to *give of oneself* in order to overcome the individual conscience and the plane of the sentiments. We have already verified this when we walked on this plane. We saw then that true love implies an attitude of submission and as this means, to the extent that it becomes effective, the suppression of the ego, love enters the field of morality.

In another essay I have also recommended the vehicle of Venus as an effective means to transport the human spirit to the divine kingdom. I would like now, however, to change the focus of this question in order to throw more light on it. I will then say that Love does not take us, strictly speaking, anywhere but rather (note this epistemological virtue) *concentrates us in the present*. He who has had the *grace* to love will be able to confirm it. Under its spell the presence of the loved one is enough to fulfil the *present* reality of the lover. Projects (future) and memories (past) are perceived then as distractions (alienations) and calculation as offensive and unpleasant (immoral). Love that is well experienced, it can be said in conclusion, transports us to the *unitive conscience* and tends to *centre us* in it. The treasure of Love is thus hidden in the present, but it provides us with the means to discover it.

The amorous relationship when inspired by Love, then, is a way to come out of ourselves and a door towards the *transcendent*. But as was expressed when we ended our journey on the animated plane, personal love, as sentiments in general seem to be in man, is unstable, impermanent, and the spirit needs *moral support* to overcome this plane and establish itself in the unitive conscience from which it will have a solid platform from which to soar to other heights. For this a wider and higher objective than that of an individual being is needed, and the first step towards this is to open one's heart to one's fellow men. For how can one open oneself up to the Being who encompasses all, which is the ultimate objective, if one has remained closed to others?

For psychosophy, love for others and for all living beings is therefore the means and condition for expanding the soul towards totality. It will be clear that this process does not consist in increasing the number of objectives on which the possessions of the ego extend, but, on the contrary, in *disintegrating* it with all its identifications, as the spirit is *integrating* itself in the World. Love, once more, is not an *accumulative* but a *unitive* knowledge; it is not a means of accumulation but of liberation.

If the human spirit, thanks to this healthy practice of loving others, has been able to overcome its egocentric radius and if it applies this noble sentiment in Divinity, that is, if it transforms human sentiment into religious sentiment, it will have created the sentimental conditions to access the *transcendent*.

Although religions in general do not express it in this way, within a psychological context, they all use these means to achieve the same end. They all preach, in effect, with relative degrees of emphasis, love thy neighbour (although in practice this principle has undergone inconceivable variations), and for all of them, whether or not they dictate it as a commandment, the ultimate unequivocal objective of the sentiments is "To love God above all things". So, this matter that is Love would not be a universal reality if it were only the legacy of our culture.

That Jesus believed that this was the most effective means to bring man closer to the divine kingdom is manifest, to the point that Christ has become the very representation (if not the incarnation) of Love, and thus an intermediary between man and God. For Plato, with whom I firmly agree on this point, human love was a preparation, a school to arrive at an understanding of Love itself. This was not an end in itself but a means to the Good, which he identified with Divinity, since the latter is not in direct contact with humans, but uses intermediaries among which Love is considered to be the most effective. This intermediary was not represented as a concrete being that came and went, but as a genius (*daimon*) who inspired human genius like a Muse, of virtues above all. Love was a generator of the virtues which establish the soul in the Good. "The object of love is the permanent possession of the good" (*Symposium* 206), that is, it tends to acquire virtue itself. The emphasis put by the father of our philosophy on this moral aspect has not been sufficiently emphasised; this is why I take up this opportunity to insist upon it. Hundreds of thinkers, in effect, have made the most daring interpretations of Plato's metaphysics without having paid greater attention to the moral *practice*, implicit in it as a *condition* for its understanding. This should be attributed to the fact that man is always ready to admit some defects, but rarely will admit that he is steeped in ignorance because of a lack of virtues. At other times our philosopher gives Love an even greater dimension, presenting it as a "great and admirable God who extends his power in the human as well as divine order" (*Symposium 186*), "so that the All is bound to itself" (*Symposium 203*).

Love and devotion, feelings and submission, the two complementary aspects for a correct religious feeling, constitute the most widespread path of liberation in India: *Bhakti Yoga.* This sentiment is first turned over to the *Guru,* the human environment and then to Isvara, the personal God in this tradition. It is not sufficient, as so many believe, only to adore Him. The teacher is there to respond to the specific requirements of the aspirant. If the latter takes the former as an end he will remain in ignorance. If the teacher presents himself as an end, he will be using the ignorance of the disciple to bloat his ego. As this path is the one that requires the least intellectual potential, it is the one that most lends itself to fundamentalism and is the one most used as an instrument of power, but the sickness of the spirit does not justify the negation of spiritual *life,* as the fundamentalist devotees of materialism claim.

But in giving explanations we have been lowering our sights. We should start our ascent again in which we caught a glimpse of Love *itself.* One last explanation to set the spirit free on its flight: In keeping with all that has been said it is not surprising that psychosophy emphasises this sentiment, but it has not drawn its knowledge from the cited doctrines, but from the same and eternal Source that has inspired man since he has been such and will continue to be so as long as there are sentient beings([1]). Nor, as has been expressed, does our discipline search for external support to sustain itself. These brief antecedents have been given so one can reflect on what has been the true function and dimension of Love in comparison with the sad use that is made of this "great and admirable god" in present times.

If the human spirit, already detached from its devotion to its ego, free in its soaring flight, allows itself to be carried away by unifying currents that become manifest at these heights, and if attracted to the love of Divinity, it will penetrate with this magnificent vehicle in Unity itself, thus accessing the experience of *Love itself,* the primary manifestation of the Spirit as revealed to sentiments. The *presence* of the loved Being will be then *sufficient,* as it encompasses *everything.* There will no longer be a lover and a loved one but only one Being; Love will have reached its consummation; the carriage of Venus will have stopped, as when it reaches its destination it becomes immutable. He who has passed through this kingdom will not need any effort to love his neighbour, as Love is (and has been so always, he will have understood) already spread over all beings.

Notes

(1) For a better understanding of this affirmation see: *The Return to the Sources.* (Ebook)

CHAPTER FOURTEEN

Some Necessary Foundations

It is feasible that no other vehicle has led more spirits to transcendence than Love has. The opening of the soul that this generates, together with the moral adjustment that a sincere devotion to the Sacred implies, can only bring forth felicitous results. However, this sentiment, even if it is conjoined with this attitude, is not enough for an unconditional liberation. It is common, in fact, amongst mystics who have only used this means that their religious experience be inconstant and that their *mystical union* be no more than a passing rapture. It is really a pity that after having soared "so high", one descends so low that the spirit is again submerged in a world of suffering, and that the sentiments make unfortunate the one who a few moments earlier was *imbued with grace* and is now forced to lament: *"What kind of death would there be that is equal / to my pitiful life, / as the more I live the more I die"* San Juan de la Cruz – *Poems*

In order to avoid this *fall,* psychosophy considers the following *foundations* as necessary: 1) *An intelligence* of the unitive experience that accompanies the elevated sentiment. 2) A transcendental philosophy or doctrine born of the experience of Unity and developed through that *constant* experience.([1]) 3) A correct and integral knowledge of psychic mechanisms and levels of consciousness. Without these *foundations* that allow for a clear perception of the unitive experience, the spirit may know that it has greatly transcended its habitual perspective, but it will barely be able to *establish* itself in this new perspective. This, in effect, will be too strange and unintelligible for it to be incorporated in its consciousness, and it will return, possibly also driven by fear of the *unknown,* to its habitual vision, thus re-establishing a subject-object relationship with Divinity, which is a *religious dualism.*

Whoever has achieved the experience of Divinity through Love and has lost it for lack of the foundation of correct understanding, *will desire* to return to that state. But in this desire, although he might have more knowledge than the common mortal, he expresses ignorance, as the desire implies a "self"; although in this attitude there is no selfishness. A correct understanding will be the advice to first get rid of this desire. This paradox fortunately has an explanation: All desire is projected onto the future, *Reality being the present*. It will be understood, however, that we are referring to a last adjustment in order to transcend time. Otherwise, man lives in time and the best he can do within it is to desire the knowledge of his own Nature, and thus achieve his liberation. By desiring it he generates the means towards this end. He generates the means, however, not the end; for the latter a direct unitive understanding is required.

The different paths that we have covered towards *the transcendent* are naturally means of liberation, but not one of them can make this aspiration effective if it excludes the others. This is so for the simple reason that in order to *integrate oneself* in the All a harmonious interrelation of *all* the faculties is needed. This *simple reason* has not been observed by many who could have had the necessary potential to achieve the said integration, not only due to the obvious difficulties that this implies, but because it is natural in man that he uses the faculties with which he has been gifted and ignore those that are alien to him. It is also common that a certain aversion is developed (not in him, but in third parties in which the said alienation is projected) for those who use the faculties that he represses. The intellectual and the devotee rarely reach an agreement, because the *agreement* has to be established for each one of the parties in *their own manner*. The fact that our contemporary culture has demonstrably repudiated sentiments can be attributed to the dominance of intellectuals in this field. Of the numerous identifications of the ego this is one of the most difficult to overcome, because despite having the sincerest will to eliminate the ego, few see the need to transcend the faculties with which it identifies. Besides, it is common that these same faculties are used to combat it, thus creating a vicious circle. It would be better to make use of the other faculties that *understand* in another way and that facilitate, for the same reason, another vision of the self.

All *primary manifestations* imply or, rather, are themselves an Order. Be it intellectual, moral or sentimental, they respond to a single

Order which is interpreted in different ways by the different faculties. It can be inferred without difficulty that in order to completely *understand* this Order these faculties will have to be fused. Any partial or relative understanding cannot, logically, make us understand the All. In a single sentence, in order to understand Unity at all levels and become One with it one has to *unify the consciousness*. Only then can we speak of liberation. This will depend on knowledge, but this will not be a "knowledge of" but an awareness. Knowledge and consciousness must become One. For this reason, psychosophy emphatically recommends keeping the spirit centred on the vital plane so that it *integrates the faculties and understanding until their total unification*.

The semi-conscious or unconscious perception of *primary manifestations*, that is, of the principles of the cosmic Order, the moral Order and Love, which affect the three central planes and, as a result, the other two planes, namely, all the planes of human understanding, are in general interpreted as a product of a universal Person or a personal God. This *representation* greatly facilitates its understanding at all levels and in all faculties, in particular discernment that can thus make an *image* of Divinity. These same manifestations have been attributed in the polytheistic religions in general to a principal God or gods in charge of Creation and destruction and of establishing justice, into which the devotee invests the sentiment of devotion; although this is also invested in minor gods who are in charge of other functions that respond to the numerous manifestations derived from the primary ones.

And yet both polytheism and monotheism which accept a God or personal gods are products of human representations, of *anthropomorphisms.* By this I do not mean that they are *entirely* human creations, far from it, these representations correspond to realities and primary manifestations. Neither do I want to say that these representations are a product of ignorance, as ignorant is the one who does not perceive these manifestations, not the one who represents them inaccurately. Since to be beyond the forms one has to achieve a state of *supra consciousness,* the most reasonable thing then would be to represent these manifestations in the most comprehensible manner possible. Being blind is very different from having a small optical error; however, the error has to be rectified. These anthropomorphic interpretations do not correspond to Reality as it is, in two fundamental aspects: one, that the First principle is not a Person but the Essence that escapes all faculties that have *composed* that deity. The other, that this would be the *representation of the manifestations* of the Essence or First principle. These are the two errors that have generated *religious dualism*.

Official Christianity has not hesitated, in the name of the supposed monotheistic–dualist "Truth", in condemning the polytheist doctrines and whenever possible in castigating with the greatest violence the followers of these supposedly *false* religions, being that, as we have seen, it falls into the same fundamental errors. We will not stop here to consider violence, it has already been said that for psychosophy violence wherever it exists, though it might emanate from the highest prelates or saints, is a product of ignorance, and ignorance in every sense; of oneself, of others, of the Order and of the very objective of religion. What is interesting to highlight here is the following: What is *decisive in understanding religious reality is not the difference between monotheism and polytheism but between monism and dualism*.

The optical error of Christianity is not, as has been expressed, very serious. Another thing, though, is the imposition of a dogma that maintains a relative truth as the ultimate truth, while denying knowledge of the true Absolute, monism, which it has condemned as a heresy, thus impeding, for two thousand years, the maximum religious experience to the aspirant. This, indeed, is very serious. Obviously, when speaking of the *imposition of dogmas* I am not speaking of the original Christianity that had very little dogmatism, but of the *official* Christianity established later by the Catholic and Protestant churches. I am excluding, however, the orthodox church whose attitude and vision are quite different.([2])

It should not be surprising that many Westerners whose idea of Divinity was not in keeping with the traditional *forms,* rejecting the dogmatic impositions, have broadened their horizons by shifting their gaze to the Far East. Buddhism like Vedanta in their most orthodox and elevated versions are *monist,* that is, for them the first Principle is not a Person but an Essence common to matter and spirit, which transcends all intellectual interpretations. Far from negating the experience of the Essence, the very objective of these doctrines is to achieve it. Besides, it is not a coincidence that these religions have not condemned the belief in a personal God or in polytheism; rather they have admitted them into their fold quite naturally, for all those of *lesser understanding*. Only he who knows the Absolute can recognise the levels of the relative.

This example of tolerance could be very useful to the West where the ultimate (relative) "truth", be it in the field of the sciences, pseudo-sciences and even, at times, science fiction, is held with as much dogmatism as vehemence, as if it were the final and inalterable absolute truth.

If I recommend the opposite of what is common, especially in our culture, in matters of religion, it should not be believed that there is only one *truth* and that all the others are *false*, as the truth, I must insist, is the *experience of each individual*, not the exclusive *belief* in a supposed truth that escapes our knowledge. Each one sees according to his level of consciousness. To pretend to see more than one sees is to show more ignorance than the average. There are no objective truths here in which everyone should believe according to their subjectivity, rather unitive truths, of which no one in their heart of hearts should doubt.

Although a monist doctrine may also be an intellectual foundation, this foundation by itself (if it is only intellectual) would be very insufficient in maintaining the unified spirit, if it can do so it is because this foundation rests on Reality itself. In other words, the doctrine will have used the intellect to express a *real experience,* and he who uses it will do so to better understand his own experience and the circumstances that present to him (not easy to order with our usual faculties). This much should be clear: monist doctrine if it is only a theory, that is, if it has been born of the intellect (which is not the case of the doctrines cited), lacks basis or will only have it as a scientific doctrine, that is, when personal experience becomes effective. In brief, he who is liberated does not lean on a theory but on Reality.

Notes

(1) The interested reader does not only have to depend on psychosophy, he can refer to the *monist* doctrines of Buddhism and Vedanta.

(2) On this theme I will be concise here, for a more detailed explanation of the same as well as with regard to monism and dualism, I refer the reader to *The Search for Universal Consciousness.* (Motilal Banarsidass Publishers, Delhi).

CHAPTER FIFTEEN

The Essential Perspective

Having affirmed these foundations, I must proceed on the premise that the aspirant is firmly settled in the unitive conscience and that the primary manifestations are now evident to him and that he is only waiting to make the last leap towards the Transcendent. For the *unitive conscience*, even with all the virtues that it encapsulates and the great distance that separates it from the individual conscience is not the last stage of the spirit if what it seeks is its unconditional liberation. This last stage should not be imagined like another step one has to climb because, to be precise, the spirit will have nothing to hold onto ahead. It will have to make the last leap into the Void, if we use a Buddhist expression, which means a reality different from the idea of a personal God or a discernible being. If it finds a grip it is because it has fallen in the same place, because where it has to fall is not in the primary manifestations, still apprehensible thanks to the unitive faculties, but in the Essence itself.

If before we tried to establish the spirit in a *unitive conscience* from which it could, through partial unifying experiences, reach the *primary manifestations*, the objective now is to establish it in a *unified conscience* through a *total vital experience*, so that it does not now perceive the said manifestations from the *outside*, I would say, but from what is *manifesting*. It is from this perspective, that I have denominated as *essential,* that the unifying energies take on their full meaning and acquire their full dimension, because they do not reveal the Essence but are their own expressions and are seen *from* it. They will be thus the *vital experiences from* this Reality that have to update the *unified conscience*.

No other knowledge can give us the *certissima scientia et clamante conscientia* that the *total unified experiences brings to us.* This is so because the *vital experience* provides us with both intellectual and emotional certitude, the truth of reason and of the heart in a single experience. This knowledge is irreducible to a scientific method that allows us an objective experience, due to the very nature of the phenomenon. This phenomenon is different because the forms of time and space are not applicable to it. For this reason, Kant had distinguished it with the name of *noumenon*. For the *noumenon*, psychosophy has found the unitive method, which is what we have been applying. The accumulative objective method, by virtue of being so, that is, for not involving the subject with its sentiments, with what to him is most intimate and loved, cannot awaken in him the *clamante conscientia,* nor urge him to an intrinsic transformation. We all know (or feel) that we might be able to accumulate objective knowledge or not, that it is always *alien* to us, despite all the interest that we might show in it, that our lives are not in play, that it does not put our being at stake. (For this reason, no one would be willing to give their life to uphold the heliocentric theory, as history demonstrates, or the truth of the rule of three).

A clarification is necessary here. It is undeniable that the emotions are an impediment at the time of knowing. No philosophers have failed to notice this and religious fanaticism is palpable proof of the inherent danger. The key to understanding this apparent contradiction is found in the distinction between individual and *unitive conscience*. In effect, while the sentiments are within the field of the former, they depend on an egocentric vision where the fears, desires and interferences of the internal plane are "natural", they will inevitably generate obstacles, but when the unity of consciousness is found in the *unitive conscience*, sentiments no longer depend on the self. They then obey altruistic interests, they tend towards the integration of the subject with the World, and they are in Order. These are the elevated sentiments that contribute to *unitive knowledge*.

In order not to err and seem hypocritical to the reader I would like to advise that we will enter into a consciousness or Reality which would require another language to be expressed, as language is created by and for discernment and to express a relative reality. External conscience cannot *represent* the content of a *unitive conscience* for the simple reason that the *unifying element* in this lacks form and we are not here "facing" the World but being One with it. To speak then a rational language with symbols that only correspond to the concrete and plural world of geometric forms or any other rational medium that I am obliged to use, is to falsify Reality, it is to make the Absolute relative, and it is also to *profane* it to the extent that the reasons extinguish the *religious sentiment* or disfigure the direct understanding of Divinity. Psychosophy does not pretend to prove anything with reasons, it only uses these as a provisional tool, the way in which it uses suggestions and metaphors as it has been obliged to do when speaking of Love and other primary manifestations. In short, the reader should be conscious of the limitations of language; an insufficiency that he can remedy by interpreting it with his unifying faculties. Otherwise, he will encounter inexplicable paradoxes. If these appear it will be because he is using an inadequate tool.

Reality is made up of both matter and Spirit (yet this is not accurate, because it is One and is not *composed;* it is the external conscience that has *decomposed*, in order to later *compose* it in its own manner; first paradox), and language is made to express concrete reality; since what is spiritual lacks form, it escapes discernment. All the sciences, thus, seeing only one side of Reality, the physical side, and this is the case with our sciences, especially the natural sciences, *denaturalise* it. As a result he who tries to express the meta-physical in the *form* of language will detract from it in some way. All metaphysics, all cosmology (that includes the spiritual side), all attempts to express the Absolute (inconceivable without including the spirit) by transcending the world of forms, will have to be *metaphorical* to some extent and will want to take us beyond our habitual understanding. This means that it will not correspond exactly to Reality on the one hand nor to discernment on the other; but not due to its being illusory, since it will express Reality in a greater or lesser measure. In order to determine what this measure is, the interested party has no other means besides his level of consciousness. Whether he believes or not, this adds nothing to his knowledge; it will only help him to adopt a posture. Man is faced with spiritual reality, as with sensible reality, face to face with a fact that he cannot avoid and has to ultimately resolve for himself. He can use religions and philosophies but he should not rely on them to the point of confusing them with realities and think that spiritual reality is reduced to a set of concepts or beliefs. He must use his own knowledge and criteria, but he will only achieve this by developing his *unitive faculties*, the only ones capable of comprehending spiritual reality; hence the insistence of psychosophy, dispensing with beliefs and of awakening the said faculties. In other words, our discipline does not ask that its vision of Reality be believed but that it be *verified.*

When speaking of unifying *energies*, the external conscience, which does not perceive them, already conditioned by its mechanical vision of the world and by the dualist and objective way of thinking, establishes (mechanically) some assumptions to which the *idea* that has made up of the said energies must adapt: that there must be a subject and an object, as well as a cause and an effect, etc. It is not surprising then that when Creation is conceived it represents a subject, God, who is the cause, and an object, the World, which is the effect. With this type of vision and mentality it is not possible to understand how the unifying energies function, much less have a vital experience of Unity, an indispensable first step prior to transcendence. As this is the ultimate objective of psychosophy, it will be understood that it warns of the limitations of this linear and relative way of representing reality. As without negating its utility for the knowledge of tangible reality, it maintains man within the limits of that reality as well as in his individual perspective, namely, in his *essential ignorance.*

I think that after all these warnings we can return to the spirit, where we left it in its soaring flight on the wings of Love. We find it as *free of desires as of fears, with the conscience calm and transparent like a high mountain lake without any kind of moral turmoil* or remorse to stir and muddy the depths of its soul, in conclusion, with a *similar* consciousness and ready to assimilate to the Reality that it contemplates.

But what is this? Perhaps the concrete world that is before its eyes? Decidedly not, because it is not with senses that it is perceived. Neither is it proved that Reality depends on things but, on the contrary, (it comes to mind for the first time) things are not real by themselves, they need *that* which transcends them and that at the same time penetrates them *in order to be*. But the spirit when it formulates these questions warns that it is trying to intellectually resolve this Unity that it contemplates, that is, that is establishing a duality, transforming this immutable Reality into a mutable Reality by wanting to resolve it in this manner. On understanding that it still has a desire, that of knowledge, it leaves it aside to only contemplate. Then it pauses and changes like the Reality itself that it contemplates and on doing so becomes One with it. But by remaining in this state it realises that it transcends all that it contemplates, that it does not depend on things, but that *it is that* on which things depend in order to *be*; it is then that it knows itself to be liberated.

It understands now that instead of having come nearer to Reality by accumulating knowledge from an erroneous perspective, it has been creating a wall as great as the Universe imagined, that *alienated* it from the Being. It understands that as an individual it could not have ever united with the world, and that all that it had to do for this was to abandon that perspective, and that it had nothing to unite except itself, as the Essence of the world, it verifies, had always had All unified. It also understands that all the efforts to unify and order the World through accumulative knowledge were motivated by the innate desire to unify, to Be–One–with–Reality.

It experiences that the Essence of the World is the Sacred itself, which it had not completely understood earlier because, despite knowing it was just Spirit, it could not have stopped thinking about it, always imagining it in some form. It understands that the Sacred cannot be contemplated, it is only possible to contemplate it from Its perspective, that is, to experience it as a Consciousness. What is then the situation of the liberated spirit? Has the human being stopped being an individual? He has not stopped being an individual but no longer sees from its perspective and neither from that of a human being, rather it has achieved plenitude as such. Is it then a duality? It depends from where one looks. From the perspective of the Essence he is One. From the unitive perspective he experiences two realities, one immutable and the other mutable, as if the Sacred had two Natures, which are also its own. The liberated spirit is then a Spectator of the World which it observes from (his) Central Consciousness.

CHAPTER SIXTEEN

The Cycle of Life

When the *external conscience* imagines the totality of a process, it represents a line that goes from α (alpha) to Ω (omega), from a beginning to an end. The experience of a totality however does not take place when α reaches Ω (although in the terminology that I have used, for the reasons given, I have so implied), but when α and Ω become One. The representation of this process would be circular, cyclical. But when the circle closes the particular spirit disappears and only the Spirit remains, the all-encompassing circle, the Absolute. Together with the individual spirit its perspective disappears and only that of the Essence remains, the essential perspective.

The Sacred (or whatever one wishes to call it now that its identity has been in some way exposed) has not *created* a concrete reality in a particular space at a given time within a linear time out of nothing. If that were so, as Heidegger correctly observed, God would have *depended on nothing* for his Creation. It is not a subject or Person that he created, but the Creative that creates in Himself, in his bosom, permanently. The Biblical version of Creation, as well as the "scientific" theory of the *Big Bang,* are born of a linear and relative vision of the World that does not explain the space-time reality that existed *before* Creation. The Creative, for its part is Eternal; but this Eternal should not be understood to be from a presumed principle, even one supposed to be unattainable, to another presumed end, from α (Alpha) to Ω (Omega), but rather it is the Eternal present (this is entirely beyond discernment and partially escapes my means of expression). The Eternal can only be understood if the two Natures of the Creative are *vitally experienced*; the space-time is only one, and flows from the Eternal present. *The Creative is the immutable Eternal, what is created is eternally renewed; this totality is what I call Reality*. The whole process, it can be said, is cyclical but the cycle begins and ends here in the present.

Nietzsche's cyclical vision is an approximation, an attempt that does not reach Reality and thus cannot be sustained. This philosopher intuits a reality to which time must submit, but which cannot overcome time; he wants to eternalise the present, but he makes this eternity depend on the future. For him the same forms and circumstances of the present will be repeated at some future moment. This theory of the *eternal return* has in its favour an entire eternity in which, apparently, anything can happen. But in order to become a reality it would be necessary for each of the individuals of the thousands of existing species to repeat this precise present (and all those present must suffer the same fate), with the same circumstances and accidents at a future moment, for which it would be sufficient for one of them not to make this cosmological date for it to have to wait a whole series of cycles, until all, *everyone,* could attend. This cannot be accepted by reason, and reason exists for something, after all.

We need not rack our brains like this thinker trying to explain the All. It is not humans who will unite the All. It is not his faculties that have to actualise Unity, but the unifying Essence. What we have to do to unify All is to change our consciousness, as Consciousness already has All unified.

It is the unifying virtue of the Essence that *inspires* man to order and unify. This universal spiritual energy flows equally over all who it inspires and attracts to a greater or lesser extent, depending on the level of sensitivity for the unifying forces and self-knowledge of the individuals, but all, consciously or unconsciously receive it. Without it each one would live only *for oneself* and no coexistence would be possible, not to mention civilisation. Without it man becomes *denaturalised,* and applies his reason to the most aberrant ends and even to his own destruction.

When I refer to the *primary manifestations in themselves,* I do not mean that they are independent of our consciousness; but this should not lead one to think that they are a *subjective reality*, because while there is an individual conscience, capable of creating a subjective reality, there is no perception of these manifestations. They are, thus, objectively transcendent to an individual conscience but, once this is transcended, they are a *unitive reality*.

The same, and with more reason, can be said of Essence *in itself.* With more reason because while the *primary manifestations* can be perceived from a *unitive conscience* in which there is still a duality, the Essence is only perceived *in Itself* from a *unified conscience* in which all duality would be an *alienation* of the Consciousness of Essence; this is perceived from its *own perspective,* the essential, from its own Consciousness, the unified. Obviously, the Essence does not look at Itself objectively, *it knows itself to be pure consciousness,* the Spectator of the World.

The Essence contemplates itself, but it does not *think itself,* because it does not *want,* it does not desire, because this would alienate it, projecting it into the future when It is the *eternal present.* The Essence is never *alienated* from Itself, otherwise it would lose its Unity and perfection. Why this is so, I do not know, my experience and knowledge reach only this far, as does, I am very much afraid, all human knowledge; I limit myself here to verifying these realities of the *unified conscience.* I am trying to be as sincere and faithful as I can. I know well that by being so I expose myself to the reasons of those who only know of reasons and nothing of this Reality, but I am not speaking for those who want to continue living in a reality of abstractions, but for those who want to better understand the Reality in which the human being lives. He who knows accommodates reasons to Reality; he who does not, accommodates what he imagines of Reality to his reasons. One thing is the Absolute and another is the why of the Absolute. I do not know the latter but I can infer that if a "why" existed, the Absolute would stop being so. Things are in It and It is in things; but without ceasing to be immutable. It is, thus, only the Essence of things but not their substance. Just as the individual Spirit preserves its independence and liberty amidst the contents of its consciousness, the Spirit preserves these in the World.

Being immutable it is practically (reasonably) impossible to establish a continued relationship between the Essence and things; but certainly before reaching them, there are subtle energies that are perceptible to the unified spirit. These emanate from the Essence, but are now a part of the mutable world. These *essential energies* are cyclical, they are born from and return to the Essence, it is they who push and attract the spirit towards its Essence; it is they that are the forces of Life of all beings; it is they who *generate the will to live.* Both the wise man and the ignoramus feed on them; but whereas the former identifies himself with Life, by making them conscious, adding his will to that of all beings, the latter only knows and worries about his own individual life. While the wise man wants to incorporate his fellow being into the Order, the ignoramus tries to make them adapt to his individual order.

Are these essential energies the same as the *unitive energies*? They are part of the same cycle of Life. When they are generators of life, as *generating energies*, they tend towards diversification and plurality. In this sense they seem opposite to the *unifying energies* that tend towards unification, but they are not so as they act simultaneously. As Life takes root, the unifying forces are sown; they are like fruit from the same tree. Both energies are thus part of the same process and interdependent. The unifying force par excellence, Love, attracts the pairs that will couple and generate descendants who will be joined by these bonds or by subtle energies like offspring to their parents. It could be said that one can only talk of the sentiment of love among higher mammals, that the other species are moved only by pure sexual instincts. I, who have lived almost all my life contemplating nature, do not believe it to be so. The care birds take for their offspring shows something more than pure instinct. But I am allowing myself to be carried away by other people's ideas, because to my mind understanding, *instinct* is a concept that only proves a fact and not the reason behind it, that is, that does not *explain* anything, is precisely generated by these energies, the generators and the unitives. If love and sex are difficult to separate in the same human being, they will be more so in other species; but, as we have seen, there are different degrees of love, the more elevated or spiritual they are, the more they evidence their unitive aspect.

The generative forces create life. What is created does not need thanatic forces, which incline towards death, to be extinguished. Their animal nature alone exhausts itself; the body returns to the elements, the spirits return to their Element: the Essence. The thanatic forces exist when the unifying forces are ignored. They come as diseases in the body, due to a lack of (spiritual) defences and like them generate destruction. Far from being opposed these essential forces maintain their equilibrium, and *it is this equilibrium of forces that makes life possible*.

The Essence of the World is, thus, a generative and a final cause. The first is projected and expands in plurality; the second causes it to be reabsorbed in Unity. The World is born as spirit, as a generating spiritual energy that is individualised and concretised. Once the individual is formed, he tends - in keeping with his potential and possibilities, including his circumstances - towards perfection, because he is attracted to and inspired by the Perfect, his Essence. When a certain grade of evolution is reached he begins to make these forces conscious and his process of spiritualisation begins, which is nothing if not the process of unification. Once a certain degree of perfection or maturity is reached, he is spiritualised, to the point of making the unifying forces fully conscious, thus discovering his Destiny, which is his Origin.

CHAPTER SEVENTEEN

The Unitive and Unified Consciences

When the conscience is *unified* a change of perspective takes place thanks to which the spirit *looks* from (its) Essence, for this reason I have called it *essential perspective.* It is this which produces a radical transformation in man. Thanks to this, *he knows himself to be liberated*, because he no longer experiences himself only as a man but as a total Being, as a universal Spirit. This change is produced not only in man but in the World, since all things, like man, lose their supposed individual being and are *integrated* in Unity, recovering their true Being. In this way the universal Spirit takes on an *ontological priority* over the tangible world which it *fills* with its *presence,* manifested not only in things but above all in the space that surrounds them, the Void itself. This apperception of the Spirit in itself and from Itself is the *transcendental aesthetic experience* of the unified spirit. The true transcendence of tangible reality does not lead to *nothing*, but to Being Itself. *Nothing* is not a reality but a concept that depends as much on things, in reference to which are thought of, as the individual perspective. From an essential perspective *nothing* disappears, while the Spirit covers the empty space and all beings, thus unifying the All. Thanks to this perspective, it becomes conscious of the *unifying virtue of the Essence*, the primary manifestation of Unity, as well as that of the other primary manifestations, as the unifying *virtue* is the *Fount of Virtue itself* which *embodies* the Order in All.

Once it knows its Essence, the spirit feels completely satisfied, it realises that what it earlier thought were needs were created by its identification with the body. Its real need, from then on, will be to return to its *centre* for tranquillity and contemplation. As the Sacred is tranquillity, the human spirit must become tranquil; as the former is silence, the latter should be silent. He who prejudges this tranquillity or silence as a numbness of the soul would be mistaken, as it is quite the opposite; it is an intense state of alertness, of pure consciousness.

All attempts to say something about Pure Consciousness would be in vain as it is the Absolute itself, which no words can describe. When consciousness penetrates it, it finds Itself. This is the Essence in itself, the limit of All, of the limitless. When this Pure Consciousness opens up to the World it manifests and experiences its own virtues. The first one that it evidences is its power of unifying Reality. This apperception generates the *unified conscience*. There are no Forms or primary manifestations here, the spirit comes *before* them. Neither is there time, there is only the *presence* of the Eternal in things. Neither is there the flow of the mind with tangible reality. The Mind is detained and silent, and is absorbed by the Immutable.

Naturally, the human spirit cannot remain indefinitely in this *state of absolute contemplation*, it must take care of the needs of the body, attend to its survival. The body will remind it of its individuality. Faced with this situation, if it has not clearly experienced its true Nature, if it is not firmly established in its *essential perspective* it will tend to return to its *individual perspective,* thus establishing a marked dualism between the two realities, and from its *unitive experience* there will only remain the memory and through this it will try to recover it. But if it is well established, if it has seen with clarity and has recognised Itself (in the manner that I have described earlier) the spirit will not lose its essential perspective but will apply this to the world in flux, it will integrate itself in the world with the light of its Essence; thanks to this, it will not exclusively identify with its individuality.

This intermediate and *balanced* state between the *unified* and the individual *conscience* is the home of the *unitive conscience*. This forms itself, thus, as a point of balance between the extremes, and this means that in order to achieve this *natural establishment*, the spirit must know (experience) the *unified conscience*, and should have acquired in it the *essential perspective*. As we saw earlier, after having achieved the *unitive conscience*, in its ascending path the spirit has access to the *primary manifestations*, thanks to which man can act correctly and express himself as an *integrated being in the World*. But while he retains his individual perspective in some measure, as small as this might be, he will not know what Liberation is; this only occurs when there is a total transformation in man, it is only possible thanks to the change in perspective.

In the *unitive conscience* the spirit finds the right measure of the whole, complete man, between the Sacred and individuality, between a state of absolute absorption in the former and a state of alienation in the latter. But it should not be forgotten that the *unitive conscience* consolidates itself thanks to a higher *unity of consciousness* and maintains itself by virtue of the perspective gained in it. By maintaining this, the spirit moves without difficulty between two higher consciousness's, so we can speak in general of a Central Consciousness. This is the true home of the human spirit, the *genuine consciousness of man*.

On affirming this, psychosophy declares man's current consciousness to be false and his external, egocentric and individual perspective to be erroneous. This in no way implies that it denies this life in the name of another, neither one extreme nor the other. When referring to the *human spirit's centre of equilibrium,* it means that thanks to it man finds his rightful position in the World, *integrating* the two realities, the material and spiritual, into a single Reality, the individual life in the universal Life, the temporal in the Eternal. For psychosophy, there is no individual psychic equilibrium, not even when one is well integrated into a given society. For it man's equilibrium is only possible in relation to the World, when he participates in the universal Order. For this discipline the individual life that we have to live is nothing more than the *great opportunity* to be integrated in Life and this integration is nothing less than *man's raison d'être*.

Immutable Totality is one with the *unified conscience*. The relationship between the Immutable and the mutable is the relationship between the unified and unitive consciences; they are two ways of being of one single Reality that correspond to two states or levels of consciousness of the same Mind.

From the perspective of discernment there is a tendency to believe that this mutable reality is as it is perceived. Nevertheless, when the spirit retains its essential perspective, what is mutable appears in two clearly differentiated moments. If he does not exceed his unitive conscience and remains centred in it, he will have neither interferences from his memory nor from his internal plane, and not even the usual ones from the external plane, the desires and projects that concern the future, that is, he will be indifferent to the past and the future. This will allow him to live in a *continuous present* in which there is no relative time, as an idea that goes from one moment to another, from one reference to another; although neither is there an absolute time as in the Absolute there is no time, only becoming, *natural time*.

When it abandons this contemplative state and exceeds this consciousness, the ideas of time and space appear and with them discernment and the multiple world, differentiated and impermanent. This state or seat of the spirit is the *mediate unifying conscience.* In this the spirit integrates the external plane as well as the memory which this uses, the accumulative, but *without being alienated from its essential perspective* that it *preserves at a vital level.* Admittedly, this is not easy because the spirit is accustomed to using discernment from its individual perspective, and thus it will tend to alienate itself in this. Only a well centred spirit that is knowledgeable of these displacements can remain *alert* using the external plane, *discerning without being exteriorised.*

To *adjust* the spirit to those levels, besides the indispensable reclusive life, the direction of an illustrious Maestro, will be required. As Mahayana Buddhism, in particular the Zen sect, has the definite objective of integrating the liberated spirit in *this life,*(1) a Maestro of this school will be surely appropriate for such an *adjustment*. One of them bluntly announces: "A true (Zen) monk should always remain the same (*centred*), whether in a monastery, on a battlefield or in a *brothel*". It will be inferred that to achieve this *integrity* one needs as much knowledge as training.(2)

We have covered the whole spectrum of the Mind in which the human spirit moves. First on its ascendant path, during which it follows a *process of unification*, then, once unified, a descending path following a *process of unitive individuation*, that is, fully aware of it. In doing so we have seen the *unitive conscience* from two perspectives: one individual, the other, essential. He who has achieved the *unitive conscience* might conserve in some way his individual perspective, but he will no longer be the same, because from this he has access to the primary manifestations, which allows him to participate in the Order and contribute to it. He is *conscious* of man's transcendental dimension and of his *universal responsibility*. For this reason, I have spoken of a *unitive perspective*. Many saints, heroes and notable men have shared this perspective which has been enough for them to achieve their greatness. Evidently it is not only this perspective that has done everything for them. The faculties that have allowed them to express themselves as philosophers, artists, etc., their will and moral integrity are no less worthy factors and these will have contributed to the said perspective. In any case, in order to awaken the *unitive conscience* exceptional talents are not required, any physically and mentally healthy person, with good faith, a lover of the truth, with good feelings and fine perception who applies himself to this, leading a mainly contemplative life, can achieve it.

This *unitive conscience* is that of the man integrated in himself and in the World. It is (or should be) the normal and natural state of the human being, thanks to which he keeps his feet firmly on the ground and his head high, he preserves his animal instinct while being aware of his spirit and its relationship with the universal Spirit. This consciousness should not be confused with the state or level which would more correctly be called *supra-consciousness*, for which it is necessary to transcend the human gaze and the world of multiplicities and reach the *essential perspective* and, thanks to this, the unified and the Transcendent.

It is to this last stage that psychosophy aspires to lead the human spirit, but, for whatever reasons, at least up until now, it has been reached by very few and it is likely to continue to be so. However, psychosophy would consider its purpose to have been attained if it could awaken in some men their correct conscience (the unitive), if it saw human beings who were *whole* and integrated in the world, manifesting the Spirit; in short, *unified men* in action.

Notes

(1) This is one of the greatest merits and, to my understanding, the most important contribution to the history of religions; a contribution that has not yet been sufficiently appreciated in the West because the beneficiaries in our culture have so far been very few.

(2) For more details on the *unitive mediate conscience*, see *The Return to the Sources.*

CHAPTER EIGHTEEN

Accumulative And Unitive Memories(1)

In the manner in which we have distinguished two kinds of knowledge, one unitive and the other accumulative, we also find two kinds of memories which the said knowledge uses, and which bear the same name.

The *accumulative memory*, which normally serves reason, stores information that has in some way been produced by reason, even if it consists of no more than simple comparisons or space-time references. Of course, abstractions and conceptualisations also belong there and make possible what we commonly call knowledge, as in the case of natural and exact sciences and technology.

The *unitive memory* registers two kinds of objectives that have, as will be seen, a common essential feature. On the one hand it stores global situations that are not filtered by reason but by feelings and unitive faculties. It recalls more the ambience of the situation than the individual components. On the other hand, it remembers in special detail objects or events that although individual, are a *complete reality* in themselves, a *totality*. This is not born of an abstraction but of *direct perception*. It is this that allows one to see details (that are generally ignored) with such clarity that they appear as evident. This memory is like a snapshot and stays registered as such similar to a photograph. Poets and artists (inherently talented, non-professional) have natural access to it and use it as material for their work. These however will not be as *aware* as a *unitive man* of the true sense and transcendence of these memory contents.

From the material registered by the *unitive memory* the internal plane (unconscious) extracts the most significant material, which it will elaborate in an irrational manner and represent symbolically in dreams. The unitive, *centred* spirit, being much more aware of these kinds of perceptions, will remember them more easily and the symbolism of the *internal plane* will be decidedly more comprehensible. Given the importance of the correct interpretation of the most significant dreams on the path to self-knowledge, the reader can, in some measure, infer the advantages derived from the correct position of the spirit.

The reader will have observed that the sense of smell, due to its ethereal constitution, has the particularity, in contrast to the other senses of perception, of not being clearly resolved by reason. This can differentiate notable concrete smells, but when dealing with subtle smells that accompany a set reality, discernment tends to give priority to the other senses, forgetting the sense of smell. However, they are still registered at the *vital level*. This also sometimes happens with indistinct sounds that apparently lack importance, but are very significant at an intimate level. Indiscernible smells and sounds can be the *unitive elements* that need a fixed reality in order *to be* something *revelatory*, thus giving the *ambience* without which, the components of that reality lack significance. This *meaning*, that *key*, is apprehended by another kind of understanding than the usual: the unitive.

Needless to say that the accumulative and *unitive memories* do not function independently but ceaselessly intertwine, but he who searches within himself, will do well to highlight in his reality the fundamental part played by the *unitive memories*.

The internal plane seems to be a confusing mass of memories, many of them ignored and forgotten by the external conscience, but which evidently has its intelligence, although rudimentary and primitive, even demonstrating a remarkable power of synthesis that resembles discernment. This and the fact that it complements this faculty reminding it, in its own way, of its oversights, shows their kinship as well as their interrelation; which makes one suppose that the external plane would be an offshoot from the internal. Like the noble Hamlet, the latter has an order in its madness; it cannot be simply equated to memory. It is used by the internal plane in a manner similar to the external. The great difference lies in the order that is used. The internal plane lacks the causes of the order of discernment; I am referring to the pure *a priori* intuitions of time and space and to the *a priori* concepts or categories that for Kant, as we saw, are those that make knowledge possible.

All of which leads me to infer that the external plane would have been born of the said intuitions, been separated then from the internal plane, and grown with the succession of concepts. Subsequently, through transcendental intuitions, conscious or unconscious, it would have extracted the rational order from Order, applying it to an individual perspective, in which it would have been progressively settling. Discernment would then be the offspring of time and space. The very conception of discernment would have been due to, as some psychologists like Fromm and Jung have thought, and as I think is generally believed, the realisation of the "self" as a separate entity, but this was not even remotely sufficient to *compose* a faculty. For this the aforesaid intuitions were necessary.

As the external conscience increased the number of concepts, it also needed to order its memories, that is, accumulate them in an ordered manner, thereby developing its *accumulative memory.* This memory, in which it stores its concepts, constitutes the relatively stable content of discernment, with which it has a necessary and interdependent relationship. For this reason discernment can only *know* if it has accumulative memory and, as a result, the ego, being identified with both cannot know things as they are, or directly.

Since there is a *unitive memory,* man would have three memories, which would correspond to the different planes of understanding: *the internal*, *the external* and *the unitive or vital*. This multiplicity of memories makes their placement in a schema of the psyche very difficult and inevitably requires certain rigidity. For this reason I have not assigned them a place in mine. I think it is illustrative nonetheless to imagine them as a single tree, whose trunk would be the unitive memory, from which there would have grown a branch which corresponds to the internal plane, and from this there would have grown what belongs to the planes of the intellect and the external. These three memories would not, then, be different nor separate, only that each one would be the result of the vision that each plane makes of reality.

I would like now to give a couple of simple examples, taken from everyday life, to illustrate some differences between these memories and also the relationship between them. We can imagine an ordinary man who walks through the centre of a city. His gaze is attracted by some jewellery in a shop window that he does not need but that awakens in him the desire to possess it and, therefore, he observes it carefully for a while. His attention, though, avoids focusing on a beggar girl sitting on the ground under the window. Once at home our character tells his spouse about the walk, he describes the district, its avenues and shops and ends up telling her about the jewellery that had caught his attention and that he can describe without difficulty. He clearly remembers all this. When referring to the jewellery, however, he feels a slight unease that goes unnoticed by his discernment so that he continues to describe the content of *his* memory and does not remember the beggar girl. The slight discomfort is a warning from his moral conscience that tries to remind him of the beggar girl. The entire, global situation that revolved around it, the tension created by the clash between the unitive and egocentric forces, was registered by the *unitive memory*; in the moral conscience there was an immediate *intelligence* and a spontaneous feeling, that is, a vital *experience* of the whole event. It is important that it be understood that it is not simply a question of two consciences with their interests and their memories, but that *what is decisive for the spirit be registered at a vital level.* Whether our character remembers the streets or not, the shops and the jewellery itself, does not affect his spirit; he can forget without consequences. This is not the case with what is perceived by the central plane. This is *vital* for himself and thus indispensable for his equilibrium and unavoidable for his self-knowledge. Being vital for the spirit, the moral conscience will strive to make the subject conscious of the event and will send messages to the external and internal planes, who will interpret them in their own way. This can generate a certain unease each time he remembers the jewellery in question, those dreamlike images that call attention to the unattended moral and vital aspect. The moral conscience will try to re-establish the psychic equilibrium broken by the selfish attitude, reminding or awakening the unitive energies that tend to harmonise with his fellow beings. For this it uses the content of the *unitive memory*.

One can understand the great advantage of the unitive man in having easy access to this memory, both to maintain his equilibrium and for his own knowledge. With the nucleus of his spirit, his *conscience* on the vital plane has a direct and natural contact with the unitive memory. The centred man will surely pay less attention to the streets, the names of shops and to jewels. He will be more "distracted" from this utilitarian aspect of reality, consequently, in all probability, he will extract fewer external advantages from it, but this will not affect him at a vital level. Thus, for example, if the subject's attention had been focused on the beggar girl and he had felt compassion and shared his humanity with her, and after having noticed the jewellery, had ignored it, there would have been no interior consequence due to his attitude. The internal plane would not, then, have tried to remind him of the jewellery, nor would the external plane have been perturbed by it.

Besides this example of the moral order, I would like to give another example to explain the relation between the aesthetic conscience and the *unitive memory*.

The awe of the common man regarding the retentive capacity of the artist, that is, his ability to remember an image, such as that of a bird in flight, for example, which is only visible for a few seconds that would in no way be sufficient for him but are enough for the painter who without haste can paint it much later in his *atelier*. The explanation can be summed up as follows: The innate artist (I include the poet here), lives (relatively speaking) in another time, far from the practical world. For this reason, to those of utilitarian mentality who lives and firmly believes in the concrete reality, it seems that the artist is distracted, vague, as if he were "in the clouds" (it is well known that philosophers also give this impression). This intellectual *alienation*, however, allows the artist to be much more attuned to *his* object, to which he is very connected and not at all alienated from. He who is established in his discernment, lives in a time without a present, and only when he is forgetful of his self, as a separate individual and of his image, as well as when he is concentrated on his work, is he oblivious to time. While the artist, who has his centre (relatively) displaced towards the vital plane, lives in a (more) 'out of time" reality, his present is, one can say, *stretched out*, it is not now a point between the past and the future but rather a line. This makes it generate another kind of perception and memory, a *unitive memory* in which the bird in flight does not (really) pass from the past to the future, but *remains* in the present (relatively free from interferences generated by utilitarian interests), sufficient to make a clear exhibition. A developed power of concentration and an innate visual memory will undoubtedly produce this result; but to my understanding, what is decisive is a greater *capacity to experience the present.* We can notice, for example, the number of *significant* details of a passing scene as experienced by a Hugo, a Turgenev or a Balzac.

The phenomenon that is observed, although not explained to my knowledge, of which some men have been the protagonists, of remembering one's whole life in times of mortal danger could be explained according to the theory of unitive memory.

This memory does not, in effect, keep a temporal sequence as it acts independently of discernment and its content is composed thanks to the perception of the *significance* of circumstances at a vital level, of global syntheses. As the moments of great vital intensity are more recorded in it and thus more patent and within reach, in a moment of extreme intensity, in which the present is something that needs to be avoided and the future is out of the question, it is viable that the spirit in a desperate effort to cling to life, as if it were trying to *save life*, submerges itself in its past life, that is, in its *unitive memory*, where it will find its most decisive experiences, those that represent life the most to him. Surely as no memory satisfies him because none can save him, he vertiginously covers several of them, which, as they are so complete in their synthesis, lead him to see, at a vital level, his whole past.

Notes

(1) This article complements the chapter *Vital or unitive memory* in *The Return to the Sources.*

CHAPTER NINETEEN

On The Control of Dreams

We can affirm that he who is firmly established in his *central consciousness* can make and control his own dreams. As this state of consciousness is the heritage of men who will surely be the last to visit an analyst, I fear that our psychologists are inclined to deny the said affirmation or express their skepticism. Even so, I would like to try and explain this matter because not only does the *central consciousness* illuminate the internal plane, but also inversely, the knowledge of dreams and the progressive control of them lead to this consciousness. It is not the interest of psychosophy to recount the marvels that accrue from true knowledge, but to lead to it.

The said control is possible in the first place because the spirit is *purified*, in the religious and psychological double meaning (this double meaning is not so for psychosophy which establishes a permanent relationship between the two). This means that, thanks to self-knowledge, a product of moral and psychic equilibrium, the spirit has overcome complexes in general. These are understood in their broadest sense, including unconscious accumulations considered "normal" by official psychology, that is, not only those capable of producing notorious behavioural disorders, but also those susceptible of generating interferences, both in the external and internal conscience, that is, distractions in the waking state and dream material in the sleeping state. This material that forms the content of the internal plane is, generally, the consequence of a lack of attention to external stimuli and, above all, to spiritual reality: religious, moral and aesthetic. This lack of attention is "normal" in the common man and gives rise to instabilities that, although minor, are nevertheless real and important since they are numerous. The said reality is conscious in the *unitive man* as his central reference is based in the philosophical–religious, moral and aesthetic conscience. This allows him to avoid the accumulation of the said material, which he achieves thanks to his favourable outlook and to his vigilance; both are necessary as distraction can lead one him to lose control of his mind. By remaining vigilant he conveniently *filters* external perceptions and prevents further internal interferences.

The control of dreams is possible in the second place, for whoever has reached his *central consciousness*, because his spirit is in the *central plane*, next to the internal plane, and thus he is better placed to control it, in such a way that he stops being absolutely unconscious (for this reason I do not call it such), to become, not conscious as we understand the waking state, but, I would say, relatively unconscious (or relatively conscious). This control also requires permanent vigilance and also a life of seclusion in order to avoid too many external stimuli (such as those generated in big modern cities, as life there implies excessive attention to practical matters, such as traffic lights and signposts in general, traffic, thieves, etc., to the point of becoming *dangerous* for he who is *distracted for being vigilant*. The modern jungle does not lend itself to these kinds of spiritual exercises).

The control of dreams, as has been said, takes place in a semi-conscious state, and is linked to the spiritual technique called *visualisation*. This is a practice of great value and efficacy as it activates the central conscience by using the memory that it depends on, which is the unitive. Visualisation, as can be verified by all who try to achieve it, does not depend on the will of the ego but on the propitious conditions created by the spirit that limits itself to evoking images. It is for this reason a *meditation*, in which accumulative memory does not intervene, as the images do not keep superimposing nor appearing as a rational sequence (conscious effort, references or conceptual relationships, etc.). It does not depend on the forms of time and space but on the simple *reappearance of what has been seen directly as it was*. Correct visualisation implies, thus, first direct perception (without the mediation of the ego) of things as they are. These are seen as a *totality* in itself, or within a global reality, a *spiritual atmosphere*, which gives them a transcendental dimension; using religious language I would say that it *sanctifies* them. The second stage of the visualisation leads one to reproduce the images seen in such a way and, above all, to *re-experience* the said reality.

It can be inferred that what I have called *correct visualisation* presupposes a relatively intimate contact with the central conscience and experiential (personally experienced) knowledge of its mechanisms, but this does not invalidate the attempts of visualisation that are made with lesser knowledge, as all visualisation that takes into account the elements cited will tend to awaken the said consciousness. Now, the spirit free from the complexes and interferences mentioned above can carry out this *correct visualisation* in a sleeping state and choose, although not in the habitual conscious manner, certain objects, landscapes or sequences experienced as was mentioned earlier, which will appear *like* dreams but without other *unconscious* interferences. This is what I called the control of dreams. I consider this form of visualisation more accurate and nutritious than the imposition of the difficult visualisation of complex *mandalas,* which were not created by our own consciousness but by others, and with an abundant content of the internal plane.

As the spirit centred in the vital plane is experienced independently of the content of the neighbouring planes, it can observe them without identifying with them. This advantageous situation is also applicable to the internal plane when the spirit finds repose during the hours of sleep. Even here it carries out a passive role, barely using its will, because if it tries to impose itself on oneiric reality it externalises itself, causing the psyche to awaken with its shifts. Many sleepless nights may be required to obtain this just measure, although I cannot generalise on this subject because I only have my own relatively limited experience.

The control of dreams requires, then, a special discipline that depends on three main factors: Firstly, an intensely (not only primarily) contemplative life; secondly, a spirit based on the vital plane and aware of its mechanisms; and thirdly, a very reduced activity of discernment. The distinction that we established earlier between this faculty and the intellect will now help us to understand this point.

Reducing the activity of discernment to the bare minimum, could seem, from the *individual perspective,* to obscure understanding in general. From the central perspective, however, it is noted that the light of understanding comes from the *pure conscience,* without negating by this that discernment illuminates the knowledge of the particulars in their extremes, *extending* the light in this way. If the knowledge of innumerable particulars is *almost* indispensable in modern society, it is not so for what is fundamental: to know ourselves. Given the interdependent connection between the intellectual plane and discernment, separating them appears to be a difficult operation; and so it is. In addition, from an individual perspective it would be a useless attempt, but from the *essential perspective* the intellect appears first and discernment later, so the spirit cannot fail to notice how far it is from its centre. He who is not firmly ensconced in the central plane should prevent discernment from *absorbing* the intellect, limiting himself to receiving intellectual intuitions without developing them logically or expressing them in a language comprehensible to third parties, as these naturally use his discernment and demand clarity. While the *language* that we use for ourselves, in what is most decisive, does not need *that* clarity, but *another;* "I understand myself", we say at times when we cannot get our message across.

An example will help to better understand what I am saying. Almost all the basic material of my book *The Return to the Sources* was written in the form of notes of these intuitions of the intellect (in turn inspired by experiences that I rarely tried to put into words). During this time, (two years in particular that I dedicated expressly to this), I could observe and generate my dreams without much difficulty, but when I started the work of ordering those notes and making them *discernible*, i.e. writing a book, the dreams began to reappear independently of my control; although in a gentle way, without becoming *messages* from the internal plane. And, reciprocally on losing control over this plane, I was less *centred*; for this reason, I said in that essay that it is very difficult to elaborate a philosophy without making the spirit lose its composure.(1)

I would like to recount a *unitive dream*. I am not, as will be noted in my work, inclined to speak about personal experiences, especially those that are of a transcendental nature. The reason is simple and it is that the Transcendent is the Sacred itself, that is, it does not *belong* to the subject, and thus there is something sacrilegious in disseminating this knowledge. On the other hand there is nothing that can be said about the Transcendent in Itself. In any case, this is only a dream that preceded this kind of experience by a couple of weeks.

I am in the forest searching for a deer to hunt. Suddenly under the light that filters through the pines (that already revealed a very suggestive *emptiness*), I see a magnificent deer with his antlers held high. On aiming at him with a rifle I observe through the telescopic sight that instead of there being a cross formed by two lines, the lines are countless and pointed in all directions, so that the whole forest, all reality is traced by these coordinates. When I say "in all directions" I want to point out that they are not in a single plane but also extended in depth. But I am no longer here gazing over there - but as happens in these unitive visions – in the place of the deer, in the *centre*, from which I see the rays of light from *any perspective*. In other words, it was not me who was looking, it was that entire reality.

This was evidently a premonitory dream, one of those that I have called *unitive*, it announced a vital experience. I have narrated this dream as proof of a theory that is precious to psychosophy, and it is that the Spirit impregnates all Reality, not only the external but also all the planes of understanding, including, as in this case, the internal plane, which is represented in this way, in part rational, (the lines and coordinates), in part symbolic (the context) and in part transcendent (experience at the vital level), the Unity in Reality.

The universal Spirit is that Unity. When the human spirit approaches it (as in that time when mine was "hunting" for the Absolute), it begins to manifest itself. Then it shows itself on the other planes, in the waking state and in external reality, which no longer is. I would not go as far to say that the Spirit "tries" to express itself, but it is a fact that becomes clear when the individual spirit *assimilates* to It. But it does not only manifest itself when it reveals itself as it Is, it illuminates all the faculties, especially the philosophic, religious, moral and aesthetic. It actually illuminates all Reality, even if this is only appreciated when it is seen in Itself.

What is recounted is a premonitory or *numinous* dream as Jung would say. But these kinds of dreams *happen* to the subject, they are not yet controlled by him.

What I understand by *control of dreams,* on the contrary, is a rememorisation or more correctly a visualisation carried out by the internal plane of a content of the *unitive memory*, provided by what is directly perceived by a pure aesthetic conscience, that is to say, without external or internal interferences, both at the time of *unitive perception* and dream visualisation. During sleep, the internal plane is in these cases, I would say, invaded by the vital plane in such a way that it would become an extension of it, as is the *mediate unitive conscience* on the external plane. It is important that it be understood that one is not dealing in any way with an abstraction or a subjective state, as there is a unitive reality: the *presence of the Essence,* which is what makes *possible* the unity of the *transcendental aesthetic experience.* Since this is as vivid as it is intense, as it captivates both the mind and the heart, it is deeply engraved in the unitive memory. This is what allows one to repeat the same experience as if it were a continuation of the same reality, in the same state, during sleep. The aesthetic pleasure in such cases is incomparable, both in waking and sleep, and thus the dream is invariably remembered upon waking, leaving an inexpressible feeling of well-being, which the soul can only feel when it has been bathing in its own Source.

Notes

(1) At first I thought of publishing the notes directly, but realising that they were written in a language foreign to modern man, similar to some *Sutras* from the East that do not include explanations, I began my great task of giving it a philosophical structure, although often interspersing the original notes. That mixture was the original manuscript that I sent to Maestro Dokushò Villalba, who would write the prologue to that book. The manuscript itself, and this is another example that illustrates the same theme, had many unintelligible passages due to the fact that my spirit did not yet have, at that time, a correct relationship with discernment, that is, it had not elaborated a *mediate unitive conscience.* But Dokushò, being a Zen Master, did not fail to understand the message; even if he warned me that I had to make it clearer, that is, more *discernible.*

CHAPTER TWENTY

The Sources of a Unitive Path of Knowledge

I am convinced that if Plato had been better understood our entire history would have been different and certainly better. I would like to clarify some aspects of his great philosophy in the light of psychosophy. On seeing the terminology of the latter in the former the reader might think that on shining this light I am transforming the object. Since it is feasible that it is so, I have no response to this objection, except this: for thirty years I have tried to understand his philosophy, and only in this light has it finally become intelligible to me; I think this is reason enough. I do not, naturally, mean that this philosopher has not been sufficiently reflected on, as possibly no other has generated so much interest and comment; but I suspect that in general he has not been examined from the correct viewpoint. Of Plato one can say the same as of the doctrines of the Far East: the precondition to study and ultimately understand him is to equip oneself with a specific level of consciousness. The recurring error that has been committed with him, as with the aforementioned doctrines, is that he has been *objectively* studied, that is, one has started from the obviously subjective belief that one was *prepared* to understand him. It is true that those who have generally ventured to comment on our philosopher have passed through universities where they have obtained degrees that apparently guaranteed them to be prepared for the study of Plato, but I do not think that Plato would have accepted this guarantee, nor the kind of teaching that is normally lavished in our universities, so different from what it would have been like in his *Republic*. The method used in our universities is, fundamentally, the same, accumulative and objective (and this is valid, despite being surprising for anyone who reflects in depth on the matter) both for the study of the exact and natural sciences and for those of philosophy and psychology even though the objectives of the studies differ radically.

At first glance, it would seem that the difference between the method used by Plato and that used by the sciences would be that between the inductive and deductive methods, as from the particular the universal is induced, then a hypothesis is ventured that would correspond to the universal, which is then applied to other particulars. To the extent that the hypothesis proves to be applicable, it will become a universal law. It should be clarified that although so denominated, several points can be left unexplained and even allow some minor contradictions; what is decisive for the sciences is that it *functions* in most cases. Plato, for his part, attends to universal knowledge before addressing himself to particulars. But the decisive difference lies in how this is attained and in its "ontological status", because, as we have seen, the sciences also use the deductive method in a certain sense once the law is established, and this aspires to be universal and permanent, although, it is from the regularity of the non-permanent that they seek the permanent. While for Plato true knowledge, which of the philosopher, is addressed to the universal and to the permanent *in itself* as a *prior condition* for other knowledge. It is thus, for example, not possible for him to establish an ethics or laws of State, that is, a harmonious society, without the knowledge of the Good *in itself;* and this is not a hypothesis or a law but what it truly *is*, the Being.

Socrates had already perfectly realised the necessary mutual correspondence between the object of study and the different states of the soul, and Plato would keep this in mind during his whole life. When the soul "uses the body to consider something", that is, when it applies the senses to the objects of the senses, "it is dragged by the body to that which is never presented in the same state and gets lost, it runs amuck and gets delirious as if it were inebriated", while "whenever it is possible for it to be alone with itself, it ceases to get lost, it always remains the same and (...) enters into contact with objects that are identical and immutable." (*Phaedo, 79*) True knowledge is, thus, born of this *symbiosis of the soul in its immutable state together with the Immutable,* which is its object. The relationship between this state and that to which meditation leads can be observed.

In order to reach the object *in itself,* it is not enough, for Plato, to study objectively; the aspirant must practice virtue until he *becomes* virtuous. It is this that will allow him to know the Good *in itself,* and it is this that generates wisdom, "because he who is not pure is afraid that it will be forbidden to reach the pure." (*Phaedo, 67b*) Plato thus proposes an *asceticism*, a purification in the manner of religions, "separating the soul as much as possible from the body and accustoming it to concentrating and enclosing itself within itself (...) and the occupation of the philosophers consists precisely in this, in the detachment and separation of the soul and the body." (*Phaedo, 67d*)

The fact that there have been and currently are so many scholars (among whom there is no lack of historians of philosophy) who wonder if Plato speaks of religion or if he is just a philosopher, makes one suspect that the nature of a religious matter and its relationship with philosophy has been ignored. Plato does not only speak of religion, but of the *purest forms of religion*, but as these *forms* seem to be unknown to them, they doubt Plato and not their own knowledge "as the common lot of people do not notice that he (the philosopher) is imbued with a divinity". (*Phaedrus, 243*)

The forms to which our later tradition have accustomed us, the symbol of a crucified Christ sacrificing himself for the salvation of our species, are accessible to even the most insensitive spirits. From this personal devotional path to the philosophical path followed by Plato; from the concrete image of God-man, to the Being *in itself,* there is some distance to be covered that must, necessarily, demand much more from the spirit. But this in no way implies that the concept of religion should adapt to those forms, to the point of questioning the doctrines that do not fit them. Truth makes its demands and this is nobody's fault, it is simply *like this,* even if it does not conform to democratic aspirations. When Plato proposes that the philosophers govern the State, he is not thinking of those who have accumulated objective knowledge but of virtuous sages.

As an *ideal* of the virtuous man he presents us with his Master, Socrates, an example of prudence, self control and Wisdom, a man *prepared...* for death. As he also corresponds to a *unitive* knowledge, as we saw when speaking about Love, he assigns it a preponderant role: "one can barely find a better collaborator for human nature than Love"

(*Symposium, 212*). This happens because "Love has as its objective the perpetual possession of what is good" (*Symposium, 207*) and it is directed towards obtaining immortality, that is, besides being a moral means it has a religious objective.

He also, naturally, considers reflection indispensable for knowledge, to the extent that in some dialogues (*Parmenides, Sophist*, in which he shows solid knowledge although these are notoriously less inspiring) he seems to want to explain everything with discernment but makes it clear that what ultimately *makes* the philosopher is experience. He even manages to identify this with the correct thought: "when (the soul) reflects alone by itself, it goes towards what is pure and has always existed and is immortal and it always presents itself in the same way"... "this experience of the soul is called thought" (*Phaedo*, 79d). This *experience of the soul* is nothing but a religious experience or, in our terminology a *unitive experience*; the ultimate objective of *unitive knowledge*.

I would not like to go so far as to put words into Plato's mouth, and he lends himself to this because there are various points that he has left unclear. In his wide-ranging work that has miraculously been preserved, in contrast to what happened to the majority of the enlightened Greeks, he had plenty of room to clarify them and did not do so. On many occasions, for example, he makes us believe that he effectively believed in his world of Forms. If this is the case, I believe that he was led to do so by his eagerness to rationalise the object of his perception until he came to identify his representations with the Idea, that is, the rational with the real; a grave error that would be taken to extremes by another distinguished idealist. On various occasions he gives the impression that in his obsession for discernment he did not notice to what extent he was entangling himself until he falls prey to the *magic of concepts*, just as the Pythagoreans (from whom he inherited this tendency) did with numbers.

His error was to create, undoubtedly through correct intuitions, an absolute "composite" Reality, or rather, a Reality made up of absolutes, in such a way that in his attempt to assimilate the specific particulars to the immutable, he was creating a static and even phantasmagorical world similar to an immense waxwork museum of perfect Forms. Therefore, it was an *intermediate* world that was neither one (absolute) Reality nor the other (tangible), but rather a world of representations. This was unnecessary as each thing does not need a perfect particular prototype for the spirit to have a perfect *idea* of it. For psychosophy, *the latent or conscious intuition of Perfection, the Essence of the World, is sufficient for the individual spirit to form ideas of perfection about particular objects.* The Essence penetrates and illuminates all things that, thus, participate in its perfection, inspiring man in this way.

CHAPTER TWENTY ONE

The Reason for the Irrationality of Myth

I am, still, very far from accepting the widespread latent belief that tends to explain the theory of Ideas as a product of Plato's ingenuity. I have reason to believe not only that there is nothing ingenuous about the Athenian genius but also to suppose that he uses his myths as a *means* to explain what he perceives at a level that transcends common sense and everyday language. For a correct understanding we should be careful not to project onto him our contemporary way of seeing (or of not seeing.)

Plato, like psychosophy, does not derive knowledge from hypotheses but from the perception of the first principles or *primary manifestations.* He uses the hypotheses as a means of approximation and explanation of a knowledge that he knows for certain. His knowledge, in essence, is not hypothetical, nor is his philosophy sustained or exhausted in his theory of Ideas. He intuited an absolute Idea (the Good, the Beautiful) on the basis of which he makes his hypotheses about particular ideas. He felt his soul "participate" in this Reality. Of this he was convinced. He advises us to be cautious of his theory, often explained in the form of myths: "Now"—he says after one of them—"forcefully sustaining that this is as I have elaborated is not what behoves a man of reason. However, the fact that it is so or something similar... I do believe that it is convenient to believe so, and I do think it is worthwhile to take the risk of believing it is so." (*Phaedo, 114*)

All this makes one think that he was trying to make this difficult knowledge accessible to men of average understanding (in several passages he suggests that he abandons approaching those of lesser understanding), for when he proposes to speak directly about the Truth, he transcends rational schemes: "Since we have to dare to tell the Truth, this is its condition"... "this reality lacks colour, form, it is impalpable and visible only to the pilot of the soul, the understanding; the fact that that reality *is* real in a way, constitutes the object of real knowledge." (*Phaedrus, 247*) The error may be, then, in those who, not being able to perceive this Reality, are left only with what Plato represents to them in his intention to make it intelligible, and thus believe that the great Athenian has exhausted his theory, when behind it there is a whole Reality that inspires it.

We can criticise Plato for having created a static world of Ideas; but we cannot fail to take into account that he eventually explained it in the form of suggestive myths and in an atmosphere too foggy for discernment, thus creating the need for intuition to penetrate it, inviting the vital experience of immutability that he knew theories could not express. Therefore, attempting to grasp Plato by the theory of Ideas is to try and take hold of the fog that he has left us in the hope of transcending it.

Truth is always experienced on a personal and vital level. We can think, once again, about love. If we are told that love exists, whether we believe in it or not, this does not essentially change anything in us. But if we fall in love, even if we cannot explain it and we are bombarded with all the possible reasons that prove its non-existence and our folly, if we are sane we will not deny our experience.

Plato, who had a fairly clear idea of Reality, verified the difficulty of both grasping and expressing it through reason. The reader of his dialogues, who is not faced with this Reality but rather with its recounting, can also attest in some way to this difficulty. He can accompany him without any problems in the secure carriage of dialectics, but before having finished his journey, when the philosopher replaces his horses for others with wings and invites him to enter the world of mythology, he finds himself disconcerted, and if he is a dogmatist of reason (as modern man generally is), he will be unwilling to follow him. But Plato had his reasons that normal reason does not discern. (Pascal rightly spoke of *reasons of the heart*).

We can represent on the external plane what our senses have seen on the exterior, and in a similar manner we can represent what our spirit has seen on the interior, as we know so many artists do. Myths are also born in this way. This is the process followed by Plato, but he did not apply these representations to the tangible world but to another world which he was filling with immutable Forms. This world was his work of art.

The reader will understand that when I speak of an *interior* reality, I am referring fundamentally to the *vital plane*, as it would be a grave error to take Platonic reality as a product of the *unconscious* and the knowledge that it expresses as *subjective*. No greater injustice could be committed to this philosopher who knew in detail the subjective mechanisms and their many inherent dangers, and who, precisely, creates his world of Ideas in a colossal effort to be objective, even at the risk of being misunderstood. And I am very much afraid that this is what ultimately happened.

Although the internal plane contributes images and fantastic associations, myths are generated on the *vital plane*; from this the spirit extracts, as we saw, its religious, ethical and aesthetic inspiration. These consciences provide what is decisive, the generative force, *the creative*, to put it correctly. Plato offers a clear example in support of this affirmation, as evidently, he could not have extracted a reality *in itself*, without forms or representations, neither from discernment nor from the internal plane; he is using a third source outside the schemas of these planes. This leads me to believe that from a psychic point of view, Plato's *intermediate* world corresponds to the central plane, *intermediate* between the external and the internal. His insistence on the moral path that structures this plane would confirm this belief. This is the plane of *understanding* on which he moves.

How far did Plato scale this plane? To talk about the level of consciousness of another naturally implies a certain risk, but I think that in this case we have enough elements to be able to judge with sufficient precision.

There is no doubt that Plato reached the highest levels of *unitive conscience*. Proof of this is the constant contact that he maintained with the *primary manifestation* which all his philosophy is inspired by, although the fact that he maintained a dualistic relationship with Divinity makes one think that he did not manage to unify his spirit. Suffice to say that this was not for lack of talent. We have already seen that this faculty is not indispensable for this purpose but, I venture to add, due to a lack of techniques directed towards this end and of doctrines in which he could have found guidance. We know that the Upanishads and the original Buddhism that preached a monist vision already existed, but these in all probability were unknown in Greece. In the West the most elevated doctrine was that of Plato himself.

The close relationship between those doctrines and the Platonic is, however, notable. As it would be excessive to elaborate a comparative analysis here it is enough to point out the common use of what in general terms can be called the *unitive method*.

I am particularly interested in reiterating that the common points between these doctrines are not due to a *cultural tradition*. Greece was at that point separated from India by an immense territory dominated by its worst enemy, the Persian Empire. Alexander the Great would later establish the connection, after having dismembered the said Empire, by establishing the Greek one (or the Macedonian, to be more precise). *The relationship is not human but divine, from spirit to Spirit.* Buddha, Plato, Jesus and all the mystics *participate* in the same inspiration; they drink from the same Source that incessantly pours its waters over all creation.

I would like to add a clarification here that to some would seem a truism but on which others need to reflect. If inspiration transcends space-time schemas, experience alone is not enough for its manifestation. Culture and the innate capacities of the subject, his philosophical, religious, artistic or poetic inclination will lead him to express it according to these tendencies and influences with greater or lesser success. If I make this clarification, it is because it is often *believed* that the founders of religions are in touch with the Truth, and being so there can be no doubt about their teachings. This means that they tend to be dogmatically accepted. But as every artist or poet knows well, the work of art is not only composed of inspiration; one has to commit it to paper or cloth, with all that this implies.

Plato will remain within the limits of a dualist conception, but there is no doubt that he tended towards Unity, nor that he was well oriented towards it as he continually establishes the correct path: the necessary purification of the soul of all lovers of wisdom. "Those who are philosophers in the full sense of the Word abstain from corporal desires" (*Phaedo,* 82); an indispensable condition for liberation. This liberation, it should be clarified, is not as psychosophy and the monist doctrines understand it to be: in present and unconditional life. Plato refers to "a pure abode" post mortem. He correctly proposes another practice essential for the *unitive path*, the "*imitation of Divinity*" (*Phaedrus,* 253) and the progressive identification of the soul with it; although he does not speak to us about a *total* identification.

The limits of his initial dualism become imprecise however in his long search and evolution, in the last dialogues he prefers to talk about *the One* and not of *the multiplicity of absolutes*, in such a way that his two realities tend to unify. In any case it is in *this* world that the creator "put intelligence in the soul and soul in the body" in such a way that "we can say that the world became a living creature endowed with soul and intelligence" (*Timaeus*). Which is, almost, a definition of pantheism.

CHAPTER TWENTY TWO

Myth, Rememorisation and Mysticism

For discernment, man needed the faculty of producing concepts that would correspond to the objects of his senses, but this did not yet provide him with knowledge. He had to develop, and has done so, a more elaborate faculty that was of much greater magnitude: the intellect, capable of creating concepts not only of things but *about* things and applicable to them; general universal syntheses, mathematical and geometrical realities. Being permanent and universal, they seem to have transcended the changeable world. This attribute must have made an impression, and in fact it did, on the Greeks (Pythagoras, Plato) when they *became* fully aware of that phenomenon. This corresponded to another perception of their spirit, to the Eternal that, thanks to those concepts, could be apprehended and made intelligible in a certain way.

In order to submerge ourselves in our inner world, as we saw, we must stop swimming on the surface of our external representations so that in this passive manner the spirit can descend naturally, without effort, to the *plane of direct perception*. Keep in mind that a passive attitude even if fundamental is not sufficient in itself. There is simultaneously in this action an active side; a state of alertness, an unusually awakened conscience is necessary so that the spirit in its descent does not fall prey to the influences of the animated plane and the reveries of the internal plane.

Once the spirit is *centred* on the *vital plane* it contemplates things as they are, that is, directly. But this does not in any way mean that the objects of the senses appear alone or disconnected, quite the contrary; only then, in fact, has the link become evident. This link is nothing but the consequence of the *unitive virtue of the Essence* to which I have already referred.

Plato intuits this link in his own way, which he tries to explain through distinctions and divisions, the similar and dissimilar, or in the manner of Heraclitus, by their opposites, obscuring the question enormously in my opinion. He calls his source of inspiration, the original link, I would say, "equality itself", an unfortunate concept with which his intellect may have been satisfied but not his usual thirst for the truth, as the same does not correspond to any reality. We should not question all his philosophy based on this antecedent, it is enough to take into account that even when dealing with basic Ideas such as these, he was capable at times, due to a lack of correct intuitions, of filling his ideal world with pure concepts.

We cannot say the same about his Ideas of aesthetic and moral perfection, the Good and the Beautiful, undoubtedly a product of correct intuitions. With this I do not want to say that even though I deny the world of "lesser" Ideas, I accept the objective existence of these "greater" Ideas, like great wax figures or as concepts etched in monumental granite by the hand of God. I accept them as spiritual realities that manifest themselves to the human being at a conscious or latent level. The Good, the Beautiful, Order and Love, when they are objects of a full apperception are not only Ideas, but *vital experiences* that take place *prior* to every *idea* and sentiment that has taken *shape.* They are realities that must be experienced in their Origen and *in statu nascendi*. We could say that they are always *attributes* of Divinity, as long as we do not imagine a *person* who possesses them in a transcendental place, but rather as manifestations of the same that are poured over all creation and, certainly, over the human spirit that they illuminate and inspire. The human *attribute* is to be able to make them *conscious.*

These Ideas, in the case of Plato, are the result of *unitive intuitions*, since everything seems to indicate that the contact he had with the Being itself was indirect, sporadic and at times even vague, rather than direct, constant and clear as would correspond to a *total unitive experience*. Proof of this lies in the fact that the link that he established between these first realities and the phenomenic world was also indirect. This mode of perception often leads him to resort to his theory of reminiscence: "According to that argument, Socrates, that you often repeat, that learning is nothing but remembering." (*Phaedo,* 73)

Although I cannot be very precise due to the very nature of the matter, I would like to throw some light on it, not only for this theory in particular, but because I believe that by doing so, other concomitant points of significant importance will also be clarified.

When the Essence is indirectly perceived, the link that the spirit establishes between itself and things is the consequence of a particular contemplative state, thanks to which time, even if not decisively transcended, recedes faraway on the horizon to the point that the reality we contemplate seems linked to a distant time, to which the spirit is transported. This means that we have the *impression that we are remembering*. But this distance, *in reality,* is not due to a past time but to a timeless time, the Eternal, only perceptible *itself* in the absolute present (unified conscience). Plato warned that his perception was not a consequence of reflection, but on the contrary, that thought had to be paused to give rise to images that, it seemed to him, came from a remote time and place. It is this kind of *understanding* that allowed him to visualise the permanent immutable reality that lit up his soul, as well as the objects of his senses. Hence his obsession with explaining the link between the two; but on trying to rationalise it his spirit was seen to have been transported to an earlier time and an imprecise place that decidedly transcended concrete reality. The framework within which he found himself then was that of the myth, to which he skilfully resorted, as this gave him greater freedom of expression and allowed him to imagine an *ideal* situation for his Ideas, and moreover to speak approximately, *as if* it were like this.

The theory of reminiscence is the strongest support that Plato uses to prove the pre-existence of the soul and hence its immortality, and on questioning this theory (as also his world of Forms), I take away this support. But it is not for this reason that I leave the thesis of the immortality of the soul unsupported. On the contrary, I think I have found a much more solid premise for it, which is *the present experience of the participation of the soul in the Eternal*. On being *present* this experience does not need to resort to an uncertain past time nor does it have to cling to the belief of a life after death, nor wait, of course, for this to confirm it. It would seem logical to look for the explanation of the immortality of the soul in the past and in the future, hence all the tests that have been tried have resorted to this; but logic has its limits, precisely those of time and space which only a *vital experience of the Eternal Present* transcends.

Plato's message is not entirely clear, but it has a purpose and corresponds *in some way* to a transcendent Reality; this is what I have tried to demonstrate in these chapters. The rich personality of this philosopher tends to be confusing because he is also a religious thinker. But I believe that this is not his obscure side, it is rather his manner of being religious, of being both a mystic and mythical; two colours of the spirit that escape the visible spectrum of modern man.

I will now try to establish the difference between these two visions of the religious. I will, however, do so in broad terms, just to underline a few points that seem to me to be of decisive importance. But I no longer have to refer to Plato. I have gone as far as I can go with him (I only hope that I have incorporated not the obscure, but the clear, from his philosophy into mine), but for this difference to be briefly stated, I will express myself directly using my own language.

We know, thanks to the works of M. Eliade,(1) that myths always refer to a particularly *significant primordial time*, which the religious man seeks, through the periodic repetition of the ritual, to update or relive; I would say *re-experience.* The relationship of myths with the Eternal is evident. Man tries through these acts to make of present time a time like *the original* that is eternal or that participates in Reality. Ritual seeks to eternalise this timeless Reality by cyclically repeating the original acts established by the gods themselves or by their chosen intermediaries. To get in touch with the *primordial*, to approach and have a certain experience of Divinity, of the Eternal, mythical man needs the ritual, which is transmitted to him by tradition, that is, which he inherits. He finds his source of inspiration in the past, and although he is conscious that he lives in a successive time, it makes sense if it is rejoined with the primordial time that makes it sacred and eternal. Ritual reproduces universal Creation or the creation of certain acts carried out by the gods significant for the culture that practises them. The mystical experience (I will refer here, to better highlight the contrast, to the maximum religious experience, the *total unitive experience*), includes the mythical experience as it provides a knowledge of the origins, not of this or that concrete task, but of the *permanent creation that takes place in each present*. While ritual tries to integrate mythical time, the mystical experience produces this effect by integrating the eternal present making everything *ipso facto* sacred, and profane time becomes sacred time. The ritual of evoking mythical time then becomes unnecessary since this *time becomes present*. When the evocation of the myth takes place, a *religious experience* is produced that, in my understanding, reaches its maximum expression in the mystical experience. In *Aspects du mythe* M. Eliade tells us "The traces of mythical behaviour are also found in the desire to find the intensity with which a thing has been experienced or known for the first time". Mystical experience actualises the said desire, as it makes *everything* seem as if it were seen for the first time, with other eyes, with another spirit. *The mythical search is none other than the search for the mystical experience.* While the myth tries to "recover the remote past, the beatific period of the beginnings" (Op. cit), the mystical experience *updates* the beatific age and the beginning. The mystic discovers *The Sources* for himself and has thus the direct experience of the *creative* itself: Divinity.

Eliade ends the cited work saying: "...it is always the same struggle against Time, the same desire to liberate oneself from the weight of dead time, from Time that crushes and kills". I am completely in agreement with him, but the decisive question still remains: Can this hope become reality? The body is necessarily linked to time and space, but not so the spirit. If the latter identifies with the former, it remains linked to the same coordinates, necessarily causing fear and desire to immediately appear, assuring the ties, while if it is identified with the Eternal, the journey to liberation has begun. There is thus a time that generates life and that kills, and another that *is* eternal Life; knowledge of the latter liberates the spirit from the former. This, in a nutshell, is what is problematic about religion. But we must understand, this is not only a matter for specialists of religion. Every human being is confronted with the alternative that he puts forward. *Behold man's great choice!*

Notes

(1) One of the few in our time who has applied himself to the study of religions with the sincere desire of discovering truths, not novelties, and, moreover, with the respect that they deserve.

CHAPTER TWENTY THREE

The Present Problem

At the beginning of this essay, I said that the human being has followed a slow but constant *process of individualisation, exteriorisation and alienation*. From the point of view of the psyche, this can be summed up thus: the process of spiritual obstruction. When the definitive obturation occurs, a phenomenon that, as we have seen, becomes manifest in the mid XIXth century, man is enclosed in the shell that he had been laboriously constructing around his individuality and, in his egocentric vision, he is externalised in his self-discernment and alienation from the universal Spirit.

This process, by radically changing man's vision, has inevitably resulted in his knowledge having to develop from this new perspective, giving rise to an *inversion of the origin of knowledge*. This *inversion*, of which Descartes would be a pioneer([1]) (as he would begin to outline a system that would definitively take shape with Feuerbach and later materialism), defines modern man in a key aspect. On this will depend his vision of reality (his way of knowing, his aspirations, his expectations, now limited to *this* world, etc.), which will clearly differentiate him from the *homo religiosus* that preceded him. Of course, with this I do not want to imply that all men of antiquity had a *correct vision*, but they had a starting point, a perspective closer to the unitive than to the individual, without having been fully conscious of it. In the same way, modern man is unaware of his present perspective, however convinced he is of his "correct vision".

I have, however, quoted Plato as an example of a *homo religiosus* fully conscious of his *unitive perspective.* For he knew that the *origin of knowledge* was in the Being itself, in the first Reality from which he drew his universal concepts, as well as those of the Good and Beautiful, the attributes of moral and aesthetic perfection that he applied to material reality. For him, these Ideas would not be *a priori* concepts, that man simply had the faculty to produce; in him, this *inversion of the origin of knowledge* had not yet occurred.

I would like to clarify that I do not think that is the historical process that has produced this inversion, as if it were a *necessary evolution*, but one of the displacements of the spirit, which does not necessarily follow a temporal or generational sequence. We find the antecedents of an individual perspective in all ages. Plato's contemporary Protagoras is an example. If I have emphasised the historical process it is because this perspective has been accentuated and generalised until it has become an accepted truth. William of Ockham could be singled out as a significant figure in this process, but I will only mention him in passing because the problem of *the universals* is only one aspect of the matter and involving ourselves in scholastic arguments here would distract us enormously.

It could be said that the turn taken by our culture in the middle of the last century, at least among those whose actions are decisive in the life of the spirit, was due to a change in beliefs, a change that could well be interpreted as a reaction to the belief system with which our culture was previously identified. But this does not express the gravity of the matter, because what really happened then is that the *intelligentsia* had begun to *believe* that reality *was* as its alienation presented it and it began to formulate, accordingly, a new vision of the world, a philosophy. Being the task and responsibility of the intellectual elite to generate and widen the scope of culture, on suffering from a serious spiritual blockage, instead of broadening culture it reduces it in what is most decisive for human beings. But this is not all because, as we have seen, man applies his ideas more than his direct perception from his individual perspective, and this allows these ideologues to acquire the magical power of demiurges, of generators not only of culture but of (supposed) "realities". All that the new ideologues have to do is to present the new ideals in an orderly manner, in keeping with the understanding of all those who suffer from the same obturation.

And it so happens that the human being, the very same who earlier denied this concrete world in the name of a spiritual world, today denies the latter for the sake of the former. Just as the religious man *believed* that he knew more than the non-believer, today the sceptic *believes* that he knows more than the believer. But both could be far from an objective or, rather, a *unitive reality*. Perhaps they are both at the same distance, they just seem to be looking in opposite directions, and nevertheless both *believe* that they are possessed of the "truth" that is, grounded in reality. The balance may, however, tip in favour of the believer [(2)] because there can be a belief founded on a religious experience, while there cannot be an experience that leads to incredulity. But the belief, in any case, only changes the *posture* of the subject, not his knowledge, and for this reason psychosophy, aspiring to knowledge, never appeals to an act of faith.

These *postures,* which according to this discipline are only relative displacements of the reference centre in the mind, generate radically different visions with huge consequences in the ways of seeing, feeling, resolving and relating to circumstances, and they determine not only the philosophies but also, in good measure, the scientific vision of contemporary man. He, in contrast to *homo religiosus,* does not view the reality in which he lives from an absolute and universal principle but from the point of view of his individuality, and thus, he inevitably feels alone and estranged, "launched into the world", like a "stranger" in it and "anguished", to use the existentialist terminology that so well expresses the new feelings caused by the aforementioned shift. It is this that has generated the unease and dissatisfaction of modern man, a disease that already in the XIXth century had spread through Europe in such a way that it was named *mal du siècle*, and which since then has been visibly worsening, expressing itself by the symptoms of *vital apathy and moral indifference* that characterise modern man. These feelings that progressively corrode man's soul (who in his alienation is more concerned with keeping the machinery he buys well oiled), are due to the fact that he is *disconnected* from the whole World, separated from the Essence or unifying and harmonising element. It is not surprising that love is a sentiment that is seriously in danger of extinction. I am convinced that once this is extinguished all the conditions will be established for Chaos to ensue, and the machinery that man produces, that generates so much hope in contemporary man, will only serve to speed up the process. Psychosophy's interest in returning this noble sentiment to man, in re-establishing Harmony, is understandable.

Disconnected from Harmony, modern man stubbornly insists on explaining his existence through mechanical laws that evidently do not satisfy him at a vital level,[(3)] and he vainly tries to find satisfaction by acquiring the new objects that technology ceaselessly procures. But alone and without spirit what other interest could he have but the acquisition of things, as these are his only reality, his only hope of satisfaction? It should be understood that modern man's greed is not really a result of his bad intentions or immorality, since for him there is no other reality but this. How can he then be faulted for desiring to have more? Without spiritual reality, morality is out of context and meaningless. Contemporary man simply does not know what he is sacrificing. For *homo religiosus*, on the other hand, the sacrifice of a concrete good made sense because with it the validity of a spiritual reality was ensured. In this way life was pumped into his soul, but whoever is alienated from it simply ignores what he has lost. In short, what modern man has lost are *the necessary references for his morality.*

Not lacking in greed and without abandoning his egocentrism, seeking (and now only seeing) the utilitarian aspect of life, man affirms himself to an increasing degree on the exterior plane, ignoring or repressing what is most intimate and vital. Determined by the vision that this plane gives to him, he assigns more and more importance to the images elaborated by discernment, to the point of believing these are more real. In this way he progressively identifies with his self-as-image. Man is, thus, far from reality and far from himself.

Having distorted and transformed all of reality, it is not surprising that his values are also altered. He desires more material goods and increasingly fears their loss, while he still does not want to know himself and does not fear this ignorance, which he does not view as alienation, as he is increasingly surrounded by utilities and luxuries, by things that support his personality and existence. He does not, thus, feel the shame of not knowing himself as he does not depend (so he thinks) on it for his existence. But he is very proud of his possessions.

The human being is following a *process of externalisation parallel to that of the obstruction suffered by the internal planes*. His inner life is more and more obscure, remote and alien.([4]) If he wants to withdraw into himself, he thinks; if he attempts to meditate, he shuts his eyes and only sees the darkness. He wants then to see, and thinks again; he no longer knows how to leave the vicious circle of externalisation. Not only has the common man fallen into this, but also the philosopher who, unable to grasp the very object of philosophy with reason, has ended up negating it or, in the best of cases, in order to maintain a metaphysical "air" (and the last breath), by reducing it to Nothing.

Just as there exists a relationship between subject and object, through which we recognise subjective and objective faculties, there is a "unity" between the subject and the object, for which we should use the appropriate faculties: the unitive ones. Just as we are objective when we are not subjective and vice versa, we can be *unitive, being*, neither the one nor the other. We should apply the corresponding faculties to the various "objects" of knowledge. If we want to remember and for this, we apply our imagination, not only will we not achieve this objective, but the more we try the farther we will be from achieving it. In the same way, in order to know ourselves we should apply the specific faculties for this, which are the unitive ones, much more subtle than reason. Imagination can transport us to the most incredible places on its magic carpet; but it will not bring us closer to memory. Reason can at times make possible what is dreamed of by imagination, it can transport us at supersonic speeds, it allows us to see remote images on a screen, etc., and it has made so many things real, it has shown itself to be so useful that it already seems indispensable for all knowledge, and we thus insist on using it. But we progressively distance ourselves from the knowledge of ourselves in the vehicle of reason.

We can be sure that of all the dogmatisms into which man has fallen, reason is the most dangerous, because he is able to see other dogmatisms objectively in the light of reason. But with what light can he see reason when he is accustomed to seeing with nothing else? If he has been developing a light that only looks outwards, how will he manage now to see what has been left in the dark? All dogmatisms are born of a lack of openness, an enclosure, an obturation. The more man externalises himself, the deafer he becomes to morality and the blinder to aesthetics, and this not only in art but in the broader sense of taste in general, and he becomes finally deaf and blind to his religious conscience. The lack of these three orders is obvious in modern society and to this lack we can unhesitatingly attribute the greatest evils that affect the human being and, by extension, the planet. The reason: *man has blocked his unitive and harmonising capacities.*

Man will happen to believe (as he happens to believe so many things, given his perspective), that restricting the activities of reason might be stupefying. Nothing is farther from the truth. What is really stupefying is occupying the mind with ceaseless abstractions that are mostly distractions, with thousands of inconsequential details, with isolated concepts or those grouped by doubtful premises; full of acquired prejudices, inherited beliefs; alienated by the preoccupation of having more, by greed, or the fear of not having. Always preoccupied in this manner he has no time to attend to what most concerns him, passing incessantly from one medium to another, his true objective becomes increasingly remote. This is not thinking, or at least not right thinking. In order to think in an ordered manner, one cannot have one's head full of this clamour, on the contrary, it has to be ordered and neat. We cannot write on the blackboard of the mind when it is crammed with inconclusive thoughts, unsatisfied desires and fantasies in general.

Thought becomes much more efficient when it can be controlled, for it is then applied when it is necessary, and when it is not, the spirit returns to its centre. It will then begin its activity from a clean base, carefree and unprejudiced. It will also be in direct contact with the sources of inspiration, in which it will find nothing but substantial matters. Always engrossed in elaborating utilities, the truly creative aspect of the mind is reduced, as a result discernment turns outwards in search of inspiration, where it finds abundant material as there are always "things" to do; but this is alienation, not inspiration.

It is necessary that the vicious circle of externalisation be understood in order to detect the danger of man's complete alienation from his Nature.

We should not *believe* that by thinking more, man becomes more intelligent, as when the spirit tries to enrich itself only with concepts, it becomes desensitised, hardened and dogmatic. For these reasons the most insensitive have the most "concrete" ideas. It is not a coincidence that they end up believing that they are the "pillars" of society. These fanatics of concepts are very dangerous because they permanently struggle to maintain the image on which they depend, well delineated with thick lines, as if they, society and reality were reduced to just a few faces, like a cube, sufficient to ensure (their) order and maintain "progress".

Externalised, man floats on the immense Ocean of the Mind. This ocean includes not only a transcendent or metaphysical reality, but also the psychic world that he calls (as this is his experience and reality) the unconscious. The motivations that are unconscious to him are numerous and permanent. However, if he had a better knowledge and control over them he would see the psychic activity that obeys these impulses greatly reduced. How much activity does man undertake to sustain the image of his ego and its projections which he must prove, corroborate, foster, and this includes relationships, work, a *status* that he has to maintain, etc.? All this is nothing more than wasted energy, useless gestures, a product only of his alienation. We have to admit that most psychic activity is spent on trifles and logic is rarely rigorous. If discernment were reduced to satisfying only what is necessary and rigorously applied, that is, having a few good reasons, it would have found its just function.

It will be understood that psychosophy is not against reason, but against the attitude of man who in his greed abuses his external faculties, especially that of discernment, his most external faculty, the least creative and the least unitive. What it tries to do is to *refine* the intellect in order to put it in touch with the *unitive faculties* and make man more receptive to *unitive forces*, since the level of understanding depends on the harmony of all the cognitive faculties.

When the intellect is used to the exclusion of the *unitive faculties*, as happens to hands that carry out heavy work, which become strong but hardened and insensitive. This is what is happening to an increasing degree. The intellect feels strong through its efficacy in using matter; but it gradually loses its subtlety. The evidence of this fact lies in the ignorance of the spirit in general, manifested in a lack of sensitivity with respect to Nature, compassion for animals, respect for the forests and seas; all of which are observed through the lens of the economy, indifferent to ecological disaster, being nothing but an extension and result of alienation.

What our discipline proposes is the integration and harmonisation of the intellect with the "rest" of the Mind in order to liberate it from the rigid schema of its concepts and put it in contact with its subtle elements. The intellect is currently being brutalised in the factory of utilities in which it lives and to this is added the danger of brute strength.

As the human being is externalised, separated from himself and the world that surrounds him, it should not surprise us that he also imagines his God to be outside of him and beyond the reality of his life. It is we who are "outside" of God. It is man who has made transcendent what is nothing but his own Nature. But one should not think here of a species that has transcended its original nature, nothing of the sort. By ignoring his Nature, one cannot speak of overcoming or evolving, but simply of ignorance and alienation. In spite of this, man suspects, foresees or intuits a reality or a *something* that transcends him and that he wants to reach, but since he presumes that his perspective is the correct one, it is almost impossible for him to accept that it is he who has "left" and that what he must do is "return" to himself.

Being already externalised (alienated), he takes as real the concrete world as he perceives it with his external faculties. He does not seek to go deeper within himself but seeks to come out of himself, he seeks the transcendent "outside", in another reality, in another time. Herein lies the danger in the belief in an external and future Reality, because even those who understand or suspect the danger of being externalised, seek in their inner soul a connection to the future in "the other" world, or with other worlds peopled with beings whose high technology enshrines all hopes. At the same time the belief (especially if it comes embedded in a dogma) in a separate *God* tends to fix the believer in his alienation. To my mind the idea of a separate God, as well as an external and future Reality, would have been born of the application of space-time forms to an intuited Reality, but which remains alien and transcendental. Although intuition has transcended those forms (as otherwise it would not have succeeded), when reason wants to grasp that Reality, it applies them, distorting and denaturalising it. This is comprehensible, but this mechanism only becomes clear when the spirit is settled in Reality and observes time and space from there. Only then does it observe how the Mind functions.

A good part of the superstructures of religions (and at times some of their pillars), have been constructed in this manner, with greater or lesser inspiration or imagination. Many inferences and steps in time and space have been made in order to construct cosmogonies, and not necessarily following a unitive or logical order. When we only intuit the Eternal, a memory remains at a vital level that, like the memory of so many dreams, does not tell us the reality that was. We then try to order an indiscernible reality with the representations that remain, but when we want to "compose" it we only decompose it as we annihilate the vital, unitive factor that formed it. It is in transcendental intuition that the spirit perceives an entire Reality as the Essence ensures that nothing is lacking, but on returning to its habitual perspective it sees only the multiple. Ontologically it is the same Reality, only now it no longer perceives the entity. The spirit is thus divided from its Nature. *It is discernment that alienates the Essence of the World.*

Thus separated two spirits appear, one individual, the other universal, and in place of a present experience there appear two beliefs: God and our soul. Then, to apprehend and understand them we apply our external attributes, our reason accompanied by its vision of the world, of the ego and its projections. And thus, the refraction has already occurred. Now they are a product of what has been elaborated. We fully enter into an anthropo–conditioned world of ideas. And so the idea of God as a person with human attributes appears. (Think of the profound Xenophanes and not of Feuerbach's "hypothesis".) [5] It is evident that as a person God cannot be infinite or free, but this does not mean that he cannot be otherwise. Precisely because he exists in some way, man tries to give him form, make him an object of concepts. On giving Him a form, he annihilates It in its true sense of Principle. What is immanent, he makes transcendent, what is vital he makes, or rather wants to make, rational.

If we try to approach our Essence from our individual perspective and with reason (normally interdependent), we are already on the wrong track, as even if reason can internalise the external world, it can hardly internalise itself in the internal world. We will then inevitably follow a negative path, and by doing so it is logically foreseeable that we arrive at a point devoid of all reality (of reason): at nothing.

Even in the exact sciences, which are the only ones that admit proofs on the plane of abstractions, these are given in view of experience. If they cannot lead us to them, they become useless. Thus, if rational proofs of the existence of God (far from the exact sciences) do not lead us to experience, they are useless. The rational proofs of the existence of God have only proven the failure of reason in the metaphysical field and, as belief depends on these proofs, they demonstrate the believer's ignorance of the subject, an ignorance of the object, of the means of achieving it and of the Nature of the subject itself. There does exist, however, a positive and effective way: the vital path. The only incontrovertible proof of the existence of the Essence (or if you prefer, of a God present and at One with me and with everything) is un-transmissible. It is not only personal, but more than personal, as it cannot be transmitted even to the discernment of the individual himself who experiences it. One only tests and proves God from His own perspective.

The more faith we have in our self the more faith we need for Divinity. By eliminating the first, the second becomes unnecessary. The faith in our self includes faith in our individual and external faculties, and faith in our capacity to represent all reality to ourselves rationally. All representations of our Essence, from the most solid like the figures of animals or humans to the most subtle concepts, are "forms" of idolatry. As long as this truth is not accepted our Nature will always be covered by an image and in a latent state, and the very subtleties of our intellect will keep us alienated. It is this same faith in a separated self that leads us to believe that our personal soul can live eternally... separated. We cannot fail to notice in this a materialist conception of the spirit born of an individual perspective that tends to affirm itself *ad infinitum*. It is the old ego that has subtly infiltrated eternal life. If I have called attention to the ego so often it is because in it we can find the roots, trunk and branches of our ignorance.

The identification of our reason on the one hand with our self-as-image, and on the other with our soul should arouse serious suspicion in us. It is evident that the external faculties belong or correspond to this changeable reality, to the individual as such which help him to survive in this concrete life. Reason in its purest state (on the intellectual plane), will be able to form concepts with divine unchangeable characteristics; but from this it does not follow (if we know how and when to best apply reason) that the faculty that produces them is unchangeable, just as we do not infer that the artist has or acquires the attributes of his work. It is comprehensible that man may as an individual want to be immortal, but this desire, which has lead him so many times to commit this simple logical error, is a misunderstanding of "his" immortality, which he perceives at latent levels. It is worth asking: What do these faculties, ideal for a world of the senses, serve for in the spiritual world? The unitive conscience makes clear that wherever the Eternal is, there are no traces of individuality, that there cannot be an eternal *person*. Only Pure Conscience, which is the Eternal itself, which is neither born nor dies, remains unchangeable.

Notes

(1) See to his effect Chap. *I think, then…* in *The Return to the Sources.*

(2) I am not speaking here of the believer of a particular doctrine, but of spiritual reality in general.

(3) With this I want to express only what is said; it would be wrong for my words to be stretched to the point of making pronouncements against the sciences and its discoveries.

(4) Art, literature and music have not strictly followed this process, but this needs a clarification that we will leave for insertion in a more appropriate context.

(5) Xenophanes maintained that "If the oxen and horses had hands and could draw like men, horses would draw images of the gods that looked like horses and oxen would draw oxen" (*Frag. 15*). This, of course, was not to ridicule God but men. As he himself said "considering the entire universe, he affirmed that Unity is God himself" (Quoted by Aristotle *Met. 986 b*). This honourable antecedent, which is the first that I have found in the West, testifies that religious *monism* is found in the very roots of our culture; psychosophy reassumes this tradition. This subject is developed in *The Search for Universal Consciousness.* (Motilal Banarsidass, Publishers, Delhi.)

Part Two

PSYCHOSOPHY AND PSYCHOLOGY

CHAPTER ONE

Psychosophy And Psychology

"We are ordinarily too easily satisfied with our intellectual achievements, which are, after all, concerned with life's periphery."

—D. T. Suzuki

When I referred to the *present problem*, I have tried to summarise, in the light of psychosophy, the evils that afflict the spirit of contemporary man. Since these evils are numerous and profound, because they affect religious, moral and aesthetic values, we can assume that we are entrenched in a *general spiritual crisis.* For a correct understanding of the problem, I reiterate that I have not said: that we are *facing,* but that we are *entrenched in* the said crisis, because it is not there, outside of us, and since our culture is so generalised and penetrated by it, we all suffer from it in some way. Only when we accept this terrible reality can we take charge of and overcome it.

Although psychology might not be in agreement with the causes that I have expressed, it has not failed to observe the symptoms of this disequilibrium that manifests itself in the form of neuroses, and has found some keys to cure and pacify them. The same internal plane (unconscious), tries, with its own means, to remind contemporary man of this *other* internal reality that has been dangerously neglected. C. G. Jung tells us, "as scientific knowledge has grown, so our world has become dehumanised. Man feels isolated in the Cosmos, because he is no longer involved with Nature and has lost his emotional unconscious identity with natural phenomena". "Modern man has freed himself from 'superstition' (or so he believes), but in the process he has lost his spiritual values to a positively dangerous degree. His moral and spiritual tradition has disintegrated, and he is now paying the price for this break-up in worldwide disorientation and disassociation". "Anthropologists have often described what happens to a primitive society when its spiritual values are exposed to the impact of modern civilisation. Its people lose the meaning of their lives, their social organisation disintegrates and they themselves morally decay. We are now in the same condition" (*Man and his Symbols*). At least in the understanding of this psychologist, psychology knows very well what are the symptoms of the disease that plagues modern man. However, as the differences between this discipline and psychosophy lie in their goals, methods and roots, the approach to solve the problem will necessarily be different. These differences are those that I intend to elaborate on below.

The reader will do well to remember what has been said about the *inversion of the origin of knowledge*, because this phenomenon has affected all modern sciences that have applied it with troubling naturalness. It has in this manner penetrated modern psychology, generating what has been called the *psychologist vision* of reality, from which an effort is made to interpret religions; a subject to be studied in this Part Two. When I use the term *Western Psychology* from now on, I will be referring to that which maintains this vision and has analytical and therapeutical experience in general as its main source of information.

Psychosophy does not claim to know man's psyche by taking him as an object, from which the subject draws conclusions according to what he manifests. It takes the opposite direction: that of self-knowledge. It does not direct its path towards hypothetical objectives but always tries to tread on firm and familiar ground through personal experience. This means that it does not advance with hypotheses supported by external cases that are considered sufficient to sustain a theory, that is, by statistics. By imposing these requisites, a gradual and apparently slow progress is required, but if we remember that in this way it avoids the infinite paths to uncertain destinations that interminable hypotheses can take, it will be seen to be the most effective route to reach its goal. This impedes the spirit from changing its ideas along the way, so that it modifies nothing on a vital level, but rather gradually transforms, refines, and progressively assimilates itself to its own Nature. This is what allows it to overcome its usual confines and enter a spiritual and religious reality, and appreciate itself from within Itself.

The objective-accumulative method, which is the one adopted by psychology, by its very nature cannot overcome the subject-object duality, because it is limited to applying the vision of the subject, which is the primary, if not exclusive, result of external faculties, to the object. The *unitive method* used by psychosophy seeks, in the first place, the integration of the psychic faculties of the subject, awakening for this the *unitive faculties*, which are also the ones which will put him in direct relation with external reality *in general*. This means that it does not pursue the partial, temporary, relative integration of the subject with a particular object, but rather the identity of the subject with all of Reality. This is achieved through the equilibrium of all the faculties, primarily the moral ones, of the subject with the *unitive forces* that also govern external reality. This implies knowledge of the internal and external mechanisms of the Mind, and thanks to this, of the personal *motivations* that *determine* the rational order, as well as the forces that, beyond the subject, urge altruism and transcendence.

As psychology aims to cure third parties, and, in the best of cases, alter the psyche of the analyst, it inevitably adheres to certain *standards* of "normality" that serve as a basic reference. Psychosophy does not start from any *standard* of normality,([1]) it has neither individuals nor the societies formed by them as a reference, but an *absolute reference* that transcends the schemas and, above all, individual *interests*. The relationship that it is primarily interested in establishing is with the universal Spirit, and it is from this absolute *essential reference* that the individual spirit will relate to other individuals. All this obviously influences the relationships and actions of the subject both in society and in the World; while psychology tries to adapt individuals to a social order, psychosophy tries to adapt them to a universal Order.([2])

Since I believe the invasion carried out by psychology in the fields of religion and philosophy is unfounded and thus illegitimate, for the reasons that I will set forth below, it can be said that psychosophy is a response in the name of these disciplines, a defence of them, with the purpose of freeing them from the psychological vision (psychologism). Nevertheless, psychosophy tries to re-establish two essential elements in philosophy and religion: experience in their premises and vitality in their practices, thus subordinating all reasoning and belief to these elements. It aspires, thus, to free them from the unnecessary intellectualism which suffocates the former and, in the West, has led to the stagnation and sclerosis that have mummified the latter.

As the objective of psychosophy is transcendence, I am not interested here in the therapeutic aspect of concrete individuals, which is what has given rise to modern psychology and around which it has centred its attention. This means, that I do not have to concern myself with the specific task of this discipline, which, through the learning provided by practice, is the inalienable legacy of professional psychologists, but rather with its limitations, with which it penetrates the field of religion.

For my purposes I have chosen three notable psychologists who seem to me to be particularly representative: S. Freud, E. Fromm and C. G. Jung. In keeping with what has been expressed, I have chosen from them only the works which deal with religion, which in the case of the first two are relatively few but, in my opinion, very significant, while in the case of Jung they are many and complex. This, and the fact that this author has founded a whole school that has ultimately completely invaded the field of religion, have made me pay more attention to him. In any case, it is not my intention to exhaust the thinking of these psychologists on this matter, but to counterpoise them sufficiently with psychosophy so as to better delineate, by contrast, the outlines of this discipline.

I have chosen these authors for the respect I have for their research and work, whose contribution in their own field I consider to be priceless; because they are outstanding figures among the most representative in Western psychology; because they have exerted a notable influence on the entire field of the humanities in the XXth century, which they, belonging to three successive generations, cover almost in its entirety. Before attending to their works, we will examine in the following chapters their field of work and the tools that they used.

Some readers will ask why I have not chosen more "up-to-date" authors in the "spiritual vein" of the end of the century. These readers will forgive me, but I am a classicist and a lover of learning and not of "novelties". It is enough to retrace a bit of history, one of the many disciplines forgotten by modern man, who looks only to the future with worrying avidity, to realise that the matters of the spirit proceed very slowly, too slowly in my opinion for a substantial change to take place in man. This is in spite of the swiftness with which a spiritual *"New Age"* will come about, as the "new" popular, spiritual leaders assure us. It is true that hope is part of the energy that propels all social movements, but it is also true that this only happens when there is a real change in individuals, that is, when these are nurtured by their own spirit and not just by hope. Besides, when there is a high level of hope, as is currently the case, it is a sign that the movement has no real basis, and that its participants have only an uncertain future as a handle, which they cling to, like a lifeline, before despairing. The "new" *spiritual market* is replete with lifelines, to which go all those who, instead of investigating the causes of their dissatisfaction, look for a "new" solution, that is, another distraction.

I am not unaware that there are new currents in psychology whose ideology would be more akin to psychosophy, as a good part of the theoretical material has been taken from the doctrines of the Far East. I confess that I have not concerned myself with seriously studying them, but from the little that I have come across I have observed that even if their authors have incorporated ideas of great importance from the East, in particular a transcendent teleology that could change (I hope) the course of psychological research, it seems that they follow the traditional Western method. This leads them, inevitably, when entering the field of religion, to the questionable domain of hypotheses. Without judging these writers, I would like to take this opportunity to warn once again about the method that the disciplines of the spirit directed towards transcendence should follow, as well as all those who *really* want to achieve their liberation.

It should be understood that if psychosophy has emphasised personal experience, it is because it considers that otherwise man will continue to depend on the mirror of the abstractions that he has created. Although it is in this mirror that he believes he has his reality, it is from this mirror that he has to come out. Otherwise, no matter how orderly and logical his theory may be, it will still only be a theory. And we can say that the more emphasis that is placed on the rational order, the more he will become attached to it and will depend on the mirror, into which he will inevitably slip without apprehending Reality.

Nothing will have changed in practice if there is no experience of an ontological transformation, neither does theory change substantially as long as no epistemological transformation occurs as a consequence of it.

Notes

(1) We would not do justice to E. Fromm if we did not remember that he tries to dispense with these standards, recognising the insufficiency of the common man to know himself.

(2) It is through Jung now that we find an honourable exception, as in his own way he tries to integrate man into the Cosmos.

CHAPTER TWO

The Sciences and Transcendence I

It will be clear that for psychosophy *the general spiritual crisis* is intimately linked to the loss of the universal Spirit in the spiritual reality of modern man. This does not mean, it should be understood, that it has been occasioned by the lack of belief in the God of the Old or New Testament in particular, but by the loss of an *essential reference* (although this might not be a direct and conscious experience) to an Absolute that comprehends reality and explains it in some way, both rationally and emotionally. Without this reference man finds himself lost in the World and without foundations. Having lost his participation in the Order, he has to make, to *create* order out of it from his *individual perspective.* It should not be surprising then that the Order is reduced to the social, and that the modern divinity is the State; symptoms that Hegel manifested and that materialism would soon incorporate.

Now, modern psychology is born within this context; although paradoxically as a remedy for this disequilibrium. In other words, from this new perspective as a consequence of the aforementioned spiritual obstruction, alienated from the universal Spirit and from Order, it seeks to restore psychic order. By ignoring the first generative causes of evil and paying attention to the evils according to how they manifest themselves in the sick, it behaves not in a preventive but rather in a curative manner, as our medicine has generally done, of which it is an offshoot. And just as medicine seeks remedies so that man can live in a polluted environment, psychology seeks to adapt individuals to a psychically and spiritually ill society.

Psychiatric and analytical experience, however, far from finding proof of the in-existence of the spiritual reality of which religions speak, has found abundant religious material, and the deeper it goes the more it discovers.

It is not this experience that leads our psychologists to incredulity but the perspective and belief which they have inherited. From here they interpret their findings in religion, in the *belief* that this approach is truer than the religious one. This approach has been named the "scientific method". And as this word has a magic power, the knowledge that wears this label will garner enormous credit and it would be very rare for someone to dare to question these "scientific facts", the holy cows of our century.

Jung himself, in his last book (*Memories, Dreams, Reflections*) in which he takes stock of his career, admits that only a third of his patients were cured, another third experienced only some improvements and an equal number remained ill. And this in the case of an analyst as remarkable as him. It will be clear that I am not trying to detract from the merit of these achievements, but this percentage is too small to be called a "scientific" result. And we are still in the proper domain of psychology, that is, where the scientific method is applicable.

A lot of harm has already been done by "scientific" interpretations of philosophy and religion. With this false label millions of people for many generations were made to believe that "Reality" *was* of a certain kind, as historical materialism concerned itself with All, even with religion, which it excluded from this reality in the name of a single premise. And it even developed with other premises, some([1]) "scientific bases" for a philosophy of history, including a future, which this prestigious label guaranteed, and which had to be fulfilled (as if it were an experiment that had been tested without any contradictory results). Admittedly, this incontrovertible theory assures us, that for the experiment not to be postponed, (as it was "something certain" that sooner or later *certus, incertus quandum* had to be fulfilled) violence was necessary, with as many victims that the "proof" required.

We will not speak here of the countless victims and the suffering and terror that this "scientific theory" generated, we simply need remember that it did not work. Despite the fact that much more blood was spilled for this "necessary sacrifice" to achieve a "promising future" than primitive religions poured onto their sacrificial altars for the same purpose; the experiment proved not to be "scientific".

This example is enough for us to be more prudent and rigorous in the future with products that are labelled "scientific". It seems strange that after five centuries of strict science in some fields, we have still not learnt what it means and what are the requirements of a science to become such. Analytical psychology wants to make even astrology out to be a "science". (2) In the light of this situation, I will dare, although it might be unnecessary to every man of science, to make a few clarifications. The scientific method does not in any way guarantee that the result be "scientific", namely, true, or with great possibilities of being so. In the first place, it is the exactitude of the theory in relation to the persistence of the *result* that makes a fact scientific. In the second, there are "objects" to which the scientific method is not applicable. Such is the case of the *noumenic,* as E. Kant maintained. In attempting an explanation psychology has made two grave mistakes: without worrying about overcoming this philosopher's definite theory of knowledge, it has simply ignored it, and to put it within the reach of the "scientific method", it has *distorted the nature* of this object by metamorphosing it in the phenomenic.

It is true that psychology promises to be less risky than Marxism, since, for now, it opposes violence; but we should not forget that it has inherited materialism. Because even if it has surpassed it in some sense, as Jung, who is possibly the one who has separated the most from that vision expresses it: "What we do know without a doubt is that empirical reality has a transcendent *background*". (*Misterium Coniuntionis*) Even he retains this *psychological vision* of reality; which clearly shows its legacy. Fortunately, the psyche is no longer a product of psychic mechanisms that blindly obey external stimuli, or a result of chemical or electrical combinations, as the theoretical fundamentalists of the sciences *believed* at the end of the XIXth century, but *the spiritual reality that continues to be rejected*, that is, the absolute values sustained by religions, thus declaring religious reality explicitly or implicitly illusory, which is, in the best of cases (Jung), nothing more than a "psychic reality", objectively inexistent. It is by virtue of this *belief* that psychology has arrogated the right to invade the territory of religion and philosophy.

Religion's "scientific" approach, which is, rational, objective and accumulative, is, to say the least, nonsensical. Religion is an *experience* and this is not *inferred*. No personal experience can be inferred. I hope I have made it clear that feelings cannot be reduced to mere *primitive emotions*, but in their highest aspect they reach the sublime, heights that the human being in general is still far from reaching. *The religious phenomenon in the historical process is something that has to be looked at forwards and not backwards.*

We give and take little or nothing regarding the spirit if we enter a temple and objectively observe the architecture and statues, lift a candlestick to see the date of manufacture, study the behaviour of the faithful and the gestures of the priest and so on. But if we adopt an attitude of respect and kneel before the gods and we give ourselves up to them we can learn something. The first attitude is that of the profane, that of the ignorant; the second is religious. In the same way, as we saw, a good theory of love can only be extracted by having passed through the experience, not by studying the behaviour of lovers; the "things" of the spirit are like this and they have to be accepted as they are. And this happens with all sentiments; one has to have them to know them. And religion is also a sentiment and it has a specific name: *religious sentiment.* It is not all sentiment, but without it we would be in a bad condition to know it. The religious "scientist" finds himself in this situation, he approaches the sacred with a profane attitude, and in general he does not do this in a respectful manner, but proclaims with his theories that his attitude is the right one and begets proselytes who adopt a new faith.

In the words of Mircea Eliade: "A religious phenomenon will only be recognised as such if it is grasped at its own level, that is to say, if it is studied as something religious. To try to grasp the essence of such phenomenon by means of physiology, psychology, sociology, economics, linguistics, art or any other study is false; it misses the one unique and irreducible element in it - the element of the sacred." (*Treatise on the History of Religions*) There is no true knowledge of the psyche if its origins are unknown, the fount that nurtures it, the Spirit that feeds it. This fount lies on sacred ground; it is the domain of religion. Whoever penetrates it finds himself *within* a reality that neither his eyes, nor his conscience, nor his feelings can deny, and he becomes *ipso facto* a *homo religiosus.* This means that whoever is not religious ignores the foundation, the motor of the psyche, his own and that of others; and the arguments that he might use to sustain his skepticism (his belief) will only prove his essential or metaphysical ignorance.

It will be understood that, being more than convinced of this and seeing that this lack of religiosity is what governs contemporary psychology in general, I have been required to develop a science of the psyche totally independent of it, which not only takes into account the said fount but also considers it an inspiration, a foundation and an objective. This is, then the cardinal difference between psychosophy and psychology.

But it is necessary to specify the question of limits more precisely so that I correctly explain myself. *Religion* is too broad a term to be encompassed by any discipline, even that of religion. With the passage of time, the same traditional religions have been accumulating numerous customs, rituals, celebrations, beliefs, *taboos*, etc., often incorporated from strange religions and even non-religious traditions which are often contrary to orthodoxy. As is well known, the Christian church has been struggling since its beginnings, sometimes using all the means at its disposal to establish an orthodoxy. It has only been able to achieve this in the theoretical field, and even then, the said elements can be found within the doctrine itself. On the other hand, when religion has been allowed to follow its natural course, as in the case of Hinduism, it has grown in *all* directions, making it almost impossible to reduce it to a few concepts. The concept of "religion" that tries to cover all religions would be even more so. In short, *religion* is a term that means so much that in the end it tells us nothing.

Most of what we understand by *religion* is a product of modest levels of conscience, by which I do not mean that they are despicable, but rather that they don't express the purest and most precious of it. Just as in the mineral world there are many metals of relative value but very useful for man and therefore the most used, and there are others which are more valuable and less common, and minerals such as semi-precious or precious stones with impurities, but pure precious stones are very rare and few possess them or have even seen them. In a similar manner, most people use the "material" that abounds in religion, that comes from the most modest levels of understanding and that constitutes the major part of religion; looking from a quantitative and not a qualitative point of view. This aspect, which would include animism, idolatry and the most popular forms of spirituality, is part of the different planes of individual conscience, in particular that of the internal. As psychology concerns itself with this plane, all these manifestations of the spirit could be the object of its study.

It would be contradictory if on the one hand I said that all this that constitutes the immense material of the religious field falls, although not entirely, under the domain of psychology, and on the other hand that what is true of religion is a matter that escapes its competence. I will clarify this issue:

On the one hand are the external manifestations of the Spirit that form the external aspect of religions, although these are found in abundance on the internal plane, and on the other are the manifestations that transcend this plane, the external and the individual conscience as a whole. This *transcendent* aspect, domain of the *unified* and *unitive conscience*, includes the *primary manifestations* and the Transcendent itself, *the manifesting*. This is what escapes the knowledge of psychology. Now, the understanding of the religious phenomenon depends on the perception of these transcendent aspects. Without them religion loses all its real sense, and thanks to them the *external manifestations* make sense. It is the experience of these transcendent aspects that makes religion *really so.* In possession of the qualitative aspect the whole of the religious phenomenon is understood and comprehended.

For this reason, studying and interpreting the external manifestations without experiencing the transcendent aspects, is nothing more than an intellectual pastime, however *interesting* it might be. There are those who are passionate about playing chess; yet they in no case believe, for that reason, that they are understanding *the first principles*.

Psychology thus has an immense field of action within the religious domain, and it is to this which it is generally applied with relative results, as certain works relating to mythology have proved. But when our psychologists have tried to go beyond their domain without having followed a religious path, that is, without having raised their level of perception or changed their perspective, they have inevitably found a clouded landscape with a reality that simply transcends its vision. In these cases it has been necessary to *give it a form* with hypotheses. The results in these cases, as to be expected, have been unfortunate as we will see in the examples selected.

It goes without saying that the limits between the psychological and the transcendent aspects are imprecise, especially in the field of mythology, but it is to be hoped that men of science will know how to pause when they stop treading on firm ground and not to venture into the beyond with questionable theories based on a supposed reality.

Notes

(1) Premises that are rather questionable that I will discuss in due course.

(2) Obviously I do not oppose research in this field, but the fact that it has become part of the same "scientific zone".

CHAPTER THREE

The Sciences and Transcendence II (Cont.)

My interest in delimiting the respective fields of action of religion and psychology is based on the conviction that if both were to adhere to their own potentialities, they could develop them to the greatest extent and always express a *true knowledge.* In this way they could also *complement* and unite their efforts instead of generating irreconcilable confrontations, as both visions hold positions that neither party is willing to change, and this paralyses the actions of both. These confrontations will be inevitable each time psychology penetrates the religious field and tries to accommodate this reality according to its vision, because in this way it distorts and profanes it. This is and will be so while it conserves the assumptions that characterise it and the methodology that defines it, adequate for its original purposes of re-establishing the mental health of troubled man, but inept to lead him to transcendence and liberation, the terrain of religion and psychosophy.

These different spheres respond to two clearly differentiated stages in man. In the first stage he has to reach maturity, overcoming the obstacles that birth, childhood and adolescence imply, that is, the traumas and fixations that they may have created, in order to start a family without passing on these traumas, and he must be able to choose a profession that is satisfactory for him and useful for society. For this, the subject must strengthen his personality and affirm his ego. In the second, if he wants to follow a spiritual path, he will have to transcend this ego and that entire stage. Psychosophy takes on the task of providing the means towards this end, it is clear that *psychosophy begins where psychology ends*, that is, with healthy and stable individuals who, not being content with this alone, are willing to go further. Considering that, undoubtedly, the aberrations that have occurred within religion were due to individuals unprepared for this stage, which perforce implies a series of sacrifices, the preparatory and complementary mission that corresponds to psychology is clear.

While psychology originates and takes its knowledge from analytical practice, religion and psychosophy have their origin in the (variable) perception of the Sacred and they obtain their knowledge from it, not from humans. These distinct points of departure, though different, should not imply a rivalry but a possible meeting at their borders that good judgment and the love of truth will make cordial and constructive; but these limits should be respected for a good understanding.

There are two paths, one from man to the *universal Mind*, the other from there to man, although strictly speaking one is dealing with a single path with two directions that the spirit takes according to its ignorance or knowledge. When the Mind is reached there is only one direction, which passes from there to the rest of creation. It can then be appreciated that there is only one single energy that emanates from The universal Mind which unceasingly creates and returns to its origin, thus closing the cycle of life; within this circle lies the Life that is One Reality.

But in order to reach this understanding one has to travel the entire ascending path, in which all the disciplines of the spirit should cooperate, each one in its corresponding sphere. The religious sphere can only be covered, as I said, if it is inspired in or by the universal Mind, and the correct path can only be indicated with certitude by him who knows the entire path and has completed the cycle of life. Not only because he already knows the path and the difficulties involved, but also because he has the beginning and the end as a permanent reference. Thanks to this he can distinguish the different faces of temptation and the nuances of the illusory. Without this reference man will continue to be identified with his body and with its perspective, and no matter how much science and technology open his horizons, he will not come out of himself.

In this period of general confusion in which anything goes and everything is put up for sale, it has been suggested that astronauts, on seeing our planet from afar, had a kind of "religious experience". Admiration for technology and the expectations that it generates border on mysticism, one wants to believe, since one no longer knows where to apply the hope of freedom that keeps hearts aflutter, that a ride on one of those devices around the earth is sufficient to understand the Whole. So, whoever can afford a *tour* that transcends the stratosphere will not need any kind of moral sacrifices or religious knowledge, he will only need money, which can buy *Everything*, to reach such heights. “El que allí llega de vero / de sí mismo desfallece, / cuanto sabía primero / mucho bajo le parece, / y su ciencia tanto crece / que se queda no sabiendo, / toda ciencia trascendiendo”. However, “The one who truly reaches there / No longer in himself remains, / And all that he had known at first / Seems base and mean to him, and wanes; / So great a knowledge then he gains / That he is left uncomprehending, / All knowledge transcending.” Thus wrote a space traveller of the XVIth Century. (San Juan de la Cruz.)

In addition, chemistry offers *voyages* that are much more accessible than physics, free of physical effort as well as moral and intellectual inputs. The sciences can thus provide a “*Brave New World*”.

After these fabulous voyages the spirit returns to the same self, the beginning and end of ignorance. To deduce from it the Whole is a vain attempt. Launching hypotheses about it without first abandoning this reference is like shooting arrows into space with the hope of hunting a bird which one has heard but not seen. And it is not that I want it to be like this, it is that Reality is like this, and even in spite of myself, because if this knowledge were accessible to the sciences I would have used the method used by them, but it is not so; here there is no other remedy other than to be “left uncomprehending, all knowledge transcending”.

It is not my intention to deny the particular discoveries made by psychology in the field of religion, what I am questioning are its premises and the result insofar as they feed man’s external faculties in detriment to the unitive ones; that is, instead of leading to a *religious experience*, they tend to eliminate it. When psychology makes of religious reality a “psychic reality”, a product of the unconscious, it reduces and minimises it to such an extent that it suffocates and extinguishes it, instead of contributing thus to the life of the spirit as it believes it is doing, it contributes to its extinction; neutralising in this way the ancient work of religions.

It is not ill will, this I take for granted, that has misled our psychologists, but two *beliefs* that underlie their thinking and research:

the first denies the existence of an objective religious reality; the second accepts the method used by the sciences in the material world as the one indicated to study the said reality. The relationship between the two is obvious. I have already referred to the origin of these beliefs, so I will not insist on it, but what should be clear is that since it is not the product of a true knowledge but rather the consequence of a lack of it, it underlies all scientific knowledge. I have termed as *latent* these kinds of beliefs that are received as a cultural legacy and accepted without being questioned and maintained as unspoken truths. As they retain this state, they tend to slide into the disciplines where they lie hidden. When these beliefs affect some lateral aspects of them, the matter is not serious because once they are noticed, the mistake is corrected without changing the whole, but when they sustain the discipline, as when they generate the method used by it, the matter is extremely grave because the whole system becomes a house of cards, a pile of reasons that sustain each other.

As psychology is a relatively young science, some defects like the one that concerns us can be explained by the pressures of youthful enthusiasm; but this matter of the method of knowledge is serious and already has a long tradition that should not be ignored or underestimated. Philosophy has developed thorough and varied theories of knowledge that psychology could have used to great advantage; but, being the child and heir of medicine, it has aligned itself since the beginning with the concrete sciences. This was correct for its original psychiatric objectives; but, when it decided to extend its domain over the ambits of philosophy and religion it should have given warning that it was using an improper method for these fields. But this was not done, and since then it has insisted on comprehending these disciplines from the outside, objectively, as if they did not know their own domain and needed external help to achieve their objectives, as if their millenary efforts were worth little or nothing; and this is assuming too much.

Philosophy that has known how to stay *within* the ambit of religion, until the aforementioned general spiritual crisis, was prepared to attend to the religious phenomenon. It was also this way because their interests and objectives are the same. Both pursue, for example, the knowledge of the Absolute; the concrete sciences on the other hand move in the world of the relative. The exact sciences know this with a mathematical perfection, and true scientists, such as Einstein himself, have been careful not to intervene in the field of the absolute, because they know that if they were to do so their theories would, *ipso facto,* stop being *scientific*. This exemplary conduct has not been adopted by psychology.

I have recognised that this discipline has harvested some fruit in the field of religion, but these are far from the true fruits, those that are the very objective of religion: the personal intimate knowledge of Divinity, and, by these means, the transcendence and liberation of the human being. Systematically and *symptomatically* our psychologists seem to forget these objectives, which are the *raison d'être* of religions, and therefore, if they are not achieved, all work in this area is a bit useless.

But this is not all. By not believing in this ultimate goal many psychologists ignore the specific means to achieve it, so they do not seek to obtain *the true fruits of religion*: temperance, kindness, love, altruism, nor be nourished by them, while these are the indispensable sustenance of the religious man. These are the fruits one has to cultivate in the field of religion, and not the novel theories that eventually take their place.

This ethical factor or nutrition is curiously ignored by our psychologists. I am not saying that they do not concern themselves with morality, but everything seems to indicate that the *capital* importance that ethics has on the path of religious understanding seems to escape them. This should be clear, if the study of religion does not produce an internal transformation, a change of attitude towards life, a *conversion* in one word, which leads one to practice a spiritual life, indispensable for establishing intimate contact with the universal Mind, it is because neither has its purpose yet been understood, nor has the religious path yet commenced. This means that, in effect, the second stage which we spoke about has not begun, that we are still on the *profane* side of reality, however many theories and published books we might have. The *objective* study of religion leads to dire slippages on the very first step and an inevitable exile from it.

Religions have always demanded a moral praxis as an irreplaceable condition and have left hypotheses, theories and arguments in general for later. And with this they have shown that they do not ignore the psyche but, on the contrary, that they know it from the inside; this is why they have given priority to the truths of the heart and the conscience, and not to those of reason. They know through experience that what is decisive is intimate experience that first moves us and then later pushes us to do good and avoid evil. They know that the manner in which we arrange the framework of reason matters little and that is of no use if with it we gain the approval and admiration of others and even fame; moreover, they have not ceased to warn against the danger and uselessness of it on the path to spiritual growth. For the same reason, because they are inconsequential, they condemn greed, pride, vanity, etc. They know, finally, that essentially each being is alone and naked before Divinity. Only when one reaches this conclusion, through the heart and with reason, and life is accordingly ordered, does the spiritual stage begin. Only then is it well guided, because the *essential perspective* is already intuited, and the *individual perspective,* having only human beings as a reference, is left behind. It is this change of reference that allows the *homo religiosus,* as history shows, to tolerate the abuses, the insults, the ill treatment and even martyrdom; in short, the ignorance of his fellow beings whom he judges from his *moral conscience.*

It is of the utmost importance for every aspirant to understand that without experience, which is the only safe guide and reference and the only *true knowledge,* this enterprise should not be undertaken, as it means venturing into an unknown world which can only be explained with uncertain conjectures. I am not trying to establish a "taboo", as certainly everyone can try the adventure that comes to mind, as long as it does not harm third parties. We are faced here with a *moral responsibility* whose reach seems to escape many anxious people who put forward a "new" hypothesis for consumption. What is at stake here is not just the theory or even the profession of some individuals, this is the least of it, but the place of the human being in the World; a *karma,* the consequences of which are unknown, is being generated. All this implies working in the field of philosophy. This leads one inevitably to assume a *professional ethics with a universal reach*; it is to this which I am appealing (although I do not know if I will be understood from an individual perspective).

If this call is not enough, I appeal, as I did at the beginning of this essay, to the authorities on Buddhism and Vedanta. For these doctrines, like I said, religious experience is the *conditio sine qua non*, prior to all demonstrations of religious matters; all the texts recognised by the orthodoxy of these doctrines are products of the said experience. Before this, according to their terminology, one is in Ignorance. The question is, then, if we accept this language: do our psychologists claim to speak of religion from the side of Ignorance or of Knowledge?

CHAPTER FOUR

Religions and the Internal Plane

In the first part of this book we covered the different paths of transcendental knowledge in keeping with the different planes of understanding but there was no special emphasis on the internal plane, despite inevitably venturing there on several occasions. In this second part while the concern is psychology we will necessarily be within the framework of this plane. It would not be possible, in fact, to deal with this discipline, or of the religious manifestations, to which we will refer below, without speaking of the unconscious. This is so because both psychology and these forms of religion depend entirely on the internal plane for their information and inspiration. This dependence is due to the fact that they have ignored or not paid sufficient attention to the other means or paths of knowledge prioritised by psychosophy.

Following these paths, we had emplaced the spirit in its *essential perspective* from which it can observe how the universal Spirit expresses itself not only in the World, but also on the different planes of understanding. It does so directly on the *plane of direct perception* and indirectly on the other planes that interpret these manifestations according to their faculties. The internal plane is a conscience that uses representations that it exposes and strives to communicate with the external plane with which it has an interdependent relationship.

Both external and internal planes have their manner of ordering, and both have, for the same purpose, the ability to synthesise the material received from the central plane. This material has first passed through the animated plane that continuously gives its opinion, which is what, at a visceral or epidermal level, makes us feel pleasure or disgust for people and objects. These are tenuous forms of love and hate that incline our spirit in an ascending or descending direction. But while the external plane uses the plane of the intellect for its synthesis, the internal plane carries out its own synthesis that takes the form of symbols. It could be said that a rudimentary intellect is used for this operation, but one still incapable of producing the forms that define the intellectual plane, in particular those of time and space. In effect, whatever happens on the internal plane, even though taking place in a time and space, indispensable factors for all representational understanding, the forms there are imprecise, arbitrary and mixed, to the point of adapting them to its understanding. This is contrary to what happens in discernment, which is *a priori* determined by these forms.

The representations that interest us for our purpose are those that *do not have their origin in the perception of the senses*, the unitive faculties of the central planes that express *the manifestations of the Spirit*. Since these manifestations lack form, the planes of representations *apply to them the forms* that the senses provide them with from the external world. But, and this is decisive, endowing them with a *meaning* that wants to express what has been perceived unitively, thus remitting the spirit to the central planes. As long as the spirit remits (or elevates) to its origin, it will experience (understand) its *meaning*. In this operation the planes of representation are forced to *anthropomorphise* or adapt to the morphology that they know is transmitted by the central planes. From this it can be inferred that without this *meaningful aspect*, that is, without a perception that *transcends* representations, any interpretation of these symbols will lack the most essential. Thus, for example, it is meaningless to say that certain people venerate monkeys, snakes, the *phallus,* etc. as is so commonly heard amongst "objective" observers; since these objects are the product of the need of these *planes of indirect perception* to in some way make intelligible what is perceived by other planes. *The meaning* of these representations is thus *the key* for he who wants to understand the religious phenomenon from the external plane.

In any case, this manner of understanding the phenomenon is *inappropriate,* as the interpretations of isolated meanings will never be able to give a meaning to the *whole* phenomenon, which is what is really interesting from a religious point of view. But even the interpretations of particular religious phenomena only acquire meaning if they are *meaningful* for me (for the interpreter), if the meaning has the *power of remitting* me to a formless reality, making me feel and experience it in some way. Even if I manage to correctly interpret (let us now suppose what we previously considered practically impossible) the phenomenon of love in third parties, I will only enjoy the benefits of Love if I fall in love. In the same way, I will only take advantage of the religious phenomenon if I experience it myself, if the meaning deeply moves me, only then will it have had an effect, as it will have made me transcend the formal and remit to the *real,* from a religious point of view.

Religions *take shape* according to different interpretations of the same phenomenon, and these depend on the planes of understanding, which are given priority for this purpose, and on the level at which the spirit is placed within the said planes. The preference, then, that individuals and peoples give to some levels of understanding, to the relative exclusion of others, determines the different forms of religion. These differences are intended to facilitate the understanding of religions and not to establish hierarchies between them, which would be very contrary to the objectives of psychosophy. These hierarchies would in any case be arbitrary, as there is no religion that has not made use of all the levels of understanding; which means that the borders between them are always blurred. The differences between them should be sought in their tendency to look for inspiration on some planes before others. *Within* each religion, one can speak of higher and purer forms, but it would be a mistake, here too, to reject these forms for others, as they are all part of the human spiritual baggage. In the same way it is not conducive to speak of higher and lower levels of understanding, as they all have their positive and negative sides.

For psychosophy, what makes for correct knowledge is the harmonious relationship and the integration of all levels of understanding and, as in psychology, it does not fail to warn of the danger that repressing the manifestations of the internal plane implies. Men and cultures should accept and know how to recognise the manifestations of this plane on which their equilibrium, religious art, and the folklore of peoples in general, so depends. One cannot, and should not, ask everyone for a philosophical (elevated, clear and measured) vision of religion. The vast majority perceive what is spiritual indirectly on the animated and internal planes, the material of which should not be repressed in the name of philosophical principles, for then they would be left with only elevated *ideas* and no experience. Each one would do well to make use of the planes that most inspire him: the sentimental character from the animated plane, the intellectual from the intellectual, the imaginative from the internal plane, and thus everyone, philosophers, artists, poets, etc., will manifest the Spirit in the best possible way.

The religions that look for inspiration mainly on the internal plane are those which Mircea Eliade has grouped under the rubric of shamanic. Even if this erudite man does not establish this psychological relationship, it is highlighted as soon as we look at these investigations in the light of psychosophy. According to this author the sources of inspiration of these religions are, in effect, dreams, visions and trances. (*Le Chamanisme*) On these depend the knowledge of the shaman, who is the one who produces and maintains this form of religion. Like the psychologist, the shaman is a doctor of souls, a *medicine man* as he is called by the North American tribes. He not only interprets his own dreams, which he has the faculty of remembering as he is attentive to them and in close contact with his internal plane, but also those of other members of the tribe. He also interprets the trances and visions, of course and as expected, the most significant being his own, not failing to value those of other members when he considers them *revelatory*. It is understandable that dreams and visions can be interpreted, while trance states due to their very nature pose some challenges. It is normal that trance states leave a gap in the memory of the protagonist, that during them he usually manifests only some spasms, or a state of unconsciousness, such as fainting. The shaman, however, interprets them.

I had the rare opportunity of witnessing various rituals of the *macumba* in Rio de Janeiro and Bahia thanks to some U.S. and Brazilian anthropologists. They were already members of the brotherhood, as their initial objective had been transformed into faith as they became internalised and exposed themselves to the practice. Since I did not expose myself like they did, perhaps due to a lack of faith, I cannot speak from personal experience([1]) but I will recount some facts that I witnessed, which I will use to supplement my lack of direct experience and that could be of interest to the reader.

In Brazil, as we know, these forms of religion were involuntarily imported by the Portuguese with the slaves, and have essentially preserved the African rituals. This was confirmed to me by a member of the brotherhood, an attaché of the embassy of a South African country who had no problem in assimilating the rituals practiced in the New World. The head priestess of ceremonies (shaman) in Brazil is, almost invariably, a woman who is given the name of *Mae* (Mother). She carefully observes the behaviour of her disciples, of which a good number, helped by a strong dose of tobacco (at times they have two cigars or cheroots in their mouths) and an insidiously repetitive dance, after a few hours and after a few spasms, go into a trance. During the first few symptoms it is usual that they cover their faces with their hands as if they were invaded from within. Then they lose consciousness which makes them continue spinning, although now as somnambulists, or fall and sit on the ground. Later they will not remember what happened, only some images that are at best confused, but the *Mother* will explain by whom they have been *possessed* and its significance. They may have been possessed by benign or evil gods or saints with their specific characteristics, which the internal plane needs to express, so that the interpretation resembles a psychoanalytical therapy.

The *Mother*, on the other hand, not only knows how to interpret her own trance states *a posteriori*, but also prepares herself and the decoration in advance to *receive* a specific spirit, which does not necessarily have to be benign.

On one occasion I was able witness a *Mae* who had laid the groundwork to receive a demon; an exclusive ritual had been arranged for it. Red and black colours were in abundance, covering a place which was already gloomy and lit by a fire and a few candles. The Mother, who had been *preparing* herself for 48 hours, made her appearance dressed in the same colours, already in a trance and very ready to dance demoniacally. The leaps, twists and turns resembled those of a young girl, but as if she was drunk (and I think she was), without grace, although on purpose and as if she were mocking the World, more than the audience, which was inexistent for her. This frenetic dance, which lasted uninterruptedly for more than two hours, would have been enough to leave an athlete exhausted. The *Mae* was almost 70 years old!

In the case of an initiation ritual for a member of the brotherhood, on the other hand, the postulant appears in virginal white, as if starting a *new life*, after having surrendered her hair, like a nun, and prepared herself mentally and physically for three days and nights. She enters the room in this way, shorn of hair, spinning like a zombie, in a trance; she doesn't seem to be aware of the ceremony. A *Mother* indicates to her what she has to do. She is *delivered.*

Two of the anthropologists who had gone to scientifically study this religion also ended up *being delivered* themselves, the third one returned to his country to continue in psychiatric treatment. They had the courage to have this experience; for better or for worse.

This religion has not only adapted itself to the official religion but has also adopted Christianity, integrating it within its tradition and tailoring it to its needs. Thus, every Christian saint, even Jesus, has an African counterpart who gives them the *meaning* that they need. This is in contrast to what happened in North America where, because of severe and systematic restrictions, people of African descent lost their language and their traditions. Nothing was left of the African religions, so the African Americans put all their faith in Christianity, but what is interesting is that they continue to apply to it their own mode of perception. Thus, dreams continue to have an outstanding importance, and it is not unusual to go into a trance at the height of religious fervour, such as when singing *spirituals,* the symptoms of which show similarities with those of Brazil. All this seems to indicate that black peoples have a special relationship with the internal plane and easy access to it. Of all the peoples that Eliade cites who continue to follow shamanic traditions, a very high percentage are of African descent and the rest are the peoples of Asia and Native Americans.

It will be clear that what I want to highlight is the mental predisposition that underlies the shamanic traditions. Now, this predisposition is not exclusive to certain peoples or races. It is also found in the most diverse individuals, and it is here that complications arise when trying to understand the phenomenon, as these individuals introduce these forms into all religions. Besides, these forms of the understanding of religious phenomena are present in all individuals. There is no shortage of cases of individuals with a high level of understanding, who are prone to entering a trance and having visions of celestial beings, such as the famous cases of Saint Teresa of Avila in the West and Ramakrishna in the East, which further complicates the matter. It would, nevertheless, be a mistake to see in these trances the real source of their knowledge. In my understanding their visions were manifestations of other planes that they knew how to awaken but not directly interpret, so they represented themselves on the internal plane, with which they undoubtedly had a singular relationship. It would be stretching reality to the point of deforming it if we *believed,* on the basis of the last two examples that all *religious experience* depends on trances of this style.

These two cases I have brought *ex profeso* to the fore in order to highlight some notable exceptions, they should be taken as such if the religious phenomenon is to be correctly understood. These are shamanic *forms* of religion, which means that they are expressions of the internal plane and thus indirect experiences that depend on non-direct representations, such as those of *the spirit centred on the vital plane*. In the former, the spirit is directed to the unconscious and in the latter towards *unitive conscience*. Experience in the latter is far from being unconscious, it is unusually conscious to the point of reaching, in the *total unitive experience,* the state of absolute conscience or Pure Conscience. In both there is a transcendence of the external plane but it may be remembered that the unitive experience transcends all individual conscience, and for this reason the internal plane.

When the experience is represented (discerned) it naturally tends to create a dual relationship between the subject and the represented object, thus awakening the religious sentiment which is one of the means, the devotional, which can take us to high levels of conscience. It is this loving relationship that Saint Teresa had with Jesus and Ramakrishna with Kali. The difference in the latter case is that he was exposed as an adult to a non-dualist doctrine by a Vedanta ascetic sage, thanks to this and his potentialities he could pass to a third stage and thus transcend the levels of representations and have the experience of Brahman, the "*Samadhi* with neither name nor form", as he himself called it. We can observe the relation between these three stages and three levels of understanding, the internal, the animated and the central. Ramakrishna would not establish himself definitively in an *absolute monism*, he would maintain his devotional relationship with the goddess whom he came to identify with Brahman; this relationship can be explained by the natural displacement of the spirit between the Unified and unitive conscience already demonstrated. Vivekananda, his disciple, who was less devotional and more prone to move between the intellectual and vital planes, and who was completely distanced from these kinds of trances (on the internal plane) would be better established in his unified conscience and would thus have a clearer vision of that admirable doctrine.

In his *History of Rome*, I. Montanelli reminds us of the origin of the central ritual of Christianity: (Due to the growing influence of the Gentiles) "the austere holy day of Saturday (in the Hebrew tradition) slowly became the happy day of Sunday. On this "day of the Lord" everyone gathered around the priest who read a passage from the Scriptures, gave the sign for prayers and ended with a sermon. This was the first and most rudimentary mass that later developed a precise and complicated ritual. In those early years, the listeners were still his protagonists, as to them was conceded the gift of *prophesying,* or expressing in a state of ecstasies concepts that the priest later had to interpret. This custom ended because it threatened to create chaos especially in questions where the Church was trying to put some order: the theological questions".

But this does not mean that Christian theology has since remained oblivious to these forms of religion. In the middle of this century, Pious XII had a dream vision in which he saw the *Mother of God* ascend to the heavens. The matter was considered by the highest Catholic dignitaries and a new dogma emerged, the "Ascension of the Virgin". This shows that the internal plane can still make itself heard and respected.

The more elementary the forms of religion, the more they take for objectively real the manifestations of the internal plane (which is why Eliade has no qualms about calling the shamanic forms "primitive"), and the more refined and elevated, the more they tend to become independent of these manifestations and approach the *manifesting*.

But, it has to be understood, the *interpretations* (representations) of the internal plane are not entirely false, as the unbelievers, guided only by the external plane for their understanding, want to believe. The internal plane represents, in its own way, spiritual reality, just as the external does with concrete reality. This spiritual reality is not, as the good listener will already have understood, the *psychic reality* that Jung tells us about. The context is radically different; it has its origin in Reality, in the Essence itself. All religions have their origin here, however rudimentary the understanding of men and however distorted their manifestations might have been; and in no way are they *spontaneous manifestations of the unconscious*. We will return to this point when we deal with this author, but in order to avoid confusion, we will call spiritual or religious realities *essential realities.*

Returning to the matter that concerns us, it will be opportune to remember at this point what was said in Part One: the two planes of representations are formed by themselves, not by realities, *both have an unreal content.* But this is not to say they do not correspond to realities; it is this correspondence that makes our knowledge, indirect in both, relatively objective in one, relatively subjective in the other. When the religious expressions of the internal plane are deprecated or minimised, as the materialist tends to do, what he does is *repress the essential reality* which this plane is trying to communicate, even if they appear on the external plane as unreal, arbitrary inventions or fantasies. Denying the reality of other planes is the dogmatism of discernment that wants to take over *all* reality. The spirit must open up and accept what is reality for the other planes of understanding; this is man's first step to integrate his psyche and knowledge.

The error, both of shamanism and of psychology, is not in seeking religious information on the internal plane, but in the exclusive utilisation of it, discarding other means or faculties due to dogmatism or ignorance.

While observing the religious content of the internal plane, some psychoanalysts have expressed that "the unconscious is religious", thus recognising, in some way, the religious nature of this plane. But they reach this far and no further, and as they cannot go further, they often make the mistake of *believing* that since they *demonstrate* that the religious manifestations *are* on the internal plane, the entire religious phenomenon is a *creation* of it. However, this plane is doing nothing other than interpreting and expressing an *essential reality* perceived and transmitted by the central planes; which is what the external plane (the psychologist) will do, on a third hand basis, with the internal plane. If our psychologists were to investigate (in the manner that we have proposed and not with their usual methods) the central planes, they would conclude that *the central planes are also religious.*

This would be the conclusion of psychosophy: *All the planes of understanding are, in their essence, religious because the Nature of the Mind, as of all things, is divine.* Modern man, alienated in his external faculty, which is the most inappropriate of all his faculties for understanding essential reality, *represses* it on all his planes of understanding, a repression that the psychoanalysts notice on the plane on which they have applied their vision.

Notes

(1) It will seem contradictory to the reader, after the emphasis I have put on personal experience, that I have not taken risks as concerns the practice of these forms of religion, but in general they require drug consumption and I am not a devotee of either these paths nor these mentors. Only in the Fiji islands, in a memorable ceremony, did I agree to drink some *soma* because I could not refuse it and because I saw that the effect on the aborigines was benign.

CHAPTER FIVE

The First Invasion: Freud

"He, who discards religion, removes the foundations of human society."

—Plato.

We have seen that moral conscience is born of the conscious or unconscious perception of Order. This is unconscious from the individual conscience; from the unitive conscience it is conscious thanks to the unitive intuitions and vital experiences; and perception is direct and indubitable from the unified conscience.

Since S. Freud looks at his moral conscience from an individual perspective, he simply does not see it; it is natural then for him to resort to the testimony of third parties. But to our surprise, in his search for the origin of moral and religious consciences, the great psychologist does not turn, as might be expected, to religious notables, philosophers or mystics who have dedicated their lives to discovering it.

We can see the testimonies that Freud is in search of: "We can risk the affirmation that if it were not possible for us to discover the origin of moral conscience through the study of obsessive neurosis we would have to renounce every hope of discovering it". (*Totem and Taboo Chap. 2*)([1]) I do not know how the reader will react on reading this assertion, but for me the fact that the pioneer of modern psychology has to resort to the mentally ill to search for the origin of (his) moral conscience, is a revelatory sign of the general *alienation* of contemporary man. Earlier, if anyone had wanted to know its origin, would he not have used the natural mechanism of introspection and self-knowledge, of his experience drawn from successive acts of conscience? Now, obsessive neurotics are asked. The result is foreseeable.

What is curious about the case is that his patients do not reveal the origin of moral conscience. They only make him establish relations between their symptoms and the expressions of the savages of some primitive tribes that observe certain taboos. Besides, this relationship seems to lie more in the ignorance of origins than in their knowledge: "This is (he says, comparing it with his neurotics) precisely what characterises the attitude of the savage with respect to the taboo, which is nothing but a commandment of his moral conscience, the transgression of which is followed by a terrible sense of guilt, as natural as it is unknown in its origin." (*T. & T. Chap. 2*)

For Freud there do not seem to be objective reasons for the moral or immoral act, they are like unjustified impulses of the psyche. Notice in this, already, the *psychologist's vision* of reality. In this way the "origin" of moral conscience would be for him a consequence of the relation between the external and internal consciences: "In this way then the moral conscience is born of an affective ambivalence inherent to determinate human relations and has as a condition the same that we have assigned to taboo and obsessive neurosis: one of the terms of the opposition remains unconscious and is maintained in a state of repression by the other which is obsessively dominant." (*T. & T. Chap. 2*) The said *ambivalence* functions approximately in this way: it is not that we do not kill someone when he causes us physical or moral pain, because it simply does not occur to us to cause so much harm, but on the contrary, the first thing that occurs to us, albeit unconsciously, is to kill him and then the self-*represses* this impulse by forbidding it. "Whenever there exists a prohibition, it is motivated by a desire, and we will admit that this tendency to kill really exists in the unconscious and that the taboo, like the *moral commandment* (emphasis mine), far from being superfluous, is explained and justified by an ambivalent attitude with respect to the impulse towards homicide." This is to say that the morally negative aspect is the positive one. "The fundamental character of this ambivalent attitude (is) that the positive desire is unconscious." (*Chap. 2*) And this is not only amongst neurotics and primitives. For all of us who want to avoid evil in society, what we really want, albeit unconsciously, is to do evil, and if we punish he who has done it is due to envy: "When an individual has managed to satisfy a repressed desire, all the other members of the community must experience the temptation to do the same; in order to repress this temptation it is necessary to punish the audacity of the one whose satisfaction is envied and, furthermore, it frequently happens that the very punishment provides to those who impose it the occasion to commit in their turn, under the guise of expiation, the same impure act." (*Chap. 2*) This could explain the behaviour of some members of the Holy Office with respect to witches, fallen women and libertines in general, and it is likely that Freud, who was no stranger to sexual motivations, was thinking of them, but he wants to establish universal laws on the basis of these premises: "This is one of the fundamental principles of the human penal order and is naturally derived from the identity of the repressed desires in the criminal and in those who are in charge of avenging the outraged society." (*T. & T. Chap. 2*)

This *ambivalence,* which for psychosophy would be another consequence of the identification of the spirit with discernment, a faculty that believes it sees clearly when it sees dualistically, Freud extends as far as he can. And this impedes him from seeing, for example, a pure love like the one we have seen at levels that transcend the individual conscience, but Freud does not leave it, so he always find a selfish, perverse counterpart. In conclusion, to all moral purposes there correspond immoral intentions, and with this our psychologist feels satisfied with the explanation that he has given on the origin of moral conscience.(2)

After these relationships between neurotics and primitives, Freud already feels enthusiastic and in full command, not only of this subject, but of practically all philosophical–religious knowledge, for which he shows us a thesis so as to substantiate an entire philosophy of history: "Humanity would have known successively, over time... three major concepts of the universe: the animist concept (mythological), the religious and the scientific". (*T. & T. Chap. 3*) Note the following regarding this thesis, surely inspired by A. Comte, who a century earlier had considered the religious stage obsolete and proposed the last stage as the positive, which is the one that corresponds to the scientific. Religion is a stage that has been *bypassed* by the *scientific* stage, in which Freud does not doubt that he is participating with this hypothesis. But he does not develop this thesis, he leaves us with the statement as if it were evidence enough, and he carries on to gather the arguments that will serve him for his true objective: the origin of religion.

It would be excessive and repetitive to reproduce here the antecedents that our psychologist uses. The reader can consult the work we are commenting on from which Freud has been able to extract the interesting work of conscientious ethnologists, although clearly directing it towards a predetermined end. These researchers, however, as even Freud concludes, do not manage to reach an agreement on the origin of totemism, a primitive form of religion; psychoanalysis will provide the necessary answers.

But for this Freud will make a leap that no attentive reader will fail to observe. None of the ethnologists, in fact, at any time mention the figure of the father in the totemic ritual, rather they seem to agree that the relationship that the totem establishes in the clan is transmitted through the maternal line. But Freud will not let himself be daunted as he already has in mind the *Oedipus complex*, a key element, well known in his psychology, with which he hopes to explain the religious phenomenon, as our psychologist starts from the *belief* that religion has to be the result of a *complex*. He will then bring to the fore other sources – in which, curiously, there is no mention of totemism – for his famous complex.

These sources are, on the one hand, Darwin and Atkinson. From the first he extracts the following passage: "The conclusion that seems to us to be the most probable, is that men lived primitively in small societies, each one generally had only one woman and sometimes many if he had great power, which he jealously defended from other men." This conjecture does not seem to be sufficient for Freud; he will thus incline towards the second which better serves his purpose: "Man need not have been a social animal and could have lived, like the gorilla, with many women that exclusively belonged to him. In these groups of animals, the presence of a single male adult has always been proved. When the young gorilla reaches a certain stage in its growth, he fights with the others for the absolute control of the group and after killing or expelling them, he becomes the supreme leader". (*Chap. 4*) Atkinson explains the exogamy of the primitive hordes from this data. It can be seen that even if Freud's main source of information for this essay is the work of J. G. Frazer, he leaves out an important caveat: "The idea that primitive monarchy is always despotic is not confirmed by the monarchies that we have been speaking about. On the contrary, the monarch lives only for his subjects." "Such a king lives as if cloistered in a system of ceremonies and protocols and prisoner of a mesh of customs and interdictions which do not seek the elevation of his dignity, nor increase in his welfare, but only inhibit him from acts that would disturb the harmony of Nature and thus cause his own loss, that of his people and that of the entire world. Far from being beneficial and pleasant, these preoccupations deprive him of all freedom and while trying to protect his life they make of it a burden and a torture".([3]) By which he refers more to a representative of Order, hence the divine character of the king, than to a monarch devoted to satisfying his egoism.

On the other hand, Freud cites two cases of children who had displaced the ambivalent relation of love and hate that they had with their parents to domestic animals. These sources, he calculates, are sufficient: "Basing ourselves on these observations, we believe we are authorised to substitute the totemic animal for the father in the totemism formula," (*Chap. 4*). This is the anticipated leap, since Freud joins together two unconnected points, the scholars of totemism do not refer to the father in one, and there is no mention of totemism in the other, but the leap has already been made and our psychologist sees his objective getting closer: "...we glimpse a hypothesis that may seem fantastic, but that gives the advantage of reducing to an unsuspected unity a series of phenomena that until now were unconnected". The hypothesis is the following: "The expelled brothers met one day, killed the father and devoured his body, putting an end to the existence of the paternal horde". (*Chap. 4*) It may be noted that Freud makes no reference to the time nor to the place where this happened, if this fact occurred one single time in the history of humanity and its consequences would have been inherited to this day by all the American, Australian, Polynesian tribes, etc., or if each of these would have experienced the same event in some remote time. Without pausing to consider these circumstances he continues: "After having suppressed and having satisfied his hatred and his desire for identification with him, charitable feelings replaced ones that were hostile and violent. As a consequence of this affective process, remorse arose and the feelings of guilt came about, and the dead father acquired a much greater power than that which he had possessed in life". (*Chap. 4*) The father thus begins to acquire a greater dimension. The alleged brothers impose on themselves certain restrictions in order to preserve the order of the tribe(s) like that of incest, and periodically repeat the parricide transferring to the totemic animal the figure of the father. Freud explains in this way not only the origin of exogamy and totemism, but also the following institutions: "Society rests on the common responsibility of collective crime, religion on the conscience of guilt and remorse, and morality on the necessities of the new society and the expiation demanded by the conscience of guilt." (*Chap. 4*)

All this according to the alleged parricide and the supposed transfer of the father to totemic animals carried out by primitive tribes who do not have in their tradition any memory of parricide nor of transference. But he still had to explain the appearance of an element in the ritual, indispensable to fully enter the domain of religion: God. But Freud has his temperament and is not intimidated by such an important character: "The answer could have been that in the interval, there would have emerged -without our knowing from where- the idea of God"... "But the psychoanalytical research of the individual has shown to us that he himself conceives of God in the image and likeness of his flesh and blood father, and that, finally God is but a sublimation of the father". (*Chap. 4*)

From this hypothesis it will not be difficult to take another leap to explain the origin of Christianity: original sin will be nothing but the *original crime*, and the redemption of the Son will be nothing but the payment of a "blood debt". "In this way in Christian doctrine humanity clearly confesses more than in any other its guilt that emanates from original crime, as only with the sacrifice of one son has a sufficient explanation been found". Nevertheless, as we all know, in this doctrine there is no mention or allusion to any crime other than that of the famous apple, but from here to a parricide there is a gap that only a tendentious vision aided by a fertile imagination can cover. Finally, Christian communion will no longer be an act of participation, of union with Divinity "but a new suppression of the father, a repetition of the necessary act of expiation" (*Chap. 4*). The only constant repetition that one sees is the systematic application of the Oedipus complex, used with such tenacity and arbitrariness that an obsessive motivation is suspected.

At the end of this work on which we have been commenting, Freud has an idea which, even if he does not develop it as Jung will later do, serves to temper these bloody events and perhaps explain the strange circumstances in which they have developed: "It could not have been hidden from anyone, that we postulate the existence of a collective soul in which the same processes develop as in the individual soul". "For this reason, the simple hostile impulses against the father and the existence of the fantasy option to kill and devour him would have been enough to provoke the moral reaction that has created totemism and taboo. In this way we would avoid the necessity of having to trace the beginnings of our civilisation to a horrible crime, contrary to all our feelings." (*Chap. 4*)

With this last hypothesis he manages to somewhat appease the hostile mood of the attentive reader, but the other hypotheses remain as before and claim to be sustaining a reality. All these entanglements and tendentious arrangements that lead nowhere and, above all, to no experience, are exposed, although it may seem incredible to anyone who knows what this label means to believe, under the sign of "scientific", as when our psychologist makes abysmal leaps, for example, from the castration complex to God. Because of all this, we believe at first that we are reading fantasy stories from the Middle East rather than a scientific essay.

Notes

(1) *Totem and Taboo.* The choice of this essay that I will comment on is not a coincidence. There is to be found here a synthesis of Freud's thought on religion, which for him had been a very significant work. He says: "I have written it with the feeling that it is my major work, perhaps my last great work". The quotes below are from the same work.

(2) On this origin see my work *The Roots of Morality*.

(3) *The Golden Bough.* Quoted by Freud in Chap. 2.

CHAPTER SIX

Freud and Moses

Freud's *belief* that the best way to unravel both religious and moral phenomena was through the study of neurotics, was not a fleeting one. Twenty-five years later and already at the end of his life, our psychologist insists on the subject and in an even more emphatic and generalising way, that is, with a more pronounced dogmatism. He informs us: (In *Moses and Monotheistic Religion*, from which I cite the following quotes.) "I have never doubted that religious phenomena are to be understood only on the model of the neurotic symptoms of the individual". And after quoting the unfortunate famous sentence from Marx, that due to its simplicity has been adopted by all those who want to avoid the troubles and obligations implied by the *practice* of religion, a *conditio sine qua non* for its comprehension: "Religion is the opium of the people", with impunity he buries the matter: "Our work brings us to the conclusion that religion is reduced to a neurosis of humanity".

The testament left by the founder of modern psychology is established: religion is the product of a collective disease; surely the most widespread in all civilisations. Freud in this way entombs all religious humanity. And he does this in such an expeditious and efficient manner that he lets no light emanate from any of the enlightened and "sages of this world", Buddha, Plato, Jesus, Handel, Bach, Rafael, Bernini, Hugo, to name but a few from an encyclopaedic list, forever condemned as neurotic in that dark den of religion.

In the first part of his *Moses*, Freud, again using the work of some historians and anthropologists, makes a historical interpretation through which he traces the Egyptian ancestors not only of the Biblical leader but also of monotheistic religion. According to it, the Judeo-Christian religion would have secured its doctrinal bases from Egypt. His hypotheses, up to this point, seem to me to be more than interesting, even legitimate. But once armed from these sources, he changes his method and henceforth makes both history and religion conform to his psychological vision.

Freud makes a new contribution in this work, which as we have seen had already been enunciated at the end of *Totem and Taboo.* It is the theory of phylogenetic inheritance.([1]) This is the existence "not only of predispositions, but also of content, of traces, of what was experienced by earlier generations". This theory is, in principle, very reasonable as it would explain the instinctive reaction of animals in their immaturity when they have not yet had time to build up experiences to justify their actions. This is the bridge that Freud had been searching for in his earlier work, that although unstable due to the great distance he wants to cover, seems to him sufficient to interpret the historical development of the religious phenomenon. "If we presume the persistence of these mnemic traces in archaic heredity, we will have laid a bridge across the abyss between individual psychology and that of the masses; we will be able to deal with people as we do with neurotic individuals." And following this, as expected, he puts this theory at the service of his obsession: the Oedipus complex. "After these elucidations, I do not hesitate to affirm that human beings have always known that in earlier times they had a primordial father and they killed him."

In this way he enunciates the two hypotheses that he will develop. The first, highly questionable, is that humanity repeats in history the stages that correspond with the ages of *neurotic* man. The traumatic experiences of the child, that is, from Antiquity, (delimited *grosso modo*) are repressed for a few years, which are centuries in history, and later manifest themselves as complexes and with the imperiousness of these that overwhelm reason, both of individuals and civilisations. The second hypothesis, similar to that expressed in *Totem and Taboo*, revolves around the supposed assassination of the *pater familiae* and tribal chief. As will be remembered, he ruled in a despotic manner and had all the women possible, provoking the envy of the young men who would ultimately kill and replace him. Remorse (whose origin is not explained) and the sublimation of the paternal figure would give rise to morality and religion.

According to one historian, Moses would in all likelihood have been assassinated. This probability (which is no more than such) is convenient for our psychologist in order to show the repetition of the primordial assassination; but by no means the fact that this leader promoted an austere religion in which monotheism was accompanied by monogamy, which would not fit within the archetype of a tribal head. Besides, according to his theory, once the primordial father had been assassinated, the existence of others who, not responding to the complex created, would in turn become fathers, would not be explained.

The attitude of the prophets is much better explained not as responding to an inherited ancestral complex, but as a *call* to Order, born as the *present* perception of the said Order, contrasted with the disorder of the community in which they live. This is clear in the case of Moses and his people.

Freud insists on stretching the Oedipus complex as far as he can with his arguments, so much so that he finds it in the history of humanity, in religions and in the origin of the mythical hero. This would not be man's struggle to transcend himself, as it is for psychosophy, but his struggle against his father. Thus, Jesus would be a successor, or the reincarnation of the supposed son who in ancient times would have killed his father to enjoy all the privileges of the tribal head: to possess all the women and absolute power. Given the Jesus's message of renunciation and love for thy neighbour, I believe that if one is not possessed by the "truth" of the Oedipus complex, that is, if one does not accept it as dogma (by which Freud tries to invalidate Christian dogma) it becomes impossible to stretch this hypothesis to these examples.

It should be added that the idea of a God generated by a projection of the father figure has a relative hold when observing the Jewish divinity of the Old Testament, but the thesis cannot claim to have a universal character. Indeed, as soon as we study the divinities of the *monistic* religions of the Far East, we see that they escape, or better, transcend all anthropomorphism, which makes it impossible for them to be reduced or compared to the paternal figure.

At the end of the first part of his *Moses*, Freud postulates an interesting hypothesis. He tells us: "A tradition founded only on the fact of being communicated, cannot be testimony to the compulsive character that corresponds to religious phenomena." In order to achieve the said character, "it is necessary for it to have gone through the fate of repression, passing through the state of permanence within the unconscious." I would agree to this with the following modifications. It is true that man represses certain impulses of a religious nature, an attitude with which he can generate complexes, but I maintain that he does so because these impulses threaten his ego, as they tend towards the overcoming and transcendence of it, that is, they point towards its ontological disintegration. The state of permanence in the unconscious is not only the result of a past event but, and mainly, of permanent stimuli that the spirit receives in the unitive centres; which causes them to be transmitted and affect all levels of knowledge. The intensity, however, is not only due to what is repressed but, and above all, to the unitive experiences, be they obvious or latent, of what is most decisive to man in his existence, and therefore what most moves and motivates him: the approach to Being itself, to the experience of Being.

Just as the calls or motives provoked by the repressed content of the internal plane are manifested, which in general terms are designated as complexes, other kinds of impulses with a repressed content are also manifested. And these should be differentiated from the former because they have a different origin and destiny. These *unitive or superior stimuli* do not have their origin in the external world, object of the external faculties, but in the transcendent reality perceived by the unitive faculties. When the latter are rejected by discernment they become, like the former, part of the repressed content.

Like our psychologists, whoever studies the internal plane from the external has no possibility of knowing the origin of the said unitive instances; he simply finds them on the internal plane. And since this content has no external origin, he will infer that they are permanent psychic realities inherited or innate from the unconscious. On the other hand, whoever has access to the elevated sectors of the vital plane will verify their transcendent origin. He will verify the transcendent origin of the moral conscience, in its complete or universal quality. Whoever has not transcended his individual conscience has no alternative and is determined to look for morality within its narrow confines. Such is the case of Freud and his successors, inheritors of the aforementioned Feuerbachian inversion, which as we saw marks the confinement and alienation of the spirit within the individual conscience. And just as for Feuerbach God was a projection of man, for Freud he would be a projection of the father figure.

As Freud is alienated from unitive drives (although, like any normal human being, he responds to their stimuli), for him everything that is an impulse, motor or cause, is a primitive force that leads us to desire and possess. Later there comes the other, the remorse for the wrong done, the interest in compensating. "Ethics is the same as a limitation of the motivational". Is the Feuerbachian inversion perceived? God, always linked to the good, is not first, but rather man with his selfish desires, who in order to compensate for the evils they generate, *creates* God. The first thing then, is the drive of the unconscious content that man always has the desire and pleasure to satisfy. If he does not do so it is because of internal or external reasons such as an implied danger. But it should not be thought that these are moved by higher motivations, or for good itself (non-existent for Freud) or for altruism, but due to internalised fear, of being punished by the father or because "he hopes in return for a compensation, to be loved by him." Moral conscience, the superego, is nothing but a "successor and surrogate of the parents (and educators) who watched over the actions of the individual in the first period of life, and continues their function almost without alteration". "Like in childhood the ego is careful of rising above the love of the master...and feels his reproaches as remorse in the moral conscience." Moral conscience, like God (the religious conscience) would also be a projection of the same father figure (which would include the educators).

In contrast to psychosophy, for Freud the drive that leads one to do good does not have its origin in the perception of the Good or of an Order, in obedience to the unitive impulses that by themselves provide satisfaction, but as a consequence of a mechanism that allows the subject to divert the original drives that are selfish and thus obtain a *substitute satisfaction*. This satisfaction, the psychologist assures us, is exalting, as the "surrender of the drive fills him with pride". I do not believe, however, that a feeling "that he (recognises) is specifically narcissistic", can raise him very high.

As I said, since Freud is alienated from the unitive forces, he cannot find a *positive* explanation of the spiritual efforts of man. "We face the phenomenon that in the development of humanity the sensual is gradually subordinated to the spiritual, and human beings feel proud and elevated for each bit of progress in this direction. But *one does not know* (the italics are mine) why it should be so. And it then happens, that the very spirituality is subordinated to the emotional phenomenon, *in all senses enigmatic* (also mine) of belief". Of which, when he does not find an explanation, attributes it to the last hypothesis possible: "It is the famous *credo quia absurdum*". Or, another no more illuminating hypothesis: "Maybe the human being declares superior that which is most difficult, and his pride is not more than the narcissism fed by the awareness of having overcome a difficulty". We see that spiritual progress, the phenomenon of belief, and the higher impulses that lead to moral action, are all an enigma for him, and the only explanations that he finds are via the absurd or negative path, through pride and narcissism.

These interpretations are notoriously insufficient. Besides, the Viennese psychologist tells us nothing of the phenomenon of extreme asceticism and even total sacrifice to which a moral conscience can lead, or the genuine states of happiness to which a religious conscience can induce. Freud, to my knowledge, does not even speak of a religious conscience. These unsatisfactory explanations, which leave a gap in these decisive issues of human nature, should be attributed as much to an erroneous perspective as to an equivocal approach.

This is clear in his late concept of the superego. For Freud this would be a product or offshoot of the ego, from which it had been separated until it acquired an autonomous existence, but it is the ego that creates it, that feeds it and makes it grow. He could barely have arrived at another conclusion having the self as a point of reference and discernment as a fundamental working tool, which is effectively structured by the ego. For Freud the moral conscience is a function of the super-ego. The latter is constituted in the first place by the internalisation of demands and prohibitions of the fathers, for which it would be an extension of the Oedipus complex; although it is forming in inverse relation with it, since it grows as the complex decreases. Even if some later psychoanalysts retrace the birth of the superego to earlier periods of childhood (M. Klein), the belief remains essentially the same: it is a cultural acquisition; which leaves the personal criteria of each individual without an explanation.

For psychology in general, (and we can also include sociology) moral conscience exists because there is a family and a society that give discernment the necessary guidelines and data to form an ethic. It seems to me that in this idea, ethics and morality are intertwined and confuse what is formed by the faculties with the faculties themselves.

Psychosophy would explain it like this: The more the self is affirmed in itself, the more alienated it is from the unitive faculties, and it perceives them vaguely and indirectly, so it is safer in terms of its behaviour to make rules, laws and customs and provide an ethic. For this it uses what has been learnt from parents, teachers, etc., a learning that confronts what is intuited from its moral conscience, all of which it weighs with its discernment. But in this process it tends to forget, because this does not occur in discernment, the said intuitions, that is, the true origin of its knowledge, the *creative* aspect of the same, and thus by structuring its ethic, *a posteriori,* it sees it solely as a product of itself and culture.

For psychosophy, a moral conscience, like all the faculties of the central plane, is a unitive mechanism so independent of the self that it would have preceded it in the development of the human psyche. The self is born in unison with the individual perspective, which is a late product of man's psychic constitution. Moral conscience is the *innate faculty to directly perceive good and evil,* and not according to my perspective, but beyond me and even beyond my environment, culture, society, race or species. And it is because there previously exists this unitive faculty capable of perceiving the universal Order, that man can avail himself of an ethics and create laws of coexistence that make human society and civilisations possible throughout history.

I do not want to leave the reader with the idea that all Freud's work that refers to religion has been useless because I am far from believing this. Freud's great discovery that the ego obeys unconscious impulses, much more so than it thinks, modifies one side of religion forever. The other side of the same coin, covered with the dust of centuries of fundamentalist closure, and already rusty and embedded in the human soul, had to be reversed; and he had the intelligence and courage to do so. From him we know that many apparently altruistic actions, even those disguised as religious, can have a selfish origin. With him vanishes the ingenuous belief that all religious action is well inspired, and that all manifestations that are apparently divine deserve respect, and that all forms of devotion are positive. Freud discovers, through obsessive neuroses, certain weak aspects of religion, and these are important contributions. The hysterical origin of those possessed by the devil, for example, is a more accurate explanation than the one previously held by theologians and exegetes of the Church. Psychoanalysis can, thus, cooperate in purging the pernicious aspects of religion and help those who are religious to relinquish them. Besides, in these cases his intervention becomes as necessary as that of a doctor facing an illness. But the fact that Freud finds an explanation for the obtuse aspects of religion does not qualify him to resolve its most elevated aspects, the higher motives by means of the lower ones, the sacred by means of the profane.

Notes

(1) There have been earlier references by the psychologist, as J. Strachey points out in his notes to the Complete Works, but he says "The analysis that Freud makes here is by far the most detailed as that which appears in his writings". It is worth noting that it is viable that at this point Freud might have been influenced by Jung, who placed so much emphasis on the same.)

CHAPTER SEVEN

On Initiation and Knowledge

Since psychosophy looks for inspiration from the same sources as do religions, it does not need to interpret any particular doctrine (much less the expressions of obsessive neurotics), in order to discover the origin of morality or religion. In keeping with this perspective, it seems much more sensible to see in the cult and myth of the hero the admiration for those who have realised the symbolic and exemplary act of the total renunciation of the ego and, as a result, the transcendence of man and his identification with Divinity. The exemplary sacrifice of heroes and saints inevitably stokes the embers of the soul in the rest of the mortals. It is the recognition of this warmth that enlivens them (not necessarily the conscious understanding of the philosophical and psychological implications), leading to the admiration and adoration of those heroes who become demigods or gods in the eyes of their admirers because, in some latent manner, they have a premonition or they intuit their participation in the divine.

It is true that the mythical forms that permeate all religions greatly depend on the symbolism which the internal plane creates in *its* interpretation of the religious phenomenon; but they are not just the legacy of this plane. The intervention of intuition, of sentiments, recognition at a vital level, even of discernment, when expressed in a poetic or artistic manner, cannot be left aside, as all these faculties *are part of the total phenomenon*. For this reason, it is an error to try to interpret myths having only the expressions of the internal plane as a source, which myths transcend in most cases, especially when they have been produced by highly sophisticated cultures like the Greek.

In my opinion, the myths that recount the episodes and sacrifices of the heroes usually express exemplary forms of initiation. M. Eliade does not go so far as to affirm this, but he does observe that cases like that of Theseus, Lycurgus, Achilles and Hephaestus "can be interpreted as initiatory proofs". (*Initiation, rites, and secret societies*) For this author, these examples that repeat, each in their exemplary manner, the essential initiatory forms; the sacrifice of the hero, his corporeal death, symbolic or real, the descent into hell, spiritual rebirth and the ascent to the world of the divinities where they are accepted, are enough to prove his argument. To this list of heroes we could easily add Hercules, Perseus, Orpheus and even Jesus, of whom tradition also says that he descended into the underworld in order to free those in purgatory.

M. Eliade maintains that all initiations tend to reproduce this process: "The aspirant begins the initiation with the objective of transcending the human condition and obtaining a higher super human mode of being". (*Op. cit.*) All these forms of religions point in the same direction to which psychosophy is directed: to the *experience of transcendence*. "One thing above all interests us: that these experiences are occasioned by rites that, in the Greco–Oriental as well as in the primitive world, are of an initiatory essence, i.e., they pursue the spiritual transmutation of the novice". (*Op. cit.*) It is clear what the purpose of all religions is, even in their rudimentary forms. It will then also be clear that without experience what is decisive for our understanding will always be lacking, no matter how many theories we might have on religion and no matter how many myths we have interpreted.

The heroes, like the gods, are there as examples, *to be imitated,* and help us in this way towards transcendence. It is this vital and real aspect which is of interest, not the intellectual and abstract one that does not take us beyond our desk. Imitating the heroes and the gods we can reproduce the same *experiences* of the transcendent, and *become* like them; this is, after all, man's only decisive task. "In all cases", maintains Eliade on *Initiations*, "there is a spiritual regeneration, a *palingenesis*, which is, a radical change of the existential regime of the initiated". (*Op. cit.*) But this implies real risks and sacrifices (that we certainly do not face at the desk), because even though everything is resolved in the psyche, not everything *occurs* there; man lives in a universal context with which he must in fact confront himself, tiring his body and risking his life, and not just *a little,* but staking all, until he feels the wings of death fanning his hair and experiences seeing everything that he *believes* to be himself disappear. It is not in the psyche of a few patients that we will understand the fury of Poseidon, but in the middle of a terrifying storm, without hope of reaching shelter. It is not by reading that we listen to the sirens, but, *by following the example* of Ulysses, in the calm of a thick fog whose surprising silence allows us to distinguish the murmur and even the voices of the nearby rocks ready to destroy us.

I have had the good fortune of knowing many *seamen*, who are forged of a different metal as compared to other mortals through their habit of solitude in the middle of the wide horizon, their courage in the face of the powerful ocean, their resignation when faced with the inevitable. They are discrete, of few words redolent of experience, with a steady gaze, not deflected by opportunism, full of confidence and capable of doing anything for a friend. They have almost always been religious and invariably respectful of the elements with which they have lived in such an intimate and intense contact, and seen in them, or through them, beyond their external aspect (which is the only one that the current common man sees), and *experience* in this way certain manifestations of the transcendent. These men know little or nothing of myths, but they live them, and to the extent that they live them, they recreate them and even create them with their strange experiences: their visions on nights lit up only by lightening during storms, in the Dawn loaded with hope, on waters with a blinding reflection, in the latent dangers below, on mysterious islands, and always under the stars with whom they have a personal relationship.

Conversing, once, with one of these men who no longer sailed the seas because of his age but still lived alone on his sailboat on an island in the Pacific, he told me: "I haven't studied much about religion but I have mine. In order to understand this world which, I have had to live in (he believed in the possibility of being born and reborn in other worlds) I try always to see it from the infinite, for this reason I have always lived by the sea, in order to have the infinite always at hand, and thus not lose myself in the different opinions of men. For the majority of them applause is sufficient to convince them of the truths they have invented". "Those who have come to the sea to compete with their peers and gain merit for themselves are not seamen, this are those who *live* in the sea, because they find in it the reason for their existence". "There is a very voracious diabolical goddess, who has many arms which are held up by her worshippers, in which she carries the medals she has won and her weighty *curriculum*; she is usually fashionably dressed; rich, fat, full of air, always floating on the surface and getting carried away by the most favourable current, but quick to burst when touched with the rocks of *reality*; this goddess is *Fame*". "If at some time you get weary of the sea, young man (I was young then), and you go back to live amongst men, do not let them distract you from the infinite".

Divinity in particular and religions in general, are either alive in us or they are dead. Either they become *creative* and inspire us in our activities, not in our "studies", but in the intimate and decisive work of our lives, in love, when faced with fear, desire or death, or they are useless junk. If gods and heroes do not incite us to imitate them, they are nothing more than statues of the past. It is not the study of the manifestations of the unconscious, which can give us an *intrinsic vision* of the religious phenomenon, but the *vital experience of the manifesting,* the inspirational aspect that *creates* the myth, not in the others and the past, but in me and the present.

The hypotheses about religion that are extracted from patients' dreams remind one of the Buddha's parables in which some blind men after groping an elephant declared the following in light of their experience. The one who had felt a leg of the pachyderm said that it was a column, the one who touched the trunk said it was a snake, and so on, each one with their own theory. In order to open one's eyes what the Buddha proposes is the awakening of the sentiment as well as religious intuition (*caruña* y *prajna*). These are the two pillars on which the theory of Buddhist knowledge rests. Principles, with their variants, which are also present in all religions. In Christianity they would be charity and faith. It would be enough to ask any Buddhist or Christian priest if it is possible to acquire real knowledge of these religions by ignoring these principles. The answer invariably would be No. Let us ask our psychologists then. Have you gone through the practice and experience of these principles before speaking to us about religion?

Psychosophy does not, like the father of modern psychology, see any tortuous origin nor even ambivalence in morality or in the psyche. It has been said that at the base of the multiple complexes that plague man, one finds an *ontological complex*, because by ignoring his true being and essence he finds himself in the World with only his external aspect, his body and external faculties that will never satisfy his need to be. As this incites him to transcendence, and he resists the sacrifice involved, what is generated in him is the incessant *desire to be and the fear of not being* (what he believes he is and to which he clings), which overwhelms him.

But, we should understand well, *the base* of complexes does not mean the base of the human spirit, because for our discipline all the complexes are relatively foreign to the essence of the soul, in which it is found to be pure, (pure conscience) and free in all senses. The ontological complex is not innate in man. It appears when he, at an early age, identifies with his individuality and unknowingly alienates himself from the unifying Essence and thus from the Whole. Man's *essential ignorance* underlies all his complexes. It is this ignorance that psychosophy would like to eradicate by shedding light on the ontological complex and, by extension, on the many complexes which are rooted in it.

From the *essential perspective*, thanks to which the spirit can see the totality of the Mind, it knows itself to be free of complexes. These complexes are, after all, *fixations* of the Ego, for which they are almost necessary; but not so for the liberated spirit, which is liberated from the ego with all its identifications and fixations.

It could be affirmed, then, that it would be enough to understand this essential ignorance to free oneself from all the complexes that are based in it, but this would be a simplistic way of posing the problem, as in order to achieve the said knowledge one must inevitably pass through the stages to which we have referred. This will lead some readers to think of Zen, whose *abrupt path* appears to skip these stages. But, unfortunately this is not so. In order to make the leap that this doctrine proposes, one has to be *prepared,* and this preparation may require, according to the same Buddhist tradition, many reincarnations, for the simple reason that the aforementioned stages imply. (One wonders to what extent the popularity of Zen in the West has depended on the erroneous interpretation of the term *abrupt,* which is confused with "easy", "practical", "simple" and other similar concepts so in keeping with the modern mentality that takes everything *lightly,* even Buddhism, possibly the most complex doctrine ever created by man). What is certain is that there is no easy path, as Divinity invariably demands, as we have seen, a sacrifice.

In fact, once the spirit is externalised it has no choice but to start from where it is, from its external conscience, and the acquired complexes have to be resolved on the way. Here there are no hypothetical leaps. The aspirant has to manage them with his present and real situation, with what he *is*, not with what he would like to be. If he has any neuroses the psychoanalyst can help him on this part of the way. In any case this should be established: psychosophy does not propose a *general therapy* that would include particular imbalances, which are the responsibility of psychology and psychiatry.

Being that from the external *conscience,* for the reasons explained, the central or vital plane is semi-conscious and even unconscious, it is only logical that not only numerous expressions of it have been attributed to the internal plane, especially the essential realities, origin of religions, but also some *functions* of the vital plane, such as the spontaneous, automatic and instinctive activities that humans carry out independently of the control of their external conscience. The reader will remember (from the chapter *The path of intuitions*), that the observation of these functions, as well as their *conscious* control, contributed to the discovery of the central plane, from which our spirit could appreciate a new corridor in the labyrinth of the psyche, which we can subsequently trace through the unitive path of self-knowledge. [(1)]

Another faculty or function of the vital plane attributed to the internal plane, are the *unitive memories*. Hazy and even unconscious from the external plane, they take on life and meaning on the central plane, to the point of becoming more *revelatory* or explanatory than customary memory.

They are, however, an indisputable legacy of the external and internal planes, as are all complexes, from the most inoffensive neuroses to the gravest psychoses, which are not in the least registered on the central plane. A doubling or splitting of the personality would be inconceivable on this plane where the spirit needs to be unified in good measure even at its most elementary levels, that is, within the area of individual conscience, where some insistent interferences (complexes) of the internal plane can still be observed. The observation and recognition of the same, facilitated by the favourable perspective that the *central plane* offers, will liberate the spirit from these obstacles; *an indispensable condition* in order to transcend individual conscience.

In conclusion, the irruption of the *central plane* within the conformation of the psyche does not change the domain or the traditional task of psychology. It only opens a new horizon which should be observed with the appropriate method.

Notes

(1) On this discovery and process see *The Return to the Sources*.

CHAPTER EIGHT

Methodological Premises

Needless to say that the search for the religious phenomenon in the unconscious has not been an arbitrary and capricious choice on the part of psychologists; the guidelines have been given to them by their patients. In reality, the great majority of human beings elaborate the said phenomenon mainly on the internal plane. This makes it subject to what has been called magical thinking, thanks to which it imagines the transcendent as something supernatural, that is, the natural sporadically modified by "miraculous" forces. This also explains why the miracle workers, conjurers (who present themselves as the enlightened), fortune tellers, and all those who awaken that magic sense of religion have many more proselytes than the authentic teachers: the sages. The human being is spiritually still in the caves, he behaves like a child when faced with the transcendent; he thus imagines the gods as supermen.

For psychosophy, the human being in general makes use of archaic devices when perceiving and manifesting religious motives. On studying these, the psychologist is forced to think of religion as a primitive affair (even Jung, as we will see, commits this mistake); but, as we have seen, religion is far from exhausting itself in these manifestations, it transcends them and, thus, also the internal plane.

When speaking of modern psychology it is common to hear that Freud has been *surpassed*. Considering that it has been more than eighty years since his passing, as well as the number of writings that have been published since then, one is tempted to believe this affirmation. However, if we observe the whole edifice of our psychology, we will see that it is built on the foundations that he left, which, inevitably determine the total structure. Some premises, of course, have changed and this has laterally extended the edifice itself; but other basic premises, on which the construction continues, are accepted without question. What happens in these cases, as has happened so often in philosophy, is that the defects of the foundations are only appreciated when the edifice begins to fail. It is also usual that those who begin to see the inclination of the building are not the specialists who work within it but those who look at it from the outside, as they have the advantage of perspective.

Although I have already referred to them separately, I will try to sum up the main points on which Western psychology has been developed that seem to me to be significantly wrong, at least when dealing with the highest spheres of the spirit. I know well that there will be psychologists who will refuse to be taken up by these points, but they will understand that my interest is not to establish a rigid system that cannot encompass the exceptions.

1st. The individual perspective, on which the different results continue to depend, has not fundamentally changed. 2nd. The research takes place in the *minds of others,* of patients who generally do not stand out for their wisdom, but for their manifest mental imbalances. 3rd. Generalisations are deduced from these cases, accepting the *statistics* derived from them. 4th. It is taken as given (latent belief) that the mind is reduced to a *separate organism.* 5th. It is assumed that psychic reality is exhausted in the *conscious-unconscious duality*, which leads us to 6th. The belief that if the unconscious were to be incorporated into the conscious, the *totality of the mind,* its unity and equilibrium, would be achieved. 7th. It is believed that this incorporation should be carried out through the analysis of the (supposed) conscious (external plane) of the unconscious (internal plane). It will be observed that all, be they latent or conscious, are beliefs.

The 4rd premise, the belief that the psyche is located inside the body and is reduced to an organism of it can be traced back to Aristotle in our culture, but it is evident that it has been affirmed in recent centuries together, naturally, with the individual perspective, until it has become an "obvious truth". Unfortunately, when this point is reached it is very difficult to turn back. Just like the edifice we spoke about earlier, it is very likely that man will only realise his mistake when he sees himself falling apart. To be precise, we must remember that Aristotle, who had a broad and open spirit, admitted the existence of a *subtle part* of the mind, a point on which I will expand later, but which I will fleetingly indicate because it has not been given sufficient attention to the extent of having fallen into oblivion. This *subtle part,* however, continues to manifest itself, although today it is interpreted by the crude *part* of the psyche. In this way, it is as if objects were brought up from a dark underground well with a small bucket, and these are the images, symbols and representations in general that the internal plane provides, which are interpreted, compared, ordered and listed on a desk, as in an archaeological study. And so, joining little bits with theories, the task of unifying the psyche is attempted. One wonders whether in this way it does not end up, on the contrary, dividing it even more.

However, in spite of the methodological weaknesses of psychology in apprehending the *subtle side of the mind*, there is no dearth of psychologists who have launched themselves like Icarus, and flying towards the transcendent with flawed wings badly held together by dubious premises. It has been a sorry sight. It seems that every psychologist, as soon as he has his own theory, runs with it; and poor bruised Icarus embarks once again on his "scientific" flight. It will be understood that my aim is not to exhibit the fractures of the unfortunate Icarus, but to avoid the useless flights of the future, which only benefit the transient prestige of the inventor of the "new" glue for the wings, but absolutely not the sciences, represented here by the legendary hero. Psychosophy's interest is to make the spirit grow wings so it can reach its true destiny. It is capable of this because, just as Freudian psychology has researched the origin and the consequences of the primitive inferior drives, psychosophy has investigated the origin and consequences of the higher essential drives; not those proceeding from man's animal needs, but from his spiritual; not from his body but from his Essence.

As we saw, the result of the first "scientific flight", elaborated by Freud was disastrous. This should not surprise us because besides the methodological limitations indicated, our psychologist added a visceral rejection of religion, so common at the turn of the century, that inclined him to see it in terms of evil and attack it with savagery. To this was added the importance he assigned to sex, which pushed him even further in his assault on Christianity. This doctrine, as we all know today, prohibited or restricted the natural use of sex with a sickly and sickening emphasis, which is what Freud had discovered. If he had limited himself to explaining the neuroses created by puritanism, evident to us today thanks to him, and which he courageously confronted, we would have little to find fault with. His mistake, like that of Icarus, was to recklessly launch himself into a flight for which he was ill prepared.

Freud's failure in this attempt has only been partly recognised by his colleagues. But this is not as decisive as is the fact that they have continued to occupy, effectively, the territory invaded by their master. Henceforth, psychology would remain installed in the field of religion by hereditary right, without questioning whether or not this is legitimate, whether or not these matters are within its competence.

With Jung we enter the field known as speculative psychology. It should be clear that even if it is inevitable that scientific and speculative psychology tangentially overlap, it is already a tradition to consider them opposites. This is so because they invariably tend to separate, in such a way that the one cannot accompany the other for more than a short distance. As a result, when the speculative dose is very high, it is inappropriate to speak of scientific psychology. This is what happens, without fail, every time psychology tries, with traditional means, to reach the heights of religion, because for this it has to distance itself from therapeutic practice. There can result from this a scientific psychology, but not a religious experience, which is the *condition sine qua non* to give the study of religion a scientific basis.

Whether conscious of this or not, the vast majority of psychologists have fortunately maintained a prudent distance from religion. Among them however we cannot include the "Jungians", whose almost religious faith in their guru's premises, makes them the most persistent invaders in this sought-after field of research.

CHAPTER NINE

The Second Invasion: Jung, an Ambiguous Being

"The greater the quantity of truth in an error the more dangerous it becomes."

—Amiel

C. G. Jung was further from the XIX century and the evils of puritanism, which no longer affected his contemporaries so much thanks to an inevitable antithetical reaction, of which the most outstanding theorist was Freud, and without his teacher's visceral hatred of religion, Jung could apply himself less prejudicially to its study. His interest in religion grew until he became so wrapped up in it that it became his obsession. Although his most extensive works deal with Christianity, some isolated texts from the Far East also came to his attention, on which he briefly commented from his particular point of view. Thanks to these studies, Jung has been seen as a bridge between East and West, and this is valid insofar as he has induced many who were searching for a distant intellectual means of approach to investigate Oriental doctrines, until then having been ignored by them. Now, whether this bridge has led them to be understood, is a subject that we will discuss.

The edifying and positive meaning that Jung found in religion led to Freud labelling this as the mystical side of his disciple. But by this we cannot conclude that we are faced with a religious person. Freud referred to it disdainfully, as if it were an atavism that Jung and the whole world should have put aside, because in general religion was a subject that had been overcome in man's evolutionary process. However, viewing the two psychologists dispassionately, we see that in most fundamental aspects Jung had been a good disciple. In fact, in spite of the desire of all those who (notwithstanding their scant knowledge about him), want to see in him a kind of mystic with a direct line to the transcendent, Jung believed throughout his life that the psyche, like everything that exists, had to respond to "natural laws". "Jung, like the early psychologists, borrowed hypotheses from physics and held the questionable view that psychic energy obeyed the first and second laws of thermodynamics." (*On Jung*, A. Stevens) This would bring him closer to the principle of self-regulation that had been applied in biology and in other fields. This principle called *homeostasis* is the "means by which all organic systems maintain themselves in a state of balance" with the objective of survival. (*Op. cit.*) "Jung was convinced that the psyche, like the body, was a system of self-regulation, and for this it strives perpetually to maintain a balance between opposing propensities". "A dynamic polarity exists between the ego and the Self, between the persona and the shadow, between the masculine consciousness and the anima, between the feminine consciousness and the animus, between extroverted and introverted attitudes, between thinking and feeling functions, between sensation and intuition and between the forces of Good and Evil." (*Op. cit*) This biological principle forms part of the premises and the structure of Jung's doctrine. Without discussing this principle, which seems very reasonable in the biological world, correctly applied by Jung in the compensatory function of dreams, it particularly interests us because our psychologist will extend it to the confines of the Cosmos and the psyche, that is, to the domain of religion, in the transcendent. "The psyche is a self-regulating system that maintains its equilibrium just as the body does". "In this sense we can take the theory of compensation as a basic law of psychic behaviour." (*C.W. 7 cit.* Stevens)

Jung's opposition to a rigid interpretation of dreams and symbols is perfectly comprehensible. He also prefers not to establish therapies that are applicable to different individuals as each patient has a singular problem. I agree with his position of giving general suggestions without committing to his theories as far as results for its application are concerned. But when it comes to establishing his "own" position with respect to some concepts that are decisive in his theory, we long for more explanations, but here he also proves to be evasive and instead of telling us: my knowledge stretches only thus far, he takes recourse to leaving us with several possible interpretations. In this way, leaving the margins blurred, he ably leaves the impression that his knowledge extends indefinitely.

It is, then, when Jung has to take a position that he becomes as slippery as a fish. With this undefined and evasive position (and we credit him with this ability), he attracts a wide and heterogeneous public, including believers (in the objective existence of God), among whom there are also those (I do not know how) who believe (although they might be confusing him with Saint Thomas Aquinas) that our psychologist had a mystical experience at the end of his days! (?) Faced with this situation, there is no choice but to catch our fish in the nets of reason, bring him to the surface and examine him at close quarters. The ambiguities that I have pointed out are not in passing or irrelevant and some have been commented on by other authors.

Thus, for example, he uses concepts such as "psychic reality". An overarching concept that extends as far as the human mind can, but when we think twice, we see that it tells us nothing. Everything, of course, is a psychic reality ... on the one hand, but on the other we want to know if it is subjective or real, if it exists "objectively" or not. But Jung opts for a middle path. On the one hand he protests: "What the majority ignores or seems incapable of understanding, is the fact that I see the psyche as something real." (*Answer to Job XIX*) But on the other hand, in another text and context in which he does not want to show his esoteric side but his scientific *persona* he tells us: "All psychological facts which cannot be verified with the help of scientific apparatus and with exact measurement are assertions and opinions, and, as such, are (only) psychic realities." (*Psyc. View of Conscience*) For him, obviously, all religious reality falls into this category.

I have nothing to object to, rather I have much to be grateful to Jung for his interpretation of the symbols expressed by the internal plane. My objections begin when, without warning, or without warning us of the distances involved, Jung passes to the field of theology; and he does this with a simple inversion of terms or of order. Instead of telling us of the symbols that God generates, he speaks to us of the symbols that this archetype expresses; which would be fine if he always adopted this position but this is not the case. If Jung is ambiguous with his terminology, he is above all ambiguous with the concept of God. Only once, and not in his writings, but in reply to a question asked when pressured to take a stand on the objective existence of God, he manages to say, "The archetype presupposes that someone has left a trace", leading one to believe that on this occasion God comes before the archetype. At other times, God is identified with the archetype, and at other times God is the symbol expressed by the archetype. So, he suits all tastes; except the most demanding. God is confused, most of the time, with other symbols of totality, such as mandalas, crosses, squares, spheres, etc. and even with flying saucers as shown by an interesting essay on them (*Flying Saucers*). Thus, although God has "a particularly important role amongst the archetypes, as he is primarily the regulator and commander of chaotic states, giving the personality the greatest unity and totality possible". (*Op. Cit. 21*) "God *is* (italics mine) a symbol of totality *par excellence,* something round, complete, perfect." (*Op. Cit. 21*) God *is* (...). like the mandala, which is a magic circle (...) symbol of the order that organises and enshrines the psychic totality". (*Op. Cit. 18*)

With the concept of individuation, which, although fundamental, as is well known in analytical psychology, we find ourselves with a series of malleable explanations that in the end do not specify the concept, on the contrary, it would seem that the more definitions that Jung gives us, the more indefinite he leaves it for us. He tells us: "I use the term *individuation* to signify the process through which a person becomes a psychological 'individual', that is, a separated, indivisible unity or whole" (*Archetypes and the Collective Unconscious*). And elsewhere, "*Individuation* means to become a single and homogenous being, and, in so far as in-dividuality, embraces our innermost, last, and incomparable uniqueness, it also implies becoming one's own self (the self of one, literally)". (*Two Essays on Analytical Psyc.*) However, although he has used in these definitions the terms: "person", "individual", "separated", "single", "incomparable uniqueness" (in the sense of untransferable *uniqueness*) and "the self"(personal, *one's self*) that, obviously refer to an ego, he does not accept this interpretation sustained by various authors: "But time and again I note that the individuation process is confused with the coming of the ego into consciousness and that the ego is in consequence identified with the self, which naturally produces a hopeless conceptual muddle. Individuation is then nothing but ego-centeredness and autoerotism. But the self comprises infinitely more than a mere ego." (*414, The Structure and Dynamics of the Psyche*) Of course, it would be erroneous to interpret it as an absolute egocentrism, that is, as a process that tends towards egoism. Nevertheless, it always enshrines a relative egocentrism as Jung never abandons the ego. In fact, for him, the ego offers the only manner of being "conscious", and it retains at all times what I have called the "individual perspective". For Jung, the ego is the conscious one and it has to do all the work in the process of individuation.

If the centre of the unity of consciousness is on the plane of representations, (the external plane), our understanding "needs" representations in order to understand. It is only logical that he directs himself to another plane of representations to complete "his knowledge" and that he believes that if only he could integrate the internal with the external plane, he would achieve his "unity". But this unity that, incidentally, is nothing but an unrealisable hypothesis, tends only towards the unity of the ego, and it is to this that Jung's process of individuation or Fromm's process of "dis-repression" are directed. And even if this union were supposedly to be reached, according to all that has been demonstrated, in no way would what we have seen, which is the Unity that includes the formless spiritual reality, be achieved. Or rather, it is this one that includes all forms. For this reason, I have elsewhere stated that Jung's individuation process has ignorance (in the Buddhist sense) as its final objective, and this is because it encloses us in the vicious circle of individual consciousness. A process of individuation is perhaps necessary in order to rescue those who are pathologically alienated and who need to acquire a personality and define themselves through it, that is, those who due to a fixation or deviation are delayed or lost in the process of becoming adults.

Jung however has greater aspirations for his individuation process. With it he aims to achieve the limits of religious knowledge. But for this, as I have already said, another method is necessary than the one adopted by Jung and psychology in general. They, in effect, try to adapt the psyche to the objective method used by psychiatry and the natural sciences, instead of creating and adapting a method that is concerned with the psyche, which would mean the inversion of this process to accommodate the subject to the object, and not the latter to the erroneous perspective of the former.

When we have reality arranged in keeping with a system of reasons, the "inversion phenomenon" occurs, from which reality begins to accommodate itself, to adapt itself to our system, and the more it adapts (or the more we make it adapt), the more we affirm ourselves in the inverse perspective, and in this way what began as a relatively objective observation becomes subjective; reality is becoming *our* vision. This inversion is "normal" when discernment is seen as the retina of the mind, in which reality is never represented *as it is,* but as a phenomenon in the Kantian sense, that is, determined by "the conditions" that the subject imposes on it.

A "system of ideas or reasons", is an extension of the basic conditions that the subject assigns to it. It can still be "thought" of as inevitable, but if this is so it is because one is seeing with this retina and not with the one that can see things as they are and, therefore, it can adapt to reality at all times without needing to fall into the inversion. That system depends, as a rule, on certain premises, on certain concepts that already have a defined meaning which are like a small system that conditions the system itself and is a "key" part of the conditions that it imposes on reality.

These premises or key concepts are the first that we must thoroughly question in a system, because it is precisely with them that the author will tend to go wrong when he takes "for granted" that the object corresponds to its definition, to the concept. This is why later we will find the enclosed object, adapted to the form of the concepts and usually deformed. Later the author will have his thousands of reasons, all of which make up his system, in order to not remove the foundations on which the whole edifice is supported. An edifice that in general has taken him a whole lifetime to construct and which is not only an external construction, but which has made him, the author, become what he "is". These premises not only sustain his edifice but also his personality; they justify an entire life. There is more than a little of the author in them, therefore far from being disposed to removing them, he would be very ready to maintain them.

Consequently, another author is usually required, one who will be committed to "his" premises and not to those of others to bring them to light and view them objectively (albeit relatively within his system) and to discover to what extent the object has been forced and deformed.

CHAPTER TEN

The Alchemical Formula: Good = Evil

Although good and evil are the constants in his work, Jung was preoccupied with finding an equilibrium amongst these forces, understandable for one whose profession it was to discover and cure psychic disequilibrium. But this does not explain why man, and Jung himself, is so worried about the moral crisis affecting our era, or why he tends towards the good or feels guilty when he chooses evil. Jung insists on putting good on an equal footing with evil, because the reality that interests him is that of the unconscious. "The Unconscious does not establish differences between Good and Evil." (*Aion*) Which is true, but can one philosophise from this premise?

I believe that the following assertion aptly summarises the constant refrain in his theory: "Everything human is relative, because everything rests on an inner polarity; for everything is a phenomenon of energy. Energy necessarily depends on a pre-existing polarity, without which there could be no energy. There must always be high and low, hot and cold, etc. (in which we can include good and evil) so that the equilibrating process, which is energy, can take place." (*Two Essays in Analitical Psyc.*) He thus expresses his admiration for "old Heraclitus who was indeed a very great sage, who discovered the most marvellous of all psychological laws: the regulative function of opposites. He called it *enantiodromia*, a running contrariwise, by which he meant that sooner or later everything runs into its opposite". (*Op. cit.*) It is true that this theory will help him to resolve the constant problem that he observes in his patients, the opposition of the conscious and the unconscious and the disequilibrium generated by the exclusion of one by the other, "as what we call madness is produced by the exclusion of the conscious by the unconscious, the exclusion of the latter by the former also generates endless complexes that sooner or later will be manifested by the law of *enantiodromia*". (*Op. cit.*)

With nothing but conscious and unconscious existing in a world of opposites, it is only logical to balance these opposing forces. For psychosophy, however, neither the psyche nor reality are exhausted in these dualisms, what is actually exhausted in them is reason. The contribution that our discipline can make to psychology is considerable, not only because it overcomes the conscious-unconscious dualism by the introduction of the central or vital plane, but also because the spirit "centred" on this plane is precisely in the best position of "equilibrium" and perspective to avoid the excesses of the external and internal planes and hence this permanent struggle of arrangements and turbulences from one extreme to the another.

I believe that Jung would have been much more satisfied to have discovered the vital plane than all the alchemical texts, because while the latter strive to proportionally mix opposites, the vital plane does so naturally for the simple fact that the spirit on it does not identify with any of the opposites. This is what allows the spirit to continue on its path without obstacles towards its Unity. It is not by uniting opposites that Unity is achieved, but by transcending them, and the best (and surely the only) way of doing so is by overcoming the dependence of the spirit on the faculties that see reality dualistically.

Once this dependence has been overcome, the spirit begins to perceive the light that illuminates the path towards its liberation, and understands that everything that leads it towards this objective is good and anything that impedes it is evil. For this reason, a light or objective is seen as being Good "in itself", but is not perceived as an Evil "in itself". The only evil is that which the subject creates out of laziness, out of desire, out of fear.

Everything, thus, is summed up in the Good, in Unity, in which there can be no opposites nor dark sides. For this reason, the man of spirit is a "good" man and that is why Jung, who puts Good and Evil on equal terms in his theory, chooses the first in the moment of action. For the motor, the energy, is not born, as he says, of those opposites like that of an electric current, but of the Good that attracts and inspires man so that he achieves his plenitude.

But, I suppose that it will be clear, this does not mean that evil or "shadows" do not exist. They exist up to the last levels of the spirit, beyond which very few reach. This means that Jung's psychology continues to be valid for the immense majority and for almost all cases. And nowhere does psychosophy, that thanks to psychology knows of the many traumas created by repressions, propose to accept only the good and the light and to repress evil, the shadows and the unconscious in general. Rather it intends not to look at good and evil from the point of view of discernment because it knows that it is this that generates the interminable struggle of opposites.

Neither does psychosophy deny, rather it corroborates, that the internal plane gives rise to the symbols of totality, it only knows that this plane does not generate them, although it might "create" them like an artist, not out of nothing, but inspired by the central plane, which is the plane of equilibrium. When this is broken, and this rupture is, often, a consequence of the alienation of the spirit from its Essence, which as we saw is the "unifying element", the symbols of totality appear in dreams as if reminding the spirit of its alienation and its objective. The fact that these dreams produce a "sensation" (*feeling*) of plenitude should not surprise, and this is not something that psychosophy discusses, but for it, these are just poor examples of what Plenitude really is. The planes of representations can become ideas of what is felt and intuited, but just as the "idea" of unity or totality that the external plane forms is not Unity or Totality, neither "are" the "ideas" such as mandalas formed by the internal plane totality. Even if these messages reach our depths because they are loaded with meaning, they are still symbols, not realities. These are found beyond the plane of representations. The spirit in these cases opens itself to other planes of conscience from which it perceives totality in a latent or unconscious way. This causes the internal plane to *interpret* this perception, and it does so in its own way, generating symbols; which are for the internal plane as the concepts are for the external plane. As Jung has no access to the plane of direct perception, he only sees the result: the symbols expressed by the internal plane. Hence, he confuses God with the symbols that represent him, the manifested with the manifesting.

A relatively complete commentary on Jung would involve an exhaustive study of his *Alchemical Studies*, which for him signify the pinnacle of his knowledge. This is not my purpose as I have already stated, and even if it was, I do not believe that I would ever have had the patience to discern the *mille nomina* of the alchemists, nor an interest in deciphering their elaborate "esoteric terminology" by stirring and separating, mixing and cataloguing until... I do not know where they wanted to reach with their concepts. With the method used by the alchemists we find ourselves at the antipodes of what is "simple," as God had (correctly) been defined as in the Middle Ages, as well as the singular exclamation, or the spontaneous gesture or silence of the Zen Master to express religious experience. With the alchemists we find ourselves enmeshed in the magical world of concepts, in which it is apparently enough to be an "initiate", that is, to know the language of alchemy and remain submerged in this world, stirring concepts so that they become reality. I cannot but see in alchemy a kind of "intellectual animism", in which the symbols produced by the unconscious are taken as reality or as an objective; where a reality presaged by these symbols is pursued, but which remains transcendent. And I fear this is what happened to Jung.

Thus Paracelsus does not seem to have reached the 700 years that man could reach according to his theories (he died at the age of 48 after writing *De Vita Longa*), nor did Gerard Dorn achieve the *unus mundus* which he had "hopes and expectations" of achieving. By this I do not mean that his theories did not in some way correspond to the total reality that he was seeking, but from there to being bearers of the "Truth", as Jung wants to present them, there is an immeasurable distance.

Jung undoubtedly felt attracted to them because his ideas are closely linked to the content of the internal plane, and this is so because his religious approach preferentially uses this plane. Hence the symbolism that he finds so familiar. But these "elementary forms" of religion have their limitations. As we have seen, the limitations offered by this plane are those of being representational, indirect and, above all, in the sense that although its manifestations are interpreted with discernment, their origin remains unconscious. This means that *in this way there is never a direct conscious experience;* hence, both in the case of alchemists and of Jung who interprets them, everything ultimately remains in a world of hypothesis.

Although Jung believes that he has gone as far with them as the spirit can reach: "It is on the one hand an endeavour to understand the archetypal world of the psyche, on the other hand a struggle against the sanity-threatening danger of fascination by the measureless heights and depths and paradoxes of psychic truth". "Here the human mind is confronted with its origins, the archetypes; the finite consciousness with its archaic foundations; the mortal ego with the immortal self, *Anthropos, purusha, atman*, or whatever else be the names that human speculation has given to that preconscious collective state from which the individual ego arose." (*Alchemical Studies, 210, Paracelsus as a spiritual phenomenon*)

This declaration is sufficient to demonstrate the grave confusion into which our psychologist had fallen, who enshrines within his schemas concepts that escape and far exceed them. In the first place, in the origins of the mind, and in unified consciousness, there is no trace of any kind of representation; not to mention pure Consciousness.

Fortunately, we do not need to submerge ourselves in the dark and abstruse world of alchemy, or decipher the interminable meanings of the *mille nomina* and compare them with Jung's terminology in order to know whether the latter corresponds to them or not. Whether there is a correlation between the *imaginatio, speculatio and phantasia* or not, we can leave this task to those who, thanks to alchemy, will live for centuries, and thus have time to untangle this web and attend to the results that our psychologist reaches after these fascinating immersions in the "measureless heights and depths and paradoxes of psychic truth" that brought him so close to delirium.

Jung has no hesitation in criticising Christianity for not having achieved its purpose in transforming humanity by following the example of Christ, but when speaking of alchemy, which according to Jung worked precisely with the element that was needed in Christianity, he forgets to apply the same yardstick. Throughout history, alchemy has, in effect, been an inconsequential movement by all accounts, a true failure; when, according to Jung's premises, this movement should have flourished extraordinarily to fill the void left by Christianity. Alchemy's failure was due to the same mistake committed by Jung, whose psychology has to follow the same destiny from the spiritual point of view, and that is that he used oneiric material too dark and abstruse to bear divine fruit. This is why neither the alchemists nor Jung managed to find the philosophers' stone.

CHAPTER ELEVEN

The Archetypes, a Psychological Determinism

Although Jung took the term and idea of *archetype* in the broad sense from Plato, it would be a grave error to superimpose their concepts onto each other because they refer to two distinct realities. For the Athenian, the archetypes are pure, beautiful, perfect Forms which, accordingly, exist in a world of Realities, while for Jung they are spontaneous products of the unconscious, a result of the marks (types) that have been left in the human psyche from typical situations repeated during their evolution. "There are as many archetypes as there are typical situations in life. Endless repetition has engraved these experiences into our psychic constitution." (*C. Works 9,99*) This seems perfectly reasonable as it would explain various of man's innate aptitudes for his survival. But for Jung, the function of archetypes does not end here, as they not only prepare us for survival but also condition us (and at times it seems that they determine us), in our way of being, thinking, loving and believing. This means that man is not really free in his choices, as his contemporaries the existentialists believed, but is marked by "types" before birth. He called this change of approach (equating it to that of Kant who had coined the expression) "Copernican inversion".

In a very early conference given by Jung (*On the Relation of Analytical Psychology to Poetry*) he tells us: "The most effective ideals are always fairly obvious variants of an archetype". Here he already seems to have inverted reality, for are the ideals variants of the archetypes or are they, as I believe, symbolic syntheses of prior ideals? Is there first the archetype of God or the idea of God? The archetype (...) "represents or personifies certain instinctive data of the dark, primitive psyche, the real but invisible roots of consciousness". (*The Psyc. of the Child Archetype*)

For Jung, such is the dependence of the human psyche on the collective unconscious, that we can say that he has supplanted religious determinism with a kind of psychological determinism.([1]) "*All* (italics mine) conscious imagination and action have evolved on the basis of these unconscious prototypes." (*Intr. to The Secret of the Golden Flower*) It is no longer God who determines man's destiny but these prototypes. It could not be any other way since God is nothing more than a prototype generated by the unconscious.

Jung rightly warns that everything is still within man: "There he is *still* (italics mine) the whole and the whole is in him..." "it is from these all-uniting depths that dreams arise." But when he refers to the mechanisms that produce the content of the unconscious, he thinks of a remote past: "The dream is a little hidden door in the innermost and most secret recesses of the soul, opening onto the cosmic night which *was* (italics mine) psyche long before there was any an ego-consciousness". Even if he verifies luminous dreams in his patients, these are strangely related to that dark and distant origin. I agree with him that primitive man was and is closer to his inner consciousness, and therefore more in touch with his dreams, which are thus more real to him, and that the same mechanisms still function in modern man. But what Jung ignores is the existence of a "central consciousness" that perceives unitively in the present and is the one that provides the raw material, which is nothing but the inspiration that the internal consciousness uses to produce these luminous dreams; not the others, the great majority of dreams, born of the habitual relationship between external and internal consciousness.

So, whereas for Freud all the content of the unconscious was dark, primitive and evil, for Jung it has a luminous side; but he still bears Freud's legacy. For Jung the unconscious represents the dark side in opposition to the conscious, and the instinctive is invariably linked to this dark, primitive and evil sector (although he does not see this evil as pernicious, but as "an evil" that has to be accepted), as opposed to the luminous spiritual.

The instinctive, like everything else in this world, also has its spiritual and luminous side. This aspect elevates the spirit; this instinct is confused with religious sentiment and can even generate it. There is a side to the instinct that is only interested in individual benefit in favour of its own survival, and there is another that is in favour of the family, the people, the species and even beyond the bonds of the self, towards transcendence. One can speak of a courageous instinct, one of sacrifice, altruism, that elevates us and brings us closer to Divinity. But these *unitive instincts* that have been settling and forming in the human being are a consequence of the *constant perception present* throughout history, of the *unitive instances*, which have been and continue to be generated by the unifying Essence. Not only because he had inherited it but because he had perceived it, Aristotle declared: "God attracts, like love does to desire".

Even if the way primitive man lived in the world was more integrated, similar to other animals, he did not perceive the absolute unity that has been a late acquisition of some exceptional men, but rather a confused, relative and variable unity. *Unity is still a project of our species that is far from being realised.*

Jung recognises that these prototypes are images that the mind has preserved from remote origins, they are primitive aspects that evolved man tends to leave behind. "A higher and wider consciousness resulting from the assimilation of the unfamiliar tends, on the other hand, towards autonomy, and rebels against the *old gods who are nothing other than those mighty, unconscious, primordial images.*" (Italics mine) Jung warns of the need to recognise these primordial images to avoid a psychic disequilibrium, as his clinical experience dictates, but he does not go further. It is for him a necessary evil of the human being while he retains this dependence.

Jung observes God in men, that is, in their unconscious, and not God in himself, as he starts from the Kantian premise that he is unknowable: "The fact that I tend towards what can be psychically experimented and reject the metaphysical (...) signifies more or less the same that Kant made one understand when he called a thing-in-itself 'bordering on a negative concept". He also adds: "Every statement about the transcendental is to be avoided, as it is only a laughable presumption on the part of the human mind, unconscious of its limitations." (*The Secret of the Golden Flower*) It is not for this that he will stop "treating" God.

As the reader will have understood by now, for psychosophy the religious experience, the unity with God and knowledge of the Divinity can be *psychically experienceable,* whenever the *psyche* is given a dimension that transcends the borders of the individual.

Everything seems to indicate that the archetype precedes God, which means that the Copernican inversion (that of Jung), is applicable to Divinity, which thus ceases to be the primary reality to become a secondary reality, a consequence. "The *self* is commonly projected onto figures or institutions perceived as possessing preeminent power and prestige, whether on human figures such as presidents, kings or queens, or supernatural entities such as the State, God, the sun, nature or the universe." (Stevens, *On Jung*)

Referring to the collective unconscious, Jung expressly tells us: "The collective unconscious should not be thought of as a self-sufficient entity. It is no more than a potentiality handed down to us from primordial times in the specific form of mnemonic images, inherited in the anatomical structure of the brain." (*On the Reference of Analytical. Psyc. to Poetry*) I believe that it is sufficiently clear that the collective unconscious should not be confused with Divinity in the religious sense which is self-sufficient by definition. Moreover, in "the theory of archetypes and collective unconscious Jung bases his psychology on biology." (Stevens, *On Jung*) (and not on religion)

Jung verifies that archetypes are inherited. However, this inheritance has been accumulated by the human being through countless generations of evolution. In other words, it is human beings who have been forming the archetypes. This being so, man has made a permanent contribution to this unconscious phenomenon. But Jung disregards this vital and present aspect in favour of the inherited stereotypical aspect, to which he attributes religious dynamism. A kind of immobile first motor, which would have saddened old Aristotle, and all those who think that twenty-three centuries have passed for "profound psychology" to have reached this version.

For psychosophy, on the contrary, God is a *present Reality*, a current experience, not inherited as a primitive residue that has stayed in some dark fold of the unconscious. It is a Reality with which every being finds himself permanently, as it is an indivisible part of current circumstances. And it maintains that the most elevated and evolved spirits come closer to Divinity and are more balanced because *Divinity is a unitive element*, a unifier par excellence. Both psychosophy and analytic psychology see a sign of mental health in the incorporation of Divinity; but both Divinity and its incorporation are seen in very different ways: while for psychology it would be like an adaptation to impositions of the unconscious, for psychosophy it would be an adaptation to the universal divine Order.

I do not deny, then, that we inherit an idea or model of God, but in life we also make ideas of the same by intuition or by conscious comparison, according to our *present* experiences of Divinity. This is not only a product of a primitive and dark unconscious, but an *eternal source of light* in all our cognitive faculties.

I consider the theories of the collective unconscious and archetypes to be great discoveries. But, as often happens with theorists, the author's shortcoming is the belief that his own particular theory is the master key with which innumerable doors can be opened; and once in possession of it one only has to use it on the desired door with the sole help of reason. This had happened to Freud with his Oedipus complex, but Jung did not learn the lesson; he believed that his was the true one. This leads to faith in our own theories, to the belief that others are false because they do not enter our field of vision. In this way Jung became convinced that his key and not Saint Peter's – which had been used by the Church for two thousand years – was the correct one and this would be the one that would let him traverse all the galleries of Christianity.

Notes

(1) It is interesting to remember the influence of Calvin in Switzerland, Jung's homeland.

CHAPTER TWELVE

Jung, Job and John

Jung found Job attractive for his temerity in judging God from a psychological point of view. Jung identifies with this Biblical character because in some way he affirms the individuality of the human being. M. Stein aptly says (in *Jung's Treatment of Christianity*), "The commitment to the judgment of the individual human being (which is Jung's most express affirmation of a psychology of the ego) barely disguises the idea of the creature surpassing his creator by a small but decisive factor"

Jung repeatedly asks (*Answer to Job,* ARK Ed.1984, London) why God wants the sacrifice of his Son, and he gives various answers, although he concludes with his theory that the sacrifice is not, in a clear allusion to Freud, the "payment of a human debt to God, but as reparation for the wrong done by God to man". (*Chap. X*) But the most obvious answer would be that the Father loves the Son, who is capable of sacrificing his individuality, his humanity for Him, which in psychological terms would mean the sacrifice of the ego and the faculties that sustain it, most notably discernment. The *sacrificium intellectus,* knowingly proposed by Saint Ignacio de Loyola, is not put forward, because this would go against his theory that maintains the ego and individuality at all times.

Since the archetype of Divinity presents a polarity (it is feasible that this is the case, but not being a psychologist by profession, I am in no position to question this), Jung insists on finding this polarity in God himself to explain the religious phenomenon. In this way if the lack of recognition of the polarity of the archetype generates a psychic disequilibrium, he "projects" this problem onto God in whom the polarity "must" be seen. "All opposites are of God, therefore man must bend to this burden, and in doing so he finds that God in his "oppositeness" (*his way of being opposite*), has taken possession of him, incarnated himself in him. He becomes a vessel filled with divine conflict." (*Chap. X*) That is, by accepting opposites man becomes like God or causes God to incarnate himself in him, because opposition is part of the intrinsic nature of Divinity. Thus, he not only projects the archetype of Divinity, but also proposes a path for the union of man with it, through the same archetype.

In my opinion, the archetype is a human configuration that needs the opposites, but not God. Jung concentrates on the God of the Old Testament, because he is sufficiently primitive to present these contradictions; but the God of the New Law does not have them, and this disorients Jung. In order to find his opposite he must look outside of himself, in Satan, with whom he tries to find kinship.

For Jung, God is an archetype whose very essence is polarity. This archetype generates an *imago Dei* in all human beings, that leads them involuntarily to believe, think and act according to it: "Because the *imago Dei* pervades the whole human sphere and makes mankind its involuntary exponent, it is just possible that the four-hundred-year-old schism in the church and the present division of the political world into two hostile camps (one of these would be Soviet Russia, that would become extinct after his death), are both expressions of the unrecognised polarity of the dominant archetype". (*Chap. X*) Thus, the entire theology of the Reformation and Counter Reformation and the beliefs of the hundreds of faithful on both sides, as well as all the philosophical, economic and political theories of Communism and capitalist liberalism, ultimately obey, like puppets, two fundamental strands that converge in the divine archetype. These strands are known only to Jung, and are ignored by all the philosophers, theologians, politicians and economists of the last four centuries. Not only does he then state too much, but he denies the knowledge of so many in the name of a questionable hypothesis. In the name of the said hypothesis, our psychologist pronounces against a basic principle held by all religions: "To believe that God is the *Summum bonum* is impossible for a reflecting consciousness." (*Chap. XI*)

When analysing the *Apocalypse of John*, Jung justifies Christianity's almost incomprehensible turnaround. I am referring to John's return to the spirit of the Old Testament, ignoring the fundamental message of the New Law. Jung explains it thus: "His (John's) Christ-image, clouded by negative feelings, has turned into a savage avenger who no longer bears any real resemblance to a saviour (...) one is not at all sure if this Christ-figure may not in the end have more of the human John in it, with his compensating shadow, than of the divine saviour who, as the *lumen de lumine*, contains 'no darkness". "Seen in the light of the gospel of love, the avenger and judge remains a most sinister figure." (*Chap. XIII*)

When he explains the psychology of Job, he seems instructive; but when he tries to analyse the psyche of God himself, with the same schemas that he uses for humans, we do not really know what kind of entity he is talking about: "Ever since John the apocalyptical first experienced the conflict into which Christianity inevitably leads, mankind (note that he does not speak of the Christian world but of 'mankind'), has groaned under this burden". "God wanted to become man, and still wants to." (*Chap. XVII*) It is not men who want to be God, but vice versa. But God, like man, has a conflictual nature: "The conflict in his nature is so great that the incarnation can only be bought by an expiatory self-sacrifice offered up to the wrath of God's dark side" (*Chap. XVII*). "God wants to reproduce himself in his own dark creature (man not redeemed from original sin)" (*Chap. XVII*). Thus, it seems that this questionable matter of Genesis is not only suffered by Buddhists and Hindus, but also by God himself. And here is another inversion: "We (humans) need more light, more goodness and moral strength, and must wash off as much of the obnoxious blackness as possible, otherwise we shall not be able to assimilate the dark God who also wants to become man". "For this all the Christian virtues are needed." (*Chap. XVII*) From this, one deduces that man does not do good to come closer to perfection and to God, (in the Christian sense of the New Law), to imitate Christ, but to be able to receive the dark side of God.

And, strictly speaking, Christ himself is part of this destiny: "Looking ahead, Christ also hinted, as I mentioned before, at a morality of evil". (?) (*Chap. XVII*) But all this effort, which goes against the grain for Jung, is to interpret the *Apocalypse of John* and the dark side, which he undoubtedly has, of the God of the Old Testament. That is to say, instead of rejecting this arbitrary and wrathful God, as might be expected from a modern critical analysis, he takes the Bible as a coherent whole, thereby committing the same error as that of the Church which refuses to see how tremendously contradictory this text is and accepts it as if it were "the word of God".

This is not the place for a critique of Christianity, which I will do elsewhere([1]), but one can deduce my position on the matter from what I have said. The New Law, of Christ, is irreconcilable with the Old Law, or it can be so only in so far as the latter conforms to the former. But this should be clear: with Christ, for he who understands, the arbitrary and wrathful God ends once and for all. I mean that the Apocalypse is a disastrous interpolation which distorts the message of Jesus; it is a backwards step towards the spirit of the Old Testament that had been surpassed by the Nazarene. But Jung accepts the whole and the chronological order. The last word is not that of Jesus but of John the apocalyptical. Jesus is only part of a process as is his gospel. "For the immediate and urgent problem in those days was not the union of opposites, which lay in the future, but the incarnation of the light and the good". The mediate, true and definitive reality is that of the Apocalypse: "The Lamb, transformed into a demonic ram, reveals a new gospel, the *Evangelium Aeternum*, which, going right beyond the love of God, has the fear of God as its main ingredient." (2) "Therefore, the Apocalypse closes, like the classical individuation process, with the symbol of the *hieros gamos*, the marriage of the son with the mother-bride". "That is the programme for the Christian aeon, which must be fulfilled before God can incarnate in the creaturely man" (*Chap. XVII*).

In this chapter, in which he summarises and concludes his interpretation of the Bible, Jung surprises the reader with his denouement. Indeed, at first it seemed that he was going to reject the tyrannical and vengeful God, but the sequence of his hypothesis does not lead to this, but, to the reader's astonishment, to an acceptance of him. "Since the Apocalypse we now know that God is not only to be loved, but also feared", because "He fills us with evil as well as good, otherwise he would not need to be feared." (*Chap. XVIII*)

I do not for a moment deny that men should assume the evil as well as the good in their bones, as the knowledge of the one leads to the other, but that it is God who "has slipped the atomic bomb and chemical weapons into his hands" (*Chap. XVIII*) seems to me to be a great leap in the field of religion and a grave error of interpretation. God no longer awakens in us the highest sentiments of love, veneration and respect as all wise and spiritually higher beings inspire, but a simple fear, a negative feeling par excellence, which generates a tyrannical and capricious being. These two feelings are not only opposed, but mutually exclusive; where fear exists, there can be no love and where the latter reigns, the former disappears. But Jung does not know this because he has not experienced the essential feeling of approaching God, that of loving him above all else, and the feeling that derives from this: that of loving like God himself, imparting Love to all beings. All religions pursue the awakening of this feeling because they know that it is the most efficient means to eradicate evil. This is essentially the message of Jesus, but for Jung it is incomplete, the message of John the apocalyptical is the *Aeternum*.

If God is both good and bad what need does man have to incarnate him in his species if he already possesses these two components? What advantages would he gain from this? While the danger of this incorporation comes to mind: that man already and definitively believes that he is God. It makes sense to believe that it is the devil that inspires evil and that man should be aware of his demonic side, with the danger involved and what could be implied after death, as man can thus assume his responsibility. While I do not believe that feeling he is the incarnation of God would make him reconsider in this way, could he perhaps believe that he would be condemned or would have to pay his debts being God himself? It gives the impression that Jung's hypothesis could be a potent fuel for the fire that he wanted to extinguish. Is the danger of these hypotheses on the historical processes that must be fulfilled understood, as I had already warned of at the beginning of this part? An erroneous interpretation of the Apocalypse can lead to its realisation.

Continuing this process preordained by the Apocalypse of John, Jung tells us: "Only in the last days will the (John's) vision of the sun-woman be fulfilled". "In recognition of this *truth* (italics mine), and evidently inspired by the workings of the Holy Ghost, the Pope has recently announced the dogma of the *Assumptio Mariae*". "This dogma is in every respect timely (...) it is a symbolic fulfilment of John's vision (....) foretells the Incarnation in creaturely man." (*Chap. XVII*) Regarding this dogma of the Ascension of the Virgin, Jung's position has its reasonable side: because if there is a God the Father and a Son it is strange that there is no Mother Goddess. Besides, as he observes, the cult of the Virgin is an indisputable fact in the hearts of Christians, as well as the increase of women's rights in modern times. In this sense the Pope knew how to interpret the spirit of the age. But the age has other meanings and also other exigencies. It is opportune to remember that this dogma, destined to dissipate chaos, in Jung's opinion, "so timely and evidently inspired by the workings of the Holy Ghost," was promulgated shortly after the Second World War by Pope Pius XII, who, as is known, also *broke bread* with fascism. Furthermore, the dogma itself as an imposed and unquestionable truth is intolerable for this liberal age. I feel it would have been enough to incorporate it as part of Catholic orthodoxy, which no longer needs, as the times demand, to be sustained by rigid, unavoidable and unappealable dogmas. Finally, the image of the Father, Son and Mother may be useful to the Church and analytic psychology in order to give shape to a popular cult, but to other higher levels of understanding the intrusion of the feminine sex in the heavens does nothing but highlight the masculine sex of the Father, when his figure at these levels tends to disappear as an icon and surpass all anthropomorphism. The interpretation of this point, both by Jung and by the Church, when sustained as an ultimate truth tends to bring religion down to a popular level and narrow the horizon of Christianity. It may partially satisfy the majority, but not the knowing minority.

Notes

(1) In *Parallel Civilisations.* (Motilal Banarsidass, New Delhi)

(2) A declaration in which we again note the influence of the fanatical Calvin.

CHAPTER THIRTEEN

Jung and Religion

As mentioned earlier, Jung locates himself between the sciences and religion which makes it very difficult for him to keep his balance. This often leads to the impression that he is trying to placate scientists as well as men of religion, but in these efforts, he cannot avoid certain ambiguous statements and even contradictions.

If we observe the process he follows, we will see that he does not start from this position. He begins with the sciences; but while investigating the religious phenomenon he progressively stretches his theories (*homeostasis* for example), because he realises time and again that the phenomenon transcends his earlier schema, which he decides not to abandon. It is this position, in which he tries to reach an always elusive objective, leaving one foot in the sciences, that makes his balance unstable.

Everything seems to indicate that Jung, (and the proverb fits him like none other) wanted to please God and the Devil at the same time, and this is a compromise that may be feasible in analytical psychology thanks to some magical or alchemical "*coniuntio*", but in science and especially in religion it is not possible because, as everyone knows (hence the saying) they are two irreconcilable beings.

If Jung had limited himself to speaking of *his* own self, then the risk of giving it other religious connotations would depend only on us, but he himself establishes connections between the aims of the Eastern religions and his theory of individuation. This is the "relationship or identity of the personal (atman) with the supra-personal atman (Hinduism) and the individual Tao with the universal Tao (Taoism)". (*Mysterium Coniunctionis*) After this assertion, there is only one thing of which we can be sure: that Jung is the only one, before and after him, who claims to have knowledge of the *Atman* and that having acquired it does not follow a religious life. (Not necessarily monastic, but yes devotional, contemplative, etc.) Thus, the objective observer, who does not know the Atman, finds himself faced with the following dilemma: Have all religious men been and continue to be wrong in ignoring that they are responding to an archetypal product of the unconscious, or is Jung at fault in taking the archetype as the first reality, which is nothing but a manifestation of what they take as Reality? In other words, is it through ignorance that they have awoken a religious feeling, or is it Jung's ignorance that keeps this feeling dormant in him?

I do not know how scientists perceive Jung. Surely as lacking in solidity, which is curiously the impression that the *homo religious* has of him. To him, psychology is represented as a highly adorned tree with many branches that is therefore striking, but when it is sounded from a religious point of view it is, deep down, hollow. It is true that in his old age Jung was gradually coming closer to God, but he never abandoned his original point of view, the individual, and most importantly for him, his personality, on which he had constructed all his psychology. His entire psychology, in fact, seemed to be adapting to the growth of his personality and *his* process of individuation, that is, it was depending on the adjustments and imbalances of his particular psychic problems. This process, undoubtedly, must be of great use to psychologists, who are interested in observing the ups and downs of the spirit, especially in the case of a notable psychologist who described them in great detail with illustrations, examples, hypotheses and conclusions. But from a scientific point of view or that of objective knowledge in general, it will be understood that it only has the relative interest of a biography. It is not at all surprising that at the end of this process we find his *Memoirs*, in which Jung makes the final adjustments to his personality, thus leaving us an admirable image: that of the child on a rock, that of the youth contemplating the vast plains of Africa from a great height, that of the old man who (he insinuates) "knows" who God is.

If he had *really* achieved a clear knowledge of Divinity and had he explained it to us, his "psychological biography" would have been of particular interest to the religious man. But alas, when he discovers that even towards the end of his days the great psychologist continues to be evasive on the subject, that the old tree still sounds hollow, he decides to leave him in the dark forest of psychology. “Does the fact that you experience God (as an archetype I suppose) mean that there must be a God for you to experience?” A. Stevens asks him, and he comments: “Jung *appears to imply* (italics mine) that there is”, and this is the answer he receives: “When I say as a psychologist that God is an archetype, I mean that the ‘type’ is in the psyche. The word ‘type’ is, as we know, derived from the Greek word typos ‘blow’ or ‘imprint’; thus an ‘archetype’ presupposes an imprinter.” (*C.W.12*) I do not know whether Jung’s admirers are satisfied with this suggestion, but I can assure them that for those who long to know God more than obtain fame and riches, this answer means nothing. And elsewhere, (also cited by Stevens who seems to have covered all Jung’s work to find these *two* cases where he makes some kind of affirmation on the subject: “I do not take His existence on belief - I know that he exists”. This should be enough for us, we should accept as a credo that Jung “knows” that God exists. But does this tell us something we do not know? There are millions who say the same thing, and not towards the end of their days but very early in life, and they are sufficiently convinced of it to start a religious *life and practice*, which is something that our indefatigable psychologist never attempted.

“...the hero archetype is about leaving home, overcoming fear and establishing personal autonomy in the world” (Stevens, *On Jung*). “For both sexes, then, initiation is a cultural strategy designed to promote severing of the bond to the parents and a public awareness that reproductive *status* has been achieved.” (*Op. cit.*) “In this way initiation functions as a psychotherapeutic measure whose purpose is to overcome the child’s regressive longings for the womb and to push him or her onwards into the next stage of life.” (*Op. cit.*) This seems to me to be a pitiful reduction of the high objectives of religion; a domestic vision for commo n people of the transcendent function of the heroic myth. Can it be claimed that all the initiated of the world are unknowingly representing this domestic archetype that leads to adulthood?

This unfortunate reduction is an inevitable consequence of Jung’s incredulousness of a transcendent ontological reality, which has been the guide of innumerable ascetics in the East for 3,000 years; it is an adaptation to his level of consciousness. All the Yogis of India know that it is not enough to interpret religions in order to achieve the transcendent; that this unfailingly implies a sacrifice. And for this they continue the mythical epic of leaving home, not of course to integrate into society, into the human world, but to leave it forever; these are the *sanyasins* (liberated in life). And even so, in spite of the great sacrifice, and the solid faith that moves them, the great majority of them fail; as it is not a task for common mortals. Why not accept, then, once and for all, the rules of the game imposed by religion, and let only those who are fully willing to follow them participate, instead of adapting (and distorting) the game to the level of those who have not surpassed their speculative planes and want to avoid the sacrifice?

We can say it once more using the words of M. Eliade: "In the case of Yoga, we are face to face with a system of beliefs, ideas and techniques, ascetic and contemplative, that tend towards transmutation, i.e., towards the *abolition of the human condition*" (italics mine). "It is important to state that this long and difficult ascetic journey develops according to the well-known signs of an initiation scenario: after all, the practice of Yoga *kills* normal man, i.e. the one that is metaphysically ignorant, a prisoner of his illusions, and *engenders* a new man, unconditioned and free." (*Initiations, Rites, Sociétés Secrètes*)

The religious or spiritual life, which is the second stage as we saw, has the destruction of the individual as its objective, and by this I understand not only the *person,* as Jung calls the image of the ego, but the entire vision of the World from the individual perspective. For this reason we can say that where the *process of individuation* ends, which leads to the formation of the personality, to the integration of the individual in family and society, which is the first necessary stage of man, *the process of dis-individuation* begins. If it follows the correct ascendant path, it should not be interpreted as retrogression or a deforma

CHAPTER FOURTEEN

The Self

The self cannot be known by study, nor by the intellect nor by listening too hard"

—(Katha Upanishad Y ii 23)

At present, Western psychology speaks, as if it were common currency, of a Self, a term that has been borrowed from the Far East, in particular from the concept of Atman, which is translated as *Self* in English, the 'Sí Mismo" in Spanish. Jung writes *Selbst* in German, without generally referring to the original Sanskrit. Oddly, he seems not to even understand the meaning of the word. There is nothing that belongs to me more than the Self, yet analytical psychology (in line with Freudian tradition), does not try to understand it from *me*, but by detecting it in third parties, in patients through their dream representations. This means that *what I truly am*, I discover in *others*. Besides, the true Self (the oriental, which I will henceforth designate with a capital letter) is not a state that I reach. On the contrary, when the Self manifests itself, I myself do not exist. Can one not see the fallacy of any hypothesis about "Myself "? Is there not an alienation of oneself when one is conjecturing it?

Jung says: "the ego is only the subject of my consciousness while the self is the subject of my total psyche which also includes the unconscious". (*The Ego and the Unconscious*) This is clearly defined and it makes us think that it is effectively so, but as we approach the core of the psyche we clearly 'see' that this definition does not go beyond a speculative level, that it is a hypothesis; however, Jung is not prudent enough to announce it as such, but rather as something definite. That Jung does not forsake discernment on enunciating this is evident from the start, since the duality, present in his entire conception of the mind and of the world, continues. As we have seen, as soon as individual consciousness is transcended, the subject disappears, and it is enough for it to appear for the spirit to return to individual consciousness. Moreover, even in the *unitive consciousness* the spirit is not yet in the nucleus of the Mind, which is the *unified consciousness,* where to speak of a subject would be a contradiction in terms. Nor is it possible to speak of a subject on the internal plane (unconscious) because here too as soon as it appears, the subject awakens. Those few unified spirits who have been able to devote years to dream control, at most, can speak of an *observer* without any identity, like a screen without a projector (although this may sound illogical to discerning minds). And when they have their spirit in the nucleus of their mind, then neither can they speak of an unconscious.

It would not be accurate to speak of an extreme egocentrism in Jung, as the individuation process is not directed towards the ego, but to a third component, the result of the relationship between the ego and the self. However, this process does not go so far as to abandon the ego at any given moment, which continues to be the *focus of human consciousness.* Therefore, it would not be correct to speak in this case of transcendence, but rather of an enrichment of the ego. In his theory this is what is in charge of modulating the unconscious inherited archetypes. "In the final analysis the decisive factor is always consciousness, which can understand the manifestations of the unconscious and take up a position toward them." (*Memories, Dreams, Reflections, 212*) Thus, without really proposing a transcendence, he claims to reach "the transcendent", which is not feasible. The individuation process never seems to end, totality is never achieved. "...the image of wholeness is itself meant to be a symbolic one, seemingly never literally or finally to be reached - a pole star that sets a direction to the traveller rather than a goal to be reached concretely." (*The Symbolic Quest*, E. C. Whitmont, Princeton Univ. Press, 135) "However, as the objective of this process, the self, is like an 'existent a priori', 'the internal God', individuation is always a route, a path, a process, a journey of work, dynamism; it is never a static or finished state at least while one lives in space and time. It is a becoming not a being." (*Op. cit.*) This, in my opinion, is badly expressed, as in this process the objective is not the self but individuation. Besides, the ego should be careful not to be absorbed by the self. "It must be reckoned a psychic catastrophe when the ego is assimilated by the self. The image of wholeness then remains in the unconscious, so that on the one hand it shares the archaic nature of the unconscious and on the other finds itself in the psychically relative space-time continuum that is characteristic of the unconscious as such." "If, therefore, the ego falls for any length of time under the control of an unconscious factor, its adaptation is disturbed and the way opened for all sorts of possible accidents. Hence it is of the greatest importance that the ego should be anchored in the world of consciousness..." (*Aion, 46*)

Here Jung clarifies that the self participates in the characteristics of the unconscious, in its "archaic nature" on the one hand and in the space-time continuum on the other. God, thus, is something archaic that we drag into the unconscious. As concerns the space-time continuum, I believe it is more a characteristic of the central than the internal plane, as on the latter these forms are only sometimes this way and sometimes not, that is, they appear arbitrarily and even chaotically but not as a regular space-time continuum. Here there is neither enlightenment nor liberation in the encounter with God, but a fall into the unconscious from which the ego must recover without delay. In my opinion, this advice from Jung could be really harmful to those who take it, as it hinders the mystical experience. It will not constitute an obstacle for he who has had a *total unitive experience*, who will be discriminating with the errors and successes of this theory, but of course it will for all those who are hovering over the religious field with isolated intuitions, because this advice will make them return to their individual perspective and remain there indefinitely: "the ego should be anchored in the world of consciousness", that is, on the external plane. This advice alone is sufficient to keep the spirit "anchored" in ignorance.

Losing the thread of his own logic, Jung himself recognises that there is no unity in the unconscious, only an undifferentiated and confused reality. "If we go so far back in the history of the mind in such a way that the distinctions between various strands of activity become invisible, we will not achieve a principle of unity that underlies them, only an early undifferentiated state in which separate activities do not exist." (*On the Relation of Analytical Psyc. to Poetry*) How, then, can the incorporation of the unconscious into the conscious generate a totality? Decidedly, Jung's self is nothing more than a hypothesis that will never be proven.

For Jung, as M. Stein comments (*Jung's Treatment of Christianity*) the responsibility of the psychologist lies in helping patients to procure a "synthesis of the conscious and the unconscious ", interpreting the "symbols that point towards the totality". This interpretation tends to integrate the parts of the self. Needless to say that the interpretation of the symbols, given their complexity, should be under a specialised analyst, that is, both man's health and totality will depend on the analysis and correct interpretation of the analyst. This more or less means that all members of society should consult psychologists specialised in religious symbolism to understand themselves and their religion.

Although the ultimate objective of the individuation process might be the union of the individual with the *unus mundus* (an idea taken from G. Dorn, who never managed to realise it), this unity should not be interpreted as a union with Divinity, as they are two distinct entities. "The *unus mundus* is the eternal ground of all empirical beings, just as the self is the ground and origin of the individual personality," (*Misterium Coniunctionis*) it is "the unitary world, the potential world of the first day of Creation, when nothing had yet become differentiated and everything was still one." (Stevens, *On Jung*)

The self, in conclusion, is a state of the psyche in which the whole is undifferentiated, in the sense of primordial chaos, which the ego with its reason puts in order. God will participate in a way that has similar characteristics. In fact, as Jung traces it from the extreme opposite, he does not see it as something finished, and thus it must follow the same individuation process or it will depend on the process followed by man to become. Since at no time does he clarify if it depends on all men, we should assume, once again, that a subjective God is being referred to. That God depends on this process should not surprise us after having heard him say: "The metaphysical process is known by the psychology of the unconscious as a process of individuation." (*Answer to Job XIX*)

God is not, for him, as any religious person of both the East and the West would say, an absolute, finished, perfect being, but an ontologically dependent being, and is not, as Hegel thought, of his universal realisation, but of man. "God himself can become whole only through man's creative confrontation with the opposites and through their synthesis in the self." (Stevens, *On Jung*) And this is what our psychologist emphasises in his *Memoirs* where he remembers contemplating the African hills, "There the cosmic sense of conscience became clear to me." "I now knew... that man is indispensable for the completion of creation; that, in fact, he himself is the second creator of the world (I do not know if in his ecstasy he thought of planet Earth or of the Universe), who alone has given to the world its objective existence - without which (...) it would have gone on in the profoundest night of non being down to its unknown end". "That is the meaning of divine service, of the service which man can render to God (here, I confess, I find it very difficult to know the ontological situation of this occasional God), that light may emerge from darkness, that the Creator may become conscious of His Creation, and man conscious of himself". Thus, "if the Creator were conscious of Himself, He would not need conscious creatures."

It was the inevitable conclusion for one who spent his whole life interpreting God through the unconscious, God is unconscious! With this declaration (and here there will be no accommodation or further adjustment, as this quotation is from the chapter entitled *Last Thoughts* from his last book) Jung shows that he basically ignored what Divinity is. Indeed, when the purified spirit reaches its highest state of consciousness, it realises that *the absolute Being is Pure Consciousness*. This does not mean that it discerns like the human being, as it does not need it, as it neither fears nor desires, it is consciousness in a state of contemplation, of peace, of absolute repose; it is then that it contemplates Himself.

Jung's conclusion was logical, but he will no longer be able to maintain the relationship of this Creator, this occasional God, with the Atman or Brahman, nor his self with the Self of the Orient, with the Purusha; a relationship that he himself establishes repeatedly. In the most orthodox and erudite strand of Hinduism, the Creator is by definition given by the *Upanishads*, and by tradition sealed by his highest exponent Shankaracharya: absolute Existence-Knowledge-Happiness (*Tat-Sit-Ananda*). In the *Taittiriya Upanishad*, in which it is maintained that the Brahman is the creator of Himself, (*Chap. VIII*) Brahman and Knowledge are spoken of as if they were inseparable. (*Chap. V*) He is also defined as Truth-Knowledge-Infinite. (II y) In the words of Shankara (in the *Kena Upanishad, IIa*), answering an objection, he very aptly says: "Brahman, like a mere substance (which is understood to be objective, not psychic) without consciousness would contradict the Vedic text". These texts begin to identify the Creator with Consciousness: "Knowledge, Happiness, and

Brahman". (*Br. III ix 28.7*) "Brahman is Consciousness itself." (*Ai. V, 3*) Moreover, it is argued whether Brahman, being pure Intelligence, could have created something material and impure: the world, but not even its consciousness is advanced. (*Brahma Sutras* 2.1.4) Even in Patanjali's *Yogasutras*, another classical orthodox text, in which the creator is called Isvara, the latter is also identified with absolute "Existence-Knowledge-Happiness". Patanjali affirms that "Omniscience is not a wonder even for Isvara" (but something natural). The *Katha Upanishad* (that speaks both of the Self as well as of Brahman), says: "The Intelligent Self is neither born nor dies". To which Shankara comments: "The intelligent One (Self) is (Immortal) because His *conscious* Nature is never lost". (*Iii 18*) We could continue interminably, as it is Jung who has come to contradict with this hypothesis the experience repeated for millennia of all those who have experienced the *true* Self.(1)

Perhaps it is not necessary to remind the reader that for psychosophy the Central Consciousness is characterised as being truly conscious, to the point of discarding what psychology calls conscious, by being semi-conscious and thus insufficient. Thus, *the Pure consciousness is the nucleus of the unified consciousness, in which the spirit becomes One with the Spirit, with the Essence of the World.*

Jung's 'awareness' (which leads him to believe that man is the only conscious being in the world and the second maker of it), is undoubtedly flattering for all those who view reality from their individual perspective, it is the definition of the realisation of this same perspective, in which everything converges and thanks to which everything makes sense. It is the old awareness of the self, to which has been added the rupture or alienation with respect to the universal Spirit that, as we have seen, occurs in the middle of the last century. It seems that we are still listening to the centrist Superman, Nietzche's *Zarathustra*: "Oh sun what would become of you without us the men who admire you!" This "Copernican inversion" is exactly the consolidation, now on behalf of psychology, of man's alienation, from the Self, from his Essence.

Notes

(1) For an ample commentary on Hinduism see my *Parallel Civilisations, Motilal Banarsidass.*

CHAPTER FIFTEEN

Jung And Christianity

I agree with Jung (and I think all psychologists agree) that it is essential to accept the evil in ourselves for our psychic equilibrium, the dark side, the "shadow" as he calls it. But he goes as far with this shadow as one can with a psychic reality. At times he even falls prey to its reasoning, and seems to forget that he does not believe in the ontological reality either of God or the Devil, and becomes irritated with Christianity because it does not give Satan the place and importance he deserves. In this way he declares himself against a positive evolution in Christianity initiated by Saint Augustine, who, inspired by Plato affirmed that evil does not exist as a reality in itself but as an absence of good. It should be noted that following the Athenian genius, this patriarch of the Church sets an important antecedent which will not be followed by the ecclesiastical orthodoxy. Moreover, Satan's existence will gain increasing reality in the centuries that follow Saint Augustine. Thus, it is not as if Christianity denies the reality of Satan, on the contrary, there he is, as we have known since the beginning of time, but this is not sufficient for Jung, he wants to grant him another *status*, as we will see. This means that instead of following the precedent of Saint Augustine, which would have been a positive modification of the trend followed by the Church, Jung tries to increase his stock, thus returning to a medieval mentality, albeit seen as a "psychic reality".

Evil does exist for psychosophy, but it is first created by the needs of survival, and later by ourselves when we create more unnecessary "needs" with our desires: greed, gluttony, etc. It is thus a product of human illusions, it does not exist by itself; while there does exist a "principle of Good", which is Divinity. It is by light, not darkness, that man can see. There is no darkness that projects itself and makes things dark. In the same way, evil contrasts with good. There is no evil in itself that projects itself on to the world; Satan does not exist, unless, as Baudelaire says, "he is so devilish as to make us believe that he does not exist". It is the lack of light; it is ignorance that leads us to evil. It is when man in his selfishness shuts himself off from all light that "the dark side" appears, the "shadows" symbolised by diabolical beings. Divinity does exist by itself, strictly speaking, it is the only Being with this virtue; and this is not only a belief, it is an experience that man can have when he comes out of himself. The devil only resides in the heart when it is closed to the unitive forces. Evil appears when the spirit blocks all light and shuts itself up in its individuality, therefore, while good is justified objectively, that is, beyond oneself, evil only finds justification subjectively. For this reason as well, man is fully responsible for the evil he does, not the devil. The devil is no more than another scapegoat, who is needed to justify man's actions that are objectively intolerable to him; while the good that he does is in spite of himself. In short, Divinity does exist as a *summun bonun*, while there is no *summun malun,* only lesser shades of light.

I personally find Jung's interpretation of religious symbols and his theory of archetypes fascinating and this, I believe, is so for most of his readers, but in our fascination, we should not go so far as to believe that, thanks to it, we have understood the essence of Christianity. Thus, for example, in his interpretation of the doctrine of the Trinity, Jung discovers that it responds to an archetype, also manifest in other religions and even in some prior to Christianity. This interpretation apparently explains the "causes" of the said doctrine, in a way that psychology seems to see beyond religion: "It was not the influence of religious or philosophical tradition that guided the minds of the Church fathers, when they elaborated the doctrine of the Trinity; it was rather a psychic factor, the archetype. In order to fully understand the doctrine of the Trinity, it is thus necessary to understand the archetypal factors that guided it and motivated the creation of the doctrine" (*Psyc. Approach to the Dogma of Trinity*).

Fascinating, is it not? But when we return to our senses once the enchantment has gone, we note that the spirit is as dissatisfied as ever, and perhaps even more restless. The psychologist, perhaps, is fine with this answer but for the religious man, as well as for the philosopher, it will be a little more difficult. They are older and more astute, and carry the heavy weight of tradition on their shoulders, and for the same reason, the recurring mania, which is now a habit, of seeking "the first principles"; Aristotle left them with this burden that they still carry. I confess that I am one of these recalcitrant old men. And we cannot help but see a problem here, which is the same that we find in the psychological interpretation of all symbols, and it is that the causes of these causes still remain. Thus, in the case of this theory we can still ask: Why does the archetype of the three divinities exist and why did it exist in the psyche? There is thus something prior to psychology that takes us back to the world of religion and philosophy. If we were to ask a theologian, he would say that it is due to divine inspiration or revelation; he would have an answer. If we posed this question to Jung, he would answer that there is no answer. "Whether this psychic structure and its elements, the archetypes, ever originated at all is a metaphysical question and therefore unanswerable" (*The Archetypes and the Collective Unconscious*). This solution is in keeping with Jung's trajectory which, as we said, in times of trouble tends towards the scientific version. But what to Jung seems "unanswerable", does not seem so to religion and philosophy, especially to the latter, whose raison d'être is to respond to the same first causes.

Without denying the power of archetypes in the human psyche, I think that Jung with his archetype tries to reduce (to avoid saying simplify) a phenomenon as complex as the persona of Jesus. "Early on ... the real Christ fades behind emotions and projections that he was assaulted with on all sides; immediately and almost without leaving a trace he was absorbed into neighbouring religious systems and moulded into their archetypal exponents" (quoted by M. Stein *Jung's Treatment of Christianity*). "Apart from the symbolic Christ, therefore, the historical Jesus has little significance, because the symbol was what attracted the peoples and nations and not the human being." (*Op. cit.*) So, with this typical psychological "turn" what is claimed is that "what is not seen" is more important than what is evident; it is not now the genius who creates the symbol around him, but the symbol around him that creates the genius. It is as if Jesus had made some gestures that correspond to his archetype and then had left this to act. As if the teachings of the Gospels were nothing more than words (thousands of symbols) that correspond to a primordial symbol and that only by virtue of this correspondence has Jesus been heard and his teachings practiced.

For those who have found salvation in Christ it is because he "has realised the idea of the self". (*Op. cit.*) But then Jung makes clear to us that this self is not really complete. "The Christ-figure... lacks the nocturnal side of the psyche's nature, the darkness of the spirit, and is also without sin." "Without the integration of evil there is no totality." (*Cit. Stein*) For Jung, not only is Christ incomplete without evil but also the Trinity; both are signs of perfection but not of totality. To be so requires the recognition of the dark side of reality.

Having reached this point Jung outlines, based on this hypothesis, a kind of philosophy of history. "The symbol of the Trinity (...) was destined to serve as a saving formula of wholeness in an epoch of change and psychic transformation" (quoted by Stein). But this wholeness seems to be insufficient. Contemporary times call for a more complete totality. And it is Jung, who realises this historical psychic need, and who has indicated the remedy, which is very difficult to swallow: the acceptance of Satan as a son of the Father, as a brother of the Son. What Jung proposes for this update of Christianity is a replacement of the Trinity with a Quaternity. In this process, he affirms, the Church has taken a first step by incorporating the Virgin with her body into Paradise. "The Assumptio Mariae paves the way...for the Quaternity. At the same time, matter is included in the metaphysical realm, together with the corrupting principle of the cosmos, evil." (*Cit. Stein*)

It is undeniable that by establishing a relationship between the Virgin (with her body), nature and the Devil, Jung expresses an extremely primitive way of thinking (which we do not know whether it is his or that of his neurotic patients). The medieval character of this mentality makes us believe that he has inherited it from his studies of alchemy. However, to our surprise, it is the model that he uses to propose a solution in *our* epoch.

It is also clear that Jung's dualist vision has done no more than extend itself to quaternity; this, in effect is two pairs of opposites, a formula that is found everywhere in his theory, even his schema of the psyche. In this way Jung takes his obsession with opposites to the heavens.

Although his purpose is not exactly to change the order of the heavens, his objective is therapeutic and is directed towards men. It is them who must accept the devil that they carry inside. And this is what he addresses immediately in his *Psychology of Quaternity* in which he concerns himself with the different stages of man towards his maturity. Since he has reached this point, Jung has landed in a field which is his domain, we do not need to follow him here, but we should return to finish tidying up the muddle he left in the heavens while officiating as a theologian.

Jung notes the evident rejection of Nature by the Christian religion and the need to recover it for man's balance with his environment. I believe that every educated person today, even if Christian, as long as they do not have an archaic vision of their religion, will agree with this proposition. But in order to update it, instead of drawing on the positive aspects of Nature, its beauty, its variety, its marvels, everything in short that could finally assimilate it with Divinity, Jung adopts the terrible Christian vision according to which the "Lord of this world" is Satan. In this way all of Nature is connected to "evil"; it is "the shadow", the dark side of reality. It is evident that the famous psychologist is accustomed to dealing with sick people or those affected by this sick conception and not with nature lovers for whom, clearly, both consciously and unconsciously, as demonstrated by so many dreams with natural elevating forms, this world is full of light or, at least it has as much light as darkness. But this uncomfortable adoption suited his logical game, as he did not have to move more than a single piece to win (according to this strange principle). Placing Satan in heaven, the Antichrist beside Christ, Nature was also incorporated and accepted by the Christian who up to then had denied it. I do not know if Jung, in his presumption of trying to arrange the order of the heavens, remembered to leave a successor of Satan in Hell, or if he took for granted that he would move to Paradise with all his cohorts. A truly new and singular Paradise, full of evils and miseries! How did he not see that what he was establishing was an earthly world in Paradise, with which it loses its raison d'être, as why would we want two worlds that are the same? Or, what amounts to the same thing, Jung is applying human psychology to the gods and thus they lose their raison d'être; his vision is very human, "too human."

Everything seems to indicate that the correct field of psychology is the human and not the divine psyche. Humans, perhaps, need to recognise their "shadow". Even if the gods have had to fight against the demons, they have freed themselves of them; as is attested in almost all mythologies. Neither in Olympus, nor in Paradise, nor in Nirvana is there a single devil left. Moreover, if any were left they would cease to be what they are, a place of Peace, contemplation, Happiness, etc. When Jung proposes his quaternary, he commits the unfortunate mistake of "projecting" the human necessities onto the gods. To suppose that Paradise needs Satan to be complete is to believe that not only does Christianity have a defect in its foundations, but also all established religions.

In Nature everything has a luminous or divine aspect and also a dark side (called demonic by religions). This, though it is what Jung apparently says, is not the case. In a definitive way he identifies certain realities of darkness, such as the feminine, the instinctive, and when it comes to generalising, all of Nature too, even though all of them have their luminous side, just as the masculine, for example, has its dark side.

If Jung has fallen into the error of conceptualisation, it is because he has given preference to symbols before reality. This error is not serious as he sees the positive, I would say, side of darkness, the potentialities that it enshrines; but it is this that leads him to put *all* the darkness, everything that is negative, together with the positive, on the path of the spirit for its "redemption". Jung uses this term, thus equating the purpose of religion with that of psychology, and although he does not explicitly say so, he repeatedly makes the suggestion that "salvation" and even "illumination" correspond to the "process of individuation". Whoever interprets it in this way, as many of his disciples have done, will have caught a drop of water that they take for the pearl of religions. In any case, they are two stages of the spirit as different as they are distanced, but Jung did not see these differences clearly, neither did he suspect the distance that separated him from the final objective of religions; although we can concede that he was convinced that he was speaking of the same thing. However, with respect to enlightenment, in the sense of a total identification of the subject with God, Jung has no qualms about interpreting it as a dangerous digression, which the Church has known how to warn against and prevent.

On this very important point, that of enlightenment, he pronounces, in effect, in favour of official Christianity against Gnosticism, whose vision is assimilated to the doctrines of the Far East. Thus, commenting on the *Acts of John* he refers to this "overweening attitude (of John) arising from an inflation caused by the fact that the enlightened John has identified with his own light and confused his ego with the 'self'". "Recognising the danger of Gnostic unrealism, the Church... has always insisted on the concretism of historical events". This is the "justification for postponing the elevation of man's *status* until after death, as this avoided the danger of Gnostic inflation". The fact that Jung interprets man's unity with the Divinity as inflation shows that he still views Divinity as an external and personal being, that is, his idea is that of the God of the Old Testament. On adopting this general attitude with respect to enlightenment and by calling it a "psychological inflation", Jung is denying not only the claims of Gnosticism but also those of Buddhism and Vedanta. At the same time he defends Christian orthodoxy, which only gives this faculty of total identification with God to Jesus, denying it *a priori* to the rest of the Christians who *should* believe that they will only achieve this solace with death, thus creating in them the anxiety of living for death and denying them the highest experience that can be had in life (psychosophy's stand on this point has been explained in the first part of this essay). This means that instead of pointing out this defect in Christianity, Jung would be affirming it from a "scientific" point of view. Let us here leave aside a minor fact, for us but not for Jung, that his arguments have also led him to deny "self" realisation.

Returning to the previous point, and on hearing me say that not all that is dark is useful on the path to salvation, the Jungians will think that I am committing the same mistake as the Christians: that of denying one part of reality; but it is not the case. There is here a confusion of which it is necessary to clarify. In the first place, let this be established once and for all: the path of salvation or liberation of religions is not the same as the one that the spirit must travel in its "individuation process", although they may be complementary on an initial level. One thing is to not use the aspects that are considered harmful on the path of salvation, and another, very different, is to deny this reality to the point of repressing it in the internal conscious (unconscious) to the point of creating a pathological state, leading us to the analyst. In such cases the analyst will notice the presence of a "shadow" that wants to manifest itself and whose recognition by the patient will act in his benefit, but to believe from this that all darkness, including everything diabolical that weighs on the soul, is useful on the path to salvation, creates a distance that can only be covered by extending this therapy to heaven. Only in the illusion of believing that the goals and results of psychoanalytic therapy are the same as those of religion can the shadow itself be installed on the divine throne.

There are some aspects of religion, it is true, that are linked with the darkness of psychic reality; Hephaestus and Dionysus, gods who live and frequent Hades are good examples. These gods are also Olympian gods, that is, they have access to the abode of the luminous gods. They are, or represent, means that man can follow to obtain such access. But Dionysus is not only darkness, he has his luminous side, and it is this luminosity that we must discover in order to go back to Olympus, because if we follow only his dark side we will end up in Hades.([1]) It would be instructive to remember how Dionysus' mother died. Being pregnant with him, she asked the father of the child, Zeus, to reveal himself not as a man but as he was "in reality". Giving in to her pleas, Zeus transformed himself into pure light and his poor lover was charred to ashes. This is ultimately the greatest god of Olympus: light. And this is, in essence Ra, Buddha, Brahman, Allah, and the Christian God; they are all simply inconceivable with a dark side. An "evil" side to them would be an aberration. In order to have access to their abode one has to *assimilate* to them, one has to become pure spirit, light, kindness and beauty.

In Plato, the Good and the Beautiful are confused with light, there is no evil nor darkness there, just as there is none in Nirvana nor in the Christian Paradise. It is true that Shiva, like Dionysus, has a dark side who appears as a black goddess, Kali or Durga, but this side is not Shiva strictly speaking, just one of his aspects. In any case it would not be correct to identify this aspect of Shiva with the Christian Devil, who symbolises low and perverse temptations, summed up as evil, the opposite of good. In Shiva it is rather the cosmic need for the end, the destruction necessary for a new rebirth. He does not provoke these evils in order to rejoice in the suffering of humans and impose evil as we imagine Satan would do. In fact there is not and has never been a religion of a certain consideration in which Jung's theory could be supported.

As it does not fit into his psychotherapy schemas, Jung does not, or does not want to, see an evident message of religions to which I referred when speaking of rituals, and it is an inevitable part of the spiritual path: the sacrifice of the ego. This is the reason for which the Son of Man sacrifices himself, to fulfil himself and to serve as an example. For Jung the son is sacrificed *by* the Father, who is also the Son, and this sacrifice is necessary because God feels guilty for having neglected his people. "God's guilt consisted in the fact that, as creator of the world and king of his creatures, he was inadequate" (*Transformation Symbolism in the Mass*). "Jung relates this theme to primitive practices in which the king, who had become impotent or who could not now guarantee the fertility of his land, was killed. The story of the murdered king is at the heart of Christianity and of the mass" (M. Stein, *Jung's Treatment of Christianity*). Given his inefficiency, God must transform himself and this transformation, and therefore this entire ritual, follows an archetype.

We cannot but see in all this Freud's legacy, except that Jung has reversed the roles, thus opposing his master, as he resolutely tried to do throughout his career; but the opposition is only superficial. Here it is now not the Son who sacrifices the Father but the Father the Son. This interpretation coincides even less with Christian doctrine which maintains that the Son sacrifices himself in order to expiate for the sins of man before God; in such a way that the doctrinal thesis is discarded and unexplained.

I think we should listen to Jung as a psychotherapist but not as a theologian. With this, however, I do not want to say what many Christians want to hear: that as religious men they should not care about the psychologist's theories, since Westerners and therefore Christianity are sick, without a doubt. All those (the great majority) who have yet to resolve their relationship with their "shadow", would be wrong to apply themselves to religious ends or those of psychosophy as they would fall prey to the same neuroses that Jung is trying to avoid; and I do not intend to create more neuroses; not even to leave things as they are, neutralising the work of psychology. Whoever rationally imposes an *imitatio Cristi*, repressing his bad side, no matter how much good he does to others, cannot avoid doing himself harm by creating possible neuroses.

Without doubt a doctrine like that of the Christian that preaches loving one's enemies can generate neurosis, as there are very few who can accept this mandate without resentment. The very idea of loving the enemy *violates* our reason and produces an intolerable internal convulsion, to the extent of our hatred. The remedy to cure hatred proposed by Jesus is extremely bitter and burns our insides, but it is a remedy for a terrible evil that destroys the spirit. But, I repeat, not everyone is ready for it and in most cases it is likely to cause more harm than good; but this is not why Jesus is going to stop giving the remedy indicated for those who are really prepared. What Jesus intends is not that we continue to taste the bitter cure all our lives, but that we are cured once and for all, that is, that we leave our *petit moi* (*little selves*), and that we *transcend* ourselves.

To this same end Zen Buddhism uses a much more uncomfortable image than that of the bitter cure: It says it is necessary to "swallow the red-hot iron ball ", a cure that no reasonable psychologist would recommend to his patients, nor any of the violent practices used by this sect. But Zen does not want to cause suffering, rather, *liberate us* from it. What Christianity wants is to prepare saints, in the same way as Buddhism wants to produce bodhisattvas and Hinduism wants to produce *sanyasins*. Yet this is not for all but, on the contrary, only for a few: "Many are called and few are chosen", warns Jesus. But the warning was not heard by the Church, which imposed the same restrictions for all, as if it wanted to make everyone saints, and it has been this imposition and the widespread self-imposition of the spiritually impotent that have created the neuroses, and as a result the excesses of Christianity that Freud and Jung observed and that we all know of.

There is an aspect of the Christian doctrine that also induces this forced neurosis-generating self-imposition. Mahayana Buddhism does not pretend to liberate only a few, since its bodhisattvas have vowed to reincarnate as many times as necessary to "liberate every last blade of grass". But while this doctrine of reincarnation provides practically infinite possibilities for all aspirants to achieve liberation, the Christian doctrine offers only one chance, and furthermore threatens cruel punishments, sometimes lasting into eternity. And to this is added another aspect of this doctrine: the unpredictable Final Judgment, which can surprise us when we are engaged precisely in "dis-repressing" a neurosis. It should also be remembered that Christianity arose in an age when it was believed that the Final Judgment was imminent; and this belief, which at first was obsessive, lasted almost the entire Middle Ages. I am not trying to say that the Buddhist doctrine is "better", but only that it is prone to fewer neuroses and, therefore, that the Christian should be attentive to them.

In my opinion, in the first place, *before becoming* a symbol and not after (the archetype that supposedly programmed the action of this hero), is Jesus the person, with his spirit, his morality and his genius. Although unfortunately we do not know anything of his years of preparation, we can imagine, as such is the case with all the great Masters of the spirit, that he must have followed a religious training, thanks to which he could reach *another* level of consciousness, allowing him to have a *direct* contact with and knowledge of Divinity (his Father). It is this knowledge that he always had *present,* and not the supposed archetype that he dragged from the past, that led him to the sacrifice (which obviously did not consist of leaving home and looking for a job to become established in society, that is, in coming of age, nor any of the other stages of life that Jung denotes for the common man), but the sacrifice of his person, of the individual, of the man of flesh and blood to completely identify himself with the Spirit. Although, naturally, he has expressed his doubts, his fears and even his desperation before and during the sacrifice. Does Jung claim that when Jesus, before the sacrifice, knelt down and prayed to his Father, he was obeying the program of an archetype, that he was talking to his unconscious, and just like the Christ all those who have prayed and continue to pray, including all the Buddhas and Bodhisattvas, do so out of an ignorance of their psyche and the true Nature of Divinity? Jesus had a real and direct knowledge of the transcendent, because he had transcended his individuality, that is, his external and internal planes and had achieved not the unity of his ego with his unconscious but his Unity with the Spirit.

Whoever follows this ascendant path to the end, with his spirit and not with his ego, as with the latter he cannot go very far, will achieve Unity, not now the unity of opposites, but the spirit with the Spirit, and he will discover that it is not the individual who establishes the union but, on the contrary, it is he who, by establishing the differences and dualities, has created his own obstacles. "When discrimination is carried out, dualism is generated, which does not lead to Nirvana" (*Sagathakam, Lankavatara Sutra*).

Notes

(1) For an explanation of the function of this Divinity I will refer to *The Quest for Universal Consciousness.* (Motilal Banarsidass, Publishers, Delhi)

CHAPTER SIXTEEN

Jung and the Orient

Jung, in spite of popular belief, never showed a *real* interest in the Orient. His passion was his European culture, and the religion that motivated him was Christianity. This attitude is well illustrated when he recalls (in his *Memoirs*) that during his only brief trip to India, accepting an invitation, when his ship docked in Bombay he did not go ashore because he was studying some alchemy texts.

In his time there were not yet many prestigious intellectuals who showed an interest in the Oriental texts that were beginning to be translated into languages other than English and for a wider public. (*The Sacred Books of the East* had reached a limited number of English readers). The growing prestige of psychology, and that of Jung, one of its greatest exponents, who had opened the doors of science to religion, led some authors and translators, and especially publishers, to offer the preface of their works to our psychologist, who did not waste the opportunity to spread his message. Because this, in truth, was Jung's interest, to demonstrate his theories and not to develop the texts that he commented on to highlight their virtues.([1]) This being Jung's interest, it is usual in these commentaries that he forces the meaning of the text, just as we saw that he did with Christian doctrine, to adapt it. In *The Secret of the Golden Flower,* Jung, who did not know any Chinese, questions Wilhelm, the translator and commentator of this text – who had spent half his life in China studying the culture – on the interpretation of some decisive concepts of the work, with the aforementioned objective: that of "bringing the waters to his own mill" (An Spanish proverb, meaning to look out for oneself at the expense of others). In the preface to the *Y Ching*, Jung limits himself to tossing the three coins and commenting on his fate. Considering that this is one of the five classic books of Chinese culture, the introduction by our representative from the West is embarrassing.

I consider it not worth dwelling on these prefaces, because Jung's lack of understanding of the substance of Oriental religions has, I believe, been made quite clear. I will only pause over a commentary written by a disciple of Jung, who translates his preface into English from the *Tibetan Book of the Dead*, because there is a mistake as big as there can be, as big as the universe itself. Jung does not commit the mistake directly, it is true, but he does not rectify his disciple, so we must assume that his silence is acquiescent. Jung's sideways acquiescence is not surprising, but I cannot say the same of Evans, the translator of the Tibetan text, a scholar of this branch of Buddhism. Evans' lack of clarification is only explicable by his ignorance of analytical psychology. Jung's disciple tells us: "The collective unconscious is the matrix of everything, it is even the matrix of the Dharmakaya". We see through this example how Jung's amphibological and suggestive language can lead to unsuspected interpretations and limitations. It would be enough for the reader to accept this comparison for him to never understand Buddhism again.

If there is a Divinity for Buddhism it is Dharmakaya. If there is *prajna* and compassion in sentient beings, the two basic forces of Buddhism, it is because they are generated by Dharmakaya. If these virtues lead to liberation, if there is liberation, it is thanks to Dharmakaya. If there is a universal Justice and Order, it is because of Dharmakaya. The karma of all beings depends on this. If the Buddha is venerated it is because he is seen as a manifestation of Dharmakaya. But the Dharmakaya "does not have a particular body, it is manifested in all places and in any place in response to the nature and conditions of things" (*Avatansaka Sutra*). For this reason, "it is capable of creating all things". (*Op. Cit.*) "It is One, it is eternal." (*Op. Cit.*) We do not find in it the dark side that Jung wants to see on earth as well as in the heavens "It is free of impurities and desires". (*Op. Cit.*) And, as befits a Divinity, in spite of Jung's emphatic position, "It is free of all oppositions and contraries, and nevertheless it is working on all things to lead them to Nirvana". (*Op. Cit.*) "Neither is its work confined to a fixed people" (a difference with the god of the Old Testament will be observed) but "works for the salvation of all things" (*Op. Cit.*), (not only of human beings, as opposed to the Old Testament). "There is no place in the universe where he is not present". "But while the universe changes; its spiritual 'Body' remains immutable" (*Op. Cit.*). I consider what has been said to be sufficient. The reader will be clear that Dharmakaya can be likened to the idea of God in his most impersonal version, but never to the collective unconscious.

One of the problems posed by the supposed confluence of Western psychology with the spiritual tradition of the Orient is the use of a common terminology, being that our psychology is born of atheistic assumptions, or pre-assumptions as I would say, while in the East the assumptions or pre-assumptions are theist. This means that, from the start, the matter is approached from very different points of view. But not only are the origins different, so are the objectives, as a consequence of the said pre-assumptions. Western psychology is born of a need in contemporary society, which is that of curing the progressive neuroses that have become evident in the eyes of the first modern psychologists. In the Orient, whether or not there are neuroses in the population, it is not a matter that has concerned them up to now. Their preoccupation is centred on achieving the aforesaid pre-assumption: Divinity. Now, this objective implies the liberation of the self, an attitude very contrary to that of Western psychology, which is interested in restructuring the dispersed self, alienated by its neuroses. For this, it applies methodologies and techniques different to those of the Orient. However, Jung's attempt, continued by many of his followers, to equate the terminology of Western psychology with that of the Orient is evident. From what I see, this attempt leads to confusion most of the time, which is to be expected from two languages born of such different contexts. The belief in *karma*, for example, is an idea that the West is still far from accepting without question. And yet the entire Orient is full of this idea, even its philosophies with atheist connotations such as the Sankhya.

The fact that Jung opines that the West should limit itself to maintaining or continuing its traditional religion betrays the psychological vision he has of religions, as well as the limitations of this vision. Jung, in fact views Christianity as an expression of the Western psyche, which already implies a falsehood, because as is well known, Christianity is not of Western origin but was born in the Middle East and was incorporated in Europe when the official religion had lost force. This proves that our culture does not need *this* religion but a doctrine with a universal character. It is this universal character of the great religions that escapes Jung, and it escapes him precisely because he views religions as groups of individuals who have certain "psychic needs" that lead them to "create" a religion, rather than from the religious perspective (in a strict sense, the unitive perspective), that begins from a Principle creator, a universal God. For this reason, in my opinion, any of the great religions which obey this universal principle could have filled the void left by the Greco-Roman religion. For what is decisive in this adoption has been the common Nature, the universal Spirit, and not this or that particular dogma that might have been incorporated into our culture and thus into our psyche. But since for Jung such a Principle is non-existent (although with his habitual astuteness he does not explicitly deny this), he prioritises certain dogmas that express certain latent symbols in our culture's unconscious. In this way he works as a reactionary against the positions adopted by the *avant-garde* religious men of almost all contemporary religions, such as Gandhi, who choose an openness towards other doctrines, the free exchange of ideas, and even the adoption of another faith when sentiment or intuition demand. In this sense Jung's attitude is tremendously contradictory, because even if he makes use of other Oriental religions, after having taken from them the material he needs for his psychology, he leaves them outside our culture, which must continue with its Western religion and not adopt (as he expressly states) an oriental religion. This, however, is not new in the history of Christianity. It is, strictly speaking, traditional to use other doctrines and later reject them as if they only had value if they are *of use* to *our* dogmas. The Aristotelian and Platonic doctrines, as is well known, were used in this way and they became denaturalised, as they were not accepted for what they really were. Jung tries to do the same with the great religions of the Orient.

But Jung has his psychological reasons. Due to his history, the Westerner has different archetypes as compared to the Easterner, and thus, for his own mental health, he has to maintain them. Jung, then, does not really ask us to be faithful to our traditional God, but to our archetype of God; who also has his "commandments". As Jung does not see beyond the symbols of the unconscious, he does not see the possibility of incorporating the religions of the Orient, for the simple reason that they have a different symbolism. It is too simple to discard the richest treasure of the Orient. For Jung, as we have seen, what does not fit into his theory is dispensable material. With which he demonstrates not only a tremendous unawareness of the consequences of his "scientific dogma", but also a lack of experience of the universality of God that transcends all frontiers and symbolism.

Jung, the son of a *Protestant* pastor, presents himself in keeping with what has been said, as a Christian "reformer". I believe that he intimately desired this image. For the purposes of psychosophy, it would be of little use to psychologically analyse Jung's relationship with his father. I believe, however, that given the immense bibliography that has sprung up around Jung, it would not hurt if someone perceptive, and with their own criteria, were to do so someday; there would be no dearth of material for this. Jung, in fact, refers to his father in various passages, even as a protagonist of his dreams, which he interprets in his own way, so our critic will have to see it from his own point of view.

I insist that I am not denying Jung's real discoveries. I am only trying to adjust the concepts that he exhaustively uses because it is his excesses that ultimately lead to confusing and denaturalising the religious phenomenon. I am trying to return his *relative* sense to his concepts and thus liberate the Absolute from the limits imposed on it by reducing it to an individual and relative perception of it, that is, from psychologism and its absolute character.

As Jung does not see the Creator, but only the created, he *projects* onto the former the attributes of the latter. Thus, just as good and evil, light and darkness exist in the created, so they will have to exist in the Creator. "Light is followed by shadow, the other side of the Creator." (*Memories, dreams, reflections 360*) Moreover, the non-recognition of the dark side of the Creator is, for him, what has brought us to the doors of catastrophe, "in the first place in the form of a threat to the conscious". This threat consists in the gigantism expressed in the assertion: "Nothing is greater than man and his actions". (*Op. cit. 360*) However, just after this, he himself tells us that man is "the second creator of the World". We can also not fail to see his own "gigantism" in his assertion: "...the service which man can render to God, that the Creator may become conscious of his creation". I agree and am grateful for his voice of alarm in the face of possible catastrophe; but for my part, I am convinced that the chaos can only be averted by going beyond the individual perspective and thus all these "gigantisms". "Here the miracle of reflecting consciousness intervenes (in the haphazard and casual transformation of species over hundreds of millions of years of devouring and being devoured) in the second cosmogony". "The importance of consciousness is so great that one cannot help suspecting the element of *meaning* to be concealed somewhere within all the monstrous, apparently senseless biological turmoil." (*Op. cit. 371*) Thus, it is man, who has to give "meaning" to this chaos that is nature. Is it not possible to see this same "gigantism" in this way of thinking, and the same current that leads it to the abyss?

If Jung had had a correct perspective he would not have seen a monstrous biological turmoil and a meaningless Nature, but on the contrary, an Order and a World full of Meaning, in which the human being has nothing to improve upon, much less help the Creator to a "second cosmogony". The ideas of the microcosms and *Anthropos*, used by Jung, sound so good to the ears of the ego, as they make one believe that a giant is inside man, but what they really have inside is "gigantism". For this reason Shankara wisely advises: "Stop worrying about the macrocosms and the microcosms, throw them out like two poisonous receptacles". (*Viveka-cudamani 289*)

If Jung had recognised the limitations of his knowledge and had said: "what follows are hypotheses that exceed my experience", which is what he should have done as a man of science, we could have continued his work only by modifying his hypotheses, but without warning he goes ahead and gets involved in realities he does not understand. "Buddha saw and grasped the cosmogonic dignity of the human consciousness; for that reason he saw clearly that if a man succeeded in extinguishing this light, the world would sink into nothingness. Schopenhauer's great achievement lay in his also recognising this" (*Memories 309*). Here he is mixing two completely different visions, his own and Schopenhauer's with that of the Buddha. The World as a representation of *my* consciousness, is the World seen from my individual consciousness; it is this that makes him say that thanks to the fact that man is conscious "the Creator can be conscious of his creation". (*Op. cit. 371*) In the state of supra-consciousness, in the unified Consciousness which I assume is the experience of the Buddha, it is not myself that becomes conscious, but through the disappearance of the self the universal Consciousness becomes manifest and not only in me, but in all beings. When the Buddha is enlightened, all beings become enlightened, states a Mahayana text.

Of course, from the individual perspective, logic would indicate that if this were the case, one Buddha would be enough, one enlightened person for everyone *ipso facto* to be so, but what this affirmation wants to say is that from the essential perspective everyone is effectively enlightened, but from the individual perspective no one is. Almost all Buddhist paradoxes obey these two perspectives. The Nature of the Buddha is inherent in all beings, including the smallest insects and the least perceptible blade of grass. The Mind of the Buddha is the legacy of all beings. "You do not know that the physical body, as well as the mountains, the rivers, the space and the immense Earth are all within the truly wonderful and brilliant minds." (*Surangama Sutra*)."Truly strange, truly strange! All beings possess the Nature of the Buddha; everyone can become a Buddha" (The words of the Buddha after his *true* awakening.)

In the Transcendent there is neither duality nor opposition of any kind. But this is not what Jung or his disciples think. For this reason, one of them adds: "God is not only the projection of the father, as Freud exclusively saw it, but father and mother carry the projections of the male and female archetypes of the divine". (E. C. Whitmont, *The Symbolic Quest*) But here is nothing like the "*complexio oppositorum*" in God. There is only opposition in God when he is a *projection* of the one who looks at him dualistically. For this reason, a Mahayana text clarifies: "Bodhisattvas are those who contemplate the nature of all things (*Dharmas*) devoid of duality like space". And a Hindu classic is of the same opinion: "To imagine the existence of dual concepts in the Atman, which is infinite Knowledge, the Absolute, is like imagining castles in the air". (Shankara, *Viveka-cudamani* 525)

Divinity is the *Creative* itself. The relationship between it and the created, between God and man takes "form" in religion. This aspect has been the object of observation and analysis by psychology. It is true that religion is "formed" by myths, but the Creative itself lacks form and is therefore *transcendent*. To interpret this according to the forms that represent it is to start from the wrong side from which one can never arrive (because it is transcendent) at the other side, which is "the beginning". From this theology, philosophy and psychosophy begin, or try to begin. Psychology's error is to assume the task of these disciplines. It could be argued that there is a rational or natural theology, whose knowledge of

Divinity begins with man, that is, it goes from man to God; but this is not strictly so, as there is or there has always been an intuition or religious feeling underlying this; this theology begins and is sustained by the same, although it may appear differently in the theoretical development.

But what are religions without all their mythology? If you were to ask me, it is precisely because one is alienated, and fragmented, because now one only sees the concrete and what is manifested. Mythology expresses common or prototypical sentiments and intuitions, but behind this is the *manifesting*, the Creative, the essential Energy itself. It is this energy that *moves* the religious man; the mythical helps him to shape this feeling, which is his religious sentiment, but it is this sentiment which is its *raison d'être* not his reasons. The "idea" of a personal God has served many who needed a personal relationship with Divinity. And yet this idea, sustained by a faith, based in turn on a dogma, makes it more difficult to understand that the Spirit is everywhere, in each and every thing, that it is omnipresent, and obviously it is in oneself. "Allah", says the Koran, "is closer to you than your jugular". And, not by reading the Koran but by hearing the same divine echo, Leibniz exclaimed: "God is closer to me than my body".(2) He is in our own consciousness, he is One with Universal Consciousness. It is to the awareness of this Truth that psychosophy tends. When it occurs the mythical aspect of religions is not important. If the interpretation of their symbols do not have a personal meaning for me, if they do not move me or lead me to understand that Truth, and to free me from my intellectual vanity, among other things, they are completely useless.

Notes

(1) His prestige at times caused the publishers to exalt his name, sometimes as much or more than that of the author. Such is the case of *The Secret of the Golden Flower*, in which the author Liu Hua-Yang goes unnoticed and does not even figure on the cover, in three languages and editions that I have before me, in which only the names of the translator and commentator and Jung appear, whereas the work abundantly shows that the only one who understands the *secret* is the author.

(2) "Gott ist mir angehöriger als der Leib".

CHAPTER SEVENTEEN

Unitive Memory and the Collective Unconscious

For Jung "psychic existence is the only category of existence of which we have immediate knowledge, as nothing can be known unless it first appears as a psychic image" (Commentary on the *Tibetan Book of the Great Liberation*). This might seem a truism to those like Jung who view reality from their external conscience but it is not strictly true. I will explain.

On the one hand, psychology ignores what I have called the *plane or conscience of direct perception*. On the other, the existence of a reality without images. This, strictly speaking, seems inconceivable. However, when the spirit attains its Centre, it experiences these two realities that simultaneously manifest themselves to such an extent that it does not know if it is this reality without images (we can use the Buddhist term of *Emptiness*), that covers objects and makes them disappear as such (objects for the subject), or if it is Consciousness that envelops them with the same result.

In this sense we are aware of the immediacy because it *occurs in our Mind.* But, it should be clear, this is not a "psychological" fact, as psychology would like to explain it, as the Mind has here a dimension that exceeds this conception; this dimension shifts consciousness to a reality where the Mind and the Sacred are confused. That is, consciousness is no longer that of the subject, and for this reason it ceases to be so, nor is the object referred to it, and for this reason it also disappears as such. There is no individual psyche (which is the view of psychology) that precedes knowledge but a *universal Mind or Consciousness* that precedes the individual, all individuals and all science.

In studying what I find the most interesting aspect of Jung's research, I have found sufficient parallels to suspect a common ground between his collective unconscious and what I have called the unitive memory. I would say that what Jung has recognised and studied with sufficient depth and clinical experience for us to accept his authority in this aspect are the symbols that this memory produces.

The Central Consciousness directly perceives the unitive "material" that will form part of the *unitive memory*. This material, which as a product of unitive experiences essentially lacks forms, is endowed with them by the internal consciousness (unconscious) as soon as it is represented for its understanding. These forms, which we can call unitive, are the archetypal symbols that Jung finds on the internal plane. I would not dare to say that all the archetypes observed by Jung are a product of unitive experiences, but certainly those related to symbols of totality: circles, mandalas, triangles, suns, moons, luminous trees, etc. The archetypal symbols discovered by Jung are thus a synthesis of the internal plane, although produced as if by decantation of repeated *unitive perceptions* and not as intellectual syntheses (like Kant's *a priori* syntheses). The power of these symbols rests on the fact that they are *full of significance*; this meaning becomes clear to the *central consciousness* as it can relive the experience that has generated them. In a similar manner, as the spirit approaches this consciousness it will be easier for it to remember these unitive contents, but as in a different memory it remembers *in another manner*; remember how it has perceived the unitive consciousness: a rationally undifferentiated reality.

Plato's vision can help us to illustrate this mechanism. He perceived things as they are, but in his eagerness to rationalise them, he differentiated them, and particularised them (the unitive perception can be concentrated in an "object" still not differentiated). They then stopped "being" what they were. But not entirely, however, they did not disappear, but remained "like" the real, without becoming so. They were like shadows, projections, reproductions; thus they *participated* in the being. Diffuse memory (of the undifferentiated and timeless that for being so cannot be clear to discernment), of that particularity that had somehow been seen in his Reality, made Plato think that he had contemplated it in another time and space. Hence the theory of reminiscence that he felt inclined to express in the form of myths, given the lack of temporal and spatial structure of that Reality.

Whoever is fully aware of his unitive perception, with a bit of practice (as he will have sufficient control of his mind and will have gone through various techniques of meditation) can visualise it, that is, repeat it internally. This image, whatever it might be, can be repeated while dreaming and will produce the *numinos* effect of Jung's archetypical images, since they also represent Reality.

These forms are unconscious adaptations that obey the structure of the human mind, thus reproducing certain prototypes, *patterns.* Even if these produce a certain unification and thus a centralisation of the spirit, they do not generate a true knowledge, the spirit remains disconnected from the Sources that originated the process that led to the production of the image. The Sources do not *form* the images but create them; yet they do not express themselves only through the said images, as they have infinite ways of manifesting themselves, the moral as well as the aesthetic (See *The Return to the Sources*).

When speaking of memory, I have said that it is feasible to consider it as one single faculty, that its content be lodged in one single container, but that for practical purposes one can talk about different memories as each plane of knowledge has its own vision of reality, its own interests. This is so because each plane is like a unit of consciousness, like a Self that feeds and "programs" memory in its own way and this makes it get different facts, as if it had its own private archive or, as I said, a separate and distinct memory.

I think that this is of extreme importance when understanding the internal plane, the primitive consciousness that has been keeping its fears and desires in its memory, its resentments and its aspirations. Since this consciousness has its origins in the most remote of times, when *homo* was still not *sapiens* but a very elementary being, an animal with confused intelligence and sentiments, a faculty with which he must have lived for a prolonged length of time, all that is accumulated in "his" memory is profoundly embedded in the human mind.

Being that, as I said, this plane or internal consciousness has an interdependent relationship with the external plane or consciousness; it drives contemporary man, *homo sapiens* to act sometimes in a very primitive manner, with violence and irrational jealousies, with profound resentments etc. These actions are sustained and are even increased by *the fear of not being and the desire to be.* On feeling the "self", in fact, ontologically insecure, he resorts to these primitive drives. Fear leads him to it, as well as the *desire to be that is substituted for his desire to possess*. I believe that as these resentments, jealousies, etc., which can go as far as finding pleasure in cruelty, are so embedded in (the memory of) the internal consciousness, which is the plane that concerns our psychologists, that they have made them think that they are an intrinsic and inseparable part of human nature. It may seem difficult to discuss this, nonetheless Freud himself had observed these urges in children, which has been corroborated by M. Klein and others. However, if we go beyond the internal plane and discover other levels of consciousness we can clarify this situation.

Firstly it is necessary to establish the limits of "human nature". If by this we understand the human animal reduced to its conscious and unconscious, which is as our psychologists see it, and we see that these primitive urges are inherited, we will conclude that they are innate and an inseparable part of our nature. But if this is extended to the levels of consciousness in which *the internal plane is transcended with its entire content* (urges, complexes, memories), we are talking about *another human Nature* that we can call spiritual or divine. On discovering this we realise that all the memories and content of the internal and external plane are "added", they are not consubstantial to the human Being but to the "human animal".

These are not, please understand, only theoretical differences, as they are full of *real* consequences that can be of great interest for psychology. Indeed, the recognition and settlement of the spirit in the *unitive consciousness* allows it to *observe* the content of the external and internal consciences as alien to its *true nature*. This cause the urges of the unconscious be represented as *strange and external*. This favourable perspective allows the spirit (of the subject) *not to identify* with the said urges, and thus when they manifest themselves, instead of diverting them to give them a dignified use, that is, to sublimate them, it *neutralises* them, and turns them off, it makes them disappear before they become actualised. And this happens effortlessly, without a struggle, as the spirit is literally beyond desire and fear, which no longer govern man. In the light of the knowledge of the *true Nature of the human being*, the roots of the primitive urges that are supposed to be intrinsic or innate to our species dry up. The "shadow", when illuminated, disappears. From then on the spirit (the subject) will be moved by the Good. The urges that motivate him will be superior.

CHAPTER EIGHTEEN

Jung as Philosopher

As we have seen, Jung is not content with just extending his theories from clinical experience to theology. From here he goes on to develop a kind of philosophy of history, venturing into the very risky extreme of teleology. Of course, in this intellectual adventure there was no risk for him. One wonders, however, if there was no risk for anyone. We find ourselves here face to face with a series of factors that are too reminiscent of the adventure undertaken by Karl Marx.

Until the last century there had been a generalised tradition that a philosopher was one who had an intimate relationship with the transcendent "thanks" to which the thinker could structure a philosophy that dealt with the two aspects of reality. The sciences, for their part, started from the other extreme, that of the particulars, of the multiple, of those who deduced its general laws, without venturing beyond them, precisely so as not to cease to be sciences. But the pseudo-philosophies and pseudo-sciences that flourished in the last century (of which there had been earlier examples but without major consequences until then) allowed themselves to break this fortunate tradition. Thus, they conceived a kind of androgyny with some elements of science, others of philosophy, others of the imagination, sustained by a series of reasons that were supported by each other, without philosophical or scientific foundations, with no other basis than some premises that responded more to the desire of the author, that reality "should be" like this, rather than reality itself. When this same desire was shared by many, the theory was put into practice in the "belief" that a rational, ordered, "scientific" exposition would guarantee a positive result.

Marx, as we know, used a philosophy that had indeed been inspired by an Idea, but which meant nothing to him, not having any experience or relationship with the transcendent. And so he discarded it and applied an ideology to fit his socioeconomic political desires. We have seen the result and millions have suffered because of it.([1])

What happened to Marx could happen to Jung. I am referring to the phenomenon of the witches of Macbeth. Once we are aware of our supreme destiny, we do not hesitate to impel events towards its realisation. Imagine a fanatic with talent and the charisma to attract multitudes (a monstrous androgyny that our species tends to produce) who, following the theories of our psychologist, creates a "new" religion in which it is proposed that the principle of evil be reintegrated and the Antichrist be placed at the right hand of Christ for history to follow its correct course. It would not be surprising, in this age of utter spiritual despair, for him to find many adepts ready to satisfy the needs of the "shadow ", to give free rein to its instincts, to do evil to compensate for the good. I will be told that this is an erroneous application of Jung's theories, with which I would agree, but it must be admitted that there is no need to diverge too far from these theories to fall into these practices. History, the very same that Jung is trying to compose, is full of examples of these kinds of diversions and slips; and even more moderate theories have been taken to unpredictable extremes, more so those that have begun at the extremes! The interpretations of history can act like witches.

When the sciences look after themselves, they can modify religion where it has gone beyond its limits, and this will be positive for both disciplines. This is the case of evolutionist theory that tangentially touched Christianity in relation to the creation myth, a puerile story that sooner or later the sciences had to dismantle. But Darwin, an exacting scientist, did not believe that this triumph gave him the right to keep advancing in the field of religion, although the conditions were right for him to do so, since his theory was better equipped than those of Marx and Jung to develop a philosophy of history. Besides, in the case of Darwin, "a true man of science" as the intransigent religious scholar Unamuno called him, there was practically no risk for third parties, as later investigations had to be carried out archaeologically, that is, with the dead, not with the living. Marx and Jung take not only the living to the laboratory but also those who will live in the future.

Darwin's and Einstein's attitude towards religion and philosophy is an example that should be followed by men of science. The matters in which the destiny of humanity is at stake must be treated with prudence, science and wisdom. And this is especially applicable for religious people, because as the limits of the sciences are more easily measurable as compared to those of religion, the latter lends itself more to fantasy and falsehoods. I do not pretend to deny any scientist the right to venture into the religious or philosophical terrain using his methods, provided that he establish that such an attempt will be neither scientific, nor religious nor philosophical; it will be infertile.

As a general evaluation of Jung's work, we can say that his contribution to psychology is undeniable, as he introduces into it the religious aspect as a regulatory element of the psyche. The vast majority of psychologists still do not fathom the importance of this fact and its implications. Thanks to this, the distance that Jung establishes from Freud is abysmal. In fact, a psychology that dispenses with a religious aspect, or even worse, that sees it as a product of a neurosis, seems inconceivable to me.

But in the field of religion itself his contribution is relative. I want to say, in a positive sense, as his research into religious symbolism; in another negative sense, in terms of following a religious path. I believe, indeed, that for all those who want to follow the second stage, the religious, strictly speaking, his work can be counterproductive, because it implies endless hypotheses that decisively *distort* the phenomenon and the religious experience. In this sense his work can be much more harmful than that of those who completely deny religious reality. This is so because once the second stage has begun, that of *dis-individuation*, the aspirant mechanically leaves behind the detractors of religion. But Jung does not present himself as such; on the contrary he presents himself as a *reformer*. He offers a new way of being religious. He illuminates the spiritual path with a lamp whose beams distort the essential reality, allowing one at times, here and there, to see some truths, which makes us believe that we are on the right path, that we are walking on realities, when in reality we are following a map, a plan traced by hypotheses with some certain points of reference, others uncertain and others false. For this reason at the end of the journey we find ourselves irredeemably lost.

Jung's fame outside the proper field of psychology can be attributed to the fact that he became, perhaps unwillingly, one of the pioneers of this wave of pseudo-science-religion that has grown in the second half of the

XX century; surely due to the general confusion and desire for novelties. This is in direct relation to man's growing dissatisfaction which will continue as long as he does not take charge of his conscience and destiny.

It has been said that religion and philosophy are not the result of deductions from data taken from concrete reality, from all that can be the object of our senses or of any machine, subtle as it might be, that sharpens them. They are born of *another reality*, manifested through revelations, transcendental intuitions, or, as I have called them, unitive experiences, it matters little what name they are given; what is important is that they *have a metaphysical origin*. Of course, this can lead to the presumption that in the name of "revelation" one claims to possess a transcendental knowledge. In this age of utter unconsciousness and irresponsibility, in which adventurers of the spirit proliferate, an evident sign of general decadence, it would not be surprising if this resource were used for "earthly" ends, and in fact this is happening. Thus, if earlier, I warned of the "scientific" label now I should do so with that of "enlightened". These dangers would naturally be avoided if we were not to dogmatically accept the label and if we knew how to look at the content with our own criteria; but I fear that at this stage it would be too much to ask. Time and again we incur the same basic problem, the ignorance of spiritual reality due to man's alienation. The remedy for this dangerous situation depends on the "degree" of alienation of contemporary man. Reality is composed of both matter and spirit. If the human being can no longer see the latter because of his growing blindness, which only allows him to see the former, it is because he is completely alienated from his own Being. This madness is not that of one who has disconnected from his ego and has remained in his unconscious, but *of the one who has disconnected from his spiritual reality and has remained in his ego*; that is, in his ill termed "conscious". For psychosophy, everyone who no longer perceives spiritual reality directly or intimately is alienated. Both those who deny spiritual reality and all who look at it through the cracks of the unconscious are alienated. Contemporary man, in general, is alienated.

Notes

(1) With this I do not want to imply in any way that I adhere to its opposite, capitalist liberal pragmatism, since what was humanistic in Marxism (which is what attracted so many intellectuals, like Fromm), is replaced here by an unscrupulous mechanical game of presumed mercantile laws that obey the interests of the capitalist.

CHAPTER NINETEEN

Psychoanalysis and Zen Buddhism

To exhaustively establish a parallel between Buddhism and psychosophy would mean leaving the framework of this work.[(1)] I consider that unnecessary at present. My intention on commenting on the work by D. T. Suzuki and E. Fromm is not to bring the waters of Buddhism to my mill, psychosophy does not need the support of this doctrine to sustain itself. This is so for the simple reason that they are rooted in the same soil; they may differ in their forms but only as trees of the same species differ.

If the reader has attentively followed the proposals expressed in the first part of this essay, he will only need his good judgement to establish the appropriate relationship between the three disciplines that are presented below. It is not my intention to show that one of these disciplines is the correct one in detriment to the others, but rather to illuminate the panorama for the reader through comparisons and clarifications.

At the beginning of the work *Psychoanalysis and Zen Buddhism,* E. Fromm recognises that the differences between these two disciplines seem to outweigh their similarities, as "Psychoanalysis is a scientific method, non-religious to its core", while "Zen is a theory and a technique to achieve enlightenment". "Psychoanalysis is a therapy for mental illness; Zen is a way to spiritual salvation". But even so, he puts his effort into highlighting the points that they seem to have in common.

The effort is worthwhile. However, I find it necessary to clarify some of these points, as they can only be superimposed if they are seen from the point of view of psychoanalysis and not from that of Zen, which starts from premises and points to objectives that are radically different. So even if the terms may be similar, or even the same, *their meaning* will inevitably be different, as if we were dealing with language dictionaries whose roots have an origin independent of each other; and this is literally the case of some terms as we shall see.

The term *liberation* depends, like all concepts, on the ideological context in which it belongs. While the liberal thinks of the liberation of the market, the Marxist thinks about the proletariat. The concept can be similar in the minds of the slave, the convict and the oppressed people; but in the three cases we are speaking of different objectives, different realities. For Freud, psychoanalysis can provide the "liberation of the human being from his neurotic symptoms, his inhibitions and abnormalities of character" (Cit. Fromm). It will be understood that this therapy can lead to the patient's normality, but hardly to liberation in a religious sense, to eternal happiness, to liberation from the laws of *karma,* to *Nirvana.*

In his follow up of common terms between psychoanalysis and Zen, Fromm continues quoting Freud to highlight some of them. "The analyst must be in a superior position.... if he is to serve as a model for the patient in certain analytical situations and in others he should act as his *teacher*". The differences between the latter and a Zen master, however, are so many and so obvious that it seems superfluous to establish them. Apart from the differences in the objectives already highlighted, we need only remember the rigorous monastery life of Buddhist monks to understand that these are two professions that could barely brush against each other tangentially. "Here, in my monastery, there is neither birth nor death", says a Zen master. Can one imagine a psychoanalyst saying: "Nor here in my study?" "We must not forget", he again quotes Freud, "that the relationship between analyst and patient is based on a *love of truth*". *Truth* is spoken of in Zen, as well as in all religions, but in these an absolute and unconditional truth is sought. Gandhi said "God is Truth". For the psychoanalyst it consists of the "acknowledgement of reality, that it precludes any kind of sham and deception". The recognition of these partial truths can help in the search of that ultimate truth, but they are put in the service of this in particular, and only then. "Those familiar with Eastern thought", as Fromm keeps insisting, "and especially with Zen Buddhism, will notice that the factors which I am going to mention are not without relation to concepts and thoughts of the Eastern mind. The principle to be mentioned here first is Freud's concept that knowledge leads to transformation, that theory and practice must not be separated, that in the very act of knowing oneself, one transforms oneself". The terms are common once again but they continue to be applied in different contexts. In one it refers to a relative transformation of the character that can lead to a better adjustment, an improvement in self-knowledge, which can influence the formation of the personality, with a greater capacity for adjustment within the family or social environment. In the other it is a knowledge not of oneself but of a reality that transcends the self to such an extent that it loses reality and disappears from the scene. The transformation here is ontological. As concerns theory and practice, the fact that there is a correlation between them does not annul the substantial distinctions that exist in them both.

After this attempt to establish the aforementioned parallels, however, Fromm ends Chap. II by admitting the insufficiency of Freudian psychoanalysis for this purpose. Referring to the problem of man's well-being, he concludes that we: "...must transcend the Freudian frame of reference and to lead to a discussion, incomplete as it must be, of the basic concept of human existence, which underlies humanistic psychoanalysis", which is what he proposes: "Only in this way can we lay the foundation for the comparison between psychoanalysis and Zen Buddhist thought".

From then onwards (*Chap. III*), he establishes certain legitimate parallels, in particular the common aspiration to give birth to the human being fully through the development of one's own awareness "to such a point that one transcends one's egocentric involvement, and arrives at a new harmony, at a new oneness with the world". Of course, this may be a common aspiration, but what is decisive is to know whether psychoanalysis can take the aspirant that far.

To do this, Fromm correctly, in my opinion, proposes the breaking of all umbilical cords, as many "remain symbiotically attached to mother, father, family, race, state, status, money, gods, etc.; they never emerge fully as themselves and thus they never become fully born". It is this path that leads to well-being. This means "to drop one's Ego, to give up greed, to cease chasing after the preservation and the aggrandisement of the Ego, to be and to experience one's self in the act of being, not in having". "Well-being means", says Fromm using a terminology that can only come from the Far East, "to arrive at the experience of oneness with all that exists". Here again the concepts and intentions seem to be common but we must look at the method of psychoanalysis to find out if it is capable of taking us to such a lofty goal, if this is an expression of desire sustained by a mere hypothesis or a reality; and we must also see if this goal is ultimately the same.

"The most characteristic element in the psychoanalytic approach", says Fromm himself, "is, without any doubt, its attempt to *make conscious the unconscious*". It is surprising; however, that after saying this he makes a definite list of the deficiencies of the conscious. He tells us: "experience can enter into awareness only under the condition that it can be perceived, related, and ordered in terms of a conceptual system and of its categories". This, by itself, signifies a series of problems. So, for example, "Every society ...develops a system of categories which determines the forms of awareness. This system works... as a socially conditioned filter". He also highlights the problems of language, "it may be said that an experience rarely comes into awareness for which the language has no word". The limitation implied is the requirement of the conscious, especially in our culture, of having to adapt the stimuli to a logical language. Later, and the discovery of this is a contribution of immense value by psychoanalysis, are the great number of stimuli that are rejected by the taboo imposed by social character. In all societies there exists "the observation of the taboos for protecting this character... the violation of which results in ostracism". I myself can testify through experience that this is a truth.

I would like to point out that consciousness seen in this way, with all these limitations, coincides with the most external faculty of reason that I have called discernment. The other more internal faculty, the intellectual plane, is not so dependent on these conditions. Through this, man at times senses that his logic is becoming too strict; that his language is insufficient to express what he *knows,* that he has given in to social pressure, that he *is* in some way other. But, of course, this intuition is only possible for those who are more *centred* on the central planes, especially on the vital.

Both Fromm and Jung ignore the existence of this plane of consciousness, and even more that this is man's true consciousness; but they open the doors to it by recognising that the unconscious harbours certain wisdom. As we saw, what psychosophy proposes is the transfer of consciousness to the central plane and *from this* to incorporate the (so called) conscious, the external plane with which the *mediate unitive consciousness* would be constituted. But Fromm, from his point of view that corresponds to the individual perspective, albeit as a man with an elevated spirit he is often inspired by *altruistic consciousness,* cannot think of another solution than to incorporate the internal plane into the external plane.

It is Freud who discovers, and this should be counted as one of his greatest achievements, that a good number of the stimuli rejected by the conscious are not lost but are stored in the unconscious. As this content is manifested in a different way, sickly in the case of neurotics, psychoanalysis can detect it and even discover it by reaching the said content. Freud called the process of rejection of the stimuli that will form part of the unconscious "repression", Fromm calls the inverse process of making them emerge into consciousness "de-repression".

It is strange that in spite of realising the insufficiencies of the conscious for understanding in general, Fromm insists that the solution for the whole of the psyche lies in such incorporation, as if this were able to change the innate condition of the faculty, its mechanisms, its possibilities, its limits. Furthermore, how can it try to incorporate the whole unconscious? By this does he mean that all its content will be incorporated, all that is accumulated in life as well as all the phylogenetic legacy, all its symbolism, its archetypes, etc., and also *be aware* of it all? This, without doubt, is a hypothesis that no one could ever prove through their own experience. Fromm's error is due to his method that in turn is determined by his perspective. This situation leads him to apply the *accumulative* method to his objective, manifest in his desire to slowly *incorporate* the content of the unconscious. I have already said that the totality can only be achieved by the unitive method, which means shedding off the ego with all its conscious and unconscious content, in order to prepare the conditions for the only vital experience capable of unifying the Whole to take place.

For the actualisation of "total man", not only the egocentric vision in Fromm's sense, that is with a selfish meaning, has to be transcended, but also any vision that converges in the self, all *individual perspective*. We must be strict with the concepts so as not to confuse ourselves. Zen Buddhism does not speak (neither does psychosophy) of the "total man", and if it does so occasionally it is not in Fromm's sense, but in the sense of Unity.

Transcendence implies the intimate certainty of having surpassed man, of having left him behind with all his personality, character, attachments, inclinations, etc.; it is the discovery of the "divine nature", of the "Nature of the Buddha" which is common to all living beings. The totality in this sense, as I have explained, is not given in me, nor is it shaped by me, but by the Unifying Essence. As long as there is a self, a man, there is no Totality.

This is what Meister Eckhart says, paradoxically quoted by Fromm himself. "In the sixth stage (man) is deformed and transformed by God's *eternal nature*" (italics mine). "He has come to full perfection and, oblivious of impermanent things and temporal life, is drawn, transported, in the image of God and become a child of God". "It is eternal rest and bliss". This is the very definition of liberation; and the liberation is that of man himself. This is inconceivable for Fromm; nature for him continues to be human. It is surprising that our psychologist believes that he is speaking of the same reality as this mystic.

After all these approaches, Fromm decides to get to the heart of the problem (Chap. V), to the very goal of Buddhism. But unfortunately, he, who proposes a path to reach it, has not himself arrived. "Since I have not experienced *satori* I can talk about Zen only in a tangential way, and not as it ought to be talked about out of the fullness of experience". And he says this after recognising that the "essence of Zen is the acquisition of enlightenment". And "one who has not had this experience can never fully understand Zen". After hearing him confess in this way we can only think that his hypothesis and method do not work, or that he is asking others to have faith in a theory that has proved insufficient for its creator. I think that he is asking too much of us, especially if we remember that Suzuki insists that "satori is the raison d'être of Zen" and "without it there is no Zen" (*Introduction to Zen Buddhism*) and that there is no way of conceptualising this experience. "The main reason for the unpredictable or surprising reason of Zen, derives from its transcendence with respect to the conceptualization" (*Zen Buddhism*).

In any case Fromm is better directed towards liberation, or at least towards a theoretical understanding of the purpose of religion than Freud, for whom mystical experience was a regression to infantile narcissism, and also than Jung, for whom enlightenment was an "inflation of the ego", which is the exact opposite of such an experience that annihilates the ego. Fromm, in the first place, humbly admits his lack of knowledge, and with this attitude in which truth precedes the ego he shows a certain understanding of the Zen path. Secondly, he proposes the overcoming not only of the ego but also its habitual identifications, such as parents, family, race, etc., a point on which he insists in other essays. Thirdly, recognising the immaturity of the contemporary common man, he confronts him with the need for transcendence. Fourthly, our psychologist is far from disqualifying enlightenment simply because he has not had it, which is the impression that Jung leaves us with when he affirms "Satori depicts an art and a way of enlightenment which is practically impossible for the European to appreciate." (Preface to the *Introduction of Zen Buddhism* by D. T. Suzuki, quoted by Fromm) Finally, Fromm warns us against the erroneous interpretation which Western psychologists tend to believe, that *satori* is a subjective state, an error that even Jung could not avoid. He says: "The imagination itself is a psychic occurrence, and therefore whether an *enlightenment* is called *real* or *imaginary* is quite immaterial. The man who has enlightenment, or alleges that he has it, thinks in any case that he is enlightened... Even if he were to lie, his lie would be a spiritual fact". Here Jung once again uses his ambiguous language. "Spiritual fact" is used here in the way that "psychic reality" is elsewhere; yet again he tries to say much but expresses little or nothing. Fortunately Fromm is not fooled, and adds mockingly: "This is of course part of Jung's general relativist position (what I would call premeditatedly ambiguous) with regard to the *truth* of religious experience. Contrary to him, I believe that a lie is never a *spiritual fact*".

The reader will remember what was said in the first part of this book about the "ethical path", and will understand that I cannot but agree with Fromm when he maintains that without ethics there can be no substantial transformation in the individual, be it in psychoanalytic treatment or on the spiritual path.

Later Fromm mentions various points of commonality between psychoanalysis and Zen, which are not exclusive to these disciplines but necessary for all spiritual evolution, such as the need not to lie, to overcome greed, to love, etc.; but all these arguments revolve around a basic error again generated by a question of terminology. The term in question is the *Unconscious* used by Dr. Suzuki who, surely, did not foresee that it could lead to misunderstandings. However, in order to avoid them

Suzuki repeatedly clarifies that the unconscious of Zen is not that of psychoanalysis: "My unconscious is meta-scientific or pre-scientific...and even antiscientific on occasions". With this single declaration he breaks apart from psychoanalysis, because, as is well known, being scientific is its stated claim. When referring to the scientific method, Suzuki highlights some of its deficiencies, similar to those we have seen in the first part of this essay. These deficiencies, moreover, will be evident to all those who might have followed a spiritual path in practice; which is not the case of the psychologists commented on here. Suzuki, who had himself undergone a rigorous Zen training, tells us: "The scientific manner kills, assassinates the object by dissecting the body and joining its parts again it tries to reproduce the original living body, which is practically impossible". "The Zen way takes life as it is lived, instead of chopping it into bits, to restore it later through intellection". "Zen gets submerged in the fount of creativity". "This source is the Unconscious of Zen". Observe the religious connotation that the capital letter implies. This *Unconscious* is not of any particular individual but of all that exists, it is cosmic, it is the Nature of the Buddha, the Dharmakaya to which I have already referred. It is in this universal context that the Zen experience should be understood. "The Universe is a great spiritual system made up of moral beings who are so many fragmentary reflexes of the Dharmakaya". (*Zen Buddhism*). What those who have not experienced Zen cannot understand that it places the spirit, *ipso facto*, within a universal conception of order; which is no less than the Order of which we spoke in the First part.

In order to demonstrate that the Buddhist conception of reality greatly transcends that of psychoanalysis, we have only to use its own language. "The Dharmakaya rejoices or is grieved by each action good or evil committed by any sentient unit (beings) of this spiritual organisation". "Individual karma, therefore, is not after all individual; it is most intimately connected with the whole". We see, then, that "the Mahayana philosophers emphasise the universal or supra-individual significance of karma". (Suzuki; *Zen Buddhism*)

After speaking about the Unconscious, and for there to be no doubt that another reality is being referred to, Suzuki elaborates greatly on the concept of the *Self.* This, fortunately, does not give rise to misconceptions because from the beginning it is clear that "The real Self is a kind of metaphysical Self in opposition to the psychological or ethical self which belongs in a finite world of relativity". It is also clear that "the scientists therefore can never reach the Self however much they desire it. They can of course speak a lot about it, but that is all". However, Fromm, who has undoubtedly noticed that this entire chapter does not serve his purpose, does not even speak of it; he clings to the previous chapter. "As Dr. Suzuki has written a chapter on the unconscious in this book, I can refer to his discussion, and thus try to clarify further the connection between the psychoanalytical and the Zen concepts". But as we have seen, it is useless, Zen's Unconscious can only be achieved through a religious path and experiences.

The term *Unconscious* has its origin in the Chinese expression *wu-hsin*, literally *no-mind*, used by some of the first Zen masters as Dr. Suzuki explains to us (in *The Zen Doctrine of No-Mind*). Others like the greatly inspired Hsi-Yun speak, although with the same meaning, only of "the Mind"; and the *Lankavatara Sutra* refers to the "Mind itself" or the "Mind-only". To discuss these texts, much more substantial than those we are commenting on, would be to deflect from the original objective. Suffice it to say that what these terms have in common, which are equivalent, is that they refer to a state of non-discrimination, in which one is outside the speculative mind, beyond that which I have called the external plane or discernment. "Reject all dualist notions and all attraction or repulsion, because all that exists is the Mind (cosmic)". (*The Doctrine of Hsi-Yun*) "When the Yogi enters the *Mind-only*, he will cease to discriminate on the external world." (270, *Sagathakem; Lankavatara Sutra*) "Maintaining the *Mind-only* the idea of reality disappears". (*Op. cit.* 280) And, to end, "*The Unconscious* (the No-Mind)", the enlightened Shen-hui tells us irrefutably "*is to be conscious* of the absolutely One".

It is evident that the texts cited do not refer to the conscious or unconscious, but to another plane of understanding and to a level of it that we are more inclined to call *supra-conscious* rather than "unconscious". In the text which we are commenting on, Suzuki is referring to a more accessible level that would correspond to the *unitive conscience* that, as we have seen, is superimposed on the *altruist conscience* that Fromm indicates. But we have also seen that it is the *experience of the unified conscience* that *shapes* the *unitive conscience*. In the cited texts of Hsi-Yun and the *Lankavatara,* as well as the sacred texts of the Orient, in general, the *unified conscience* is referred to, which is nothing if not the Mind-only, the

Mind. But let us return to the levels of consciousness accessible to all the speculative planes in order to follow Fromm.

Our psychologist is impatient to arrive at an identity with Zen and wonders if the state of de-repression would not correspond to that of enlightenment. The question, for those who have traversed even a stretch of the spiritual path, is extremely ambitious or ingenuous. But he wants to be convinced of this correspondence to the point of using Buddhist terminology. He says: "To become conscious of the unconscious (...) means to awaken, to see reality as it is. The man who awakens is the liberated man". Liberated from what, perhaps from the human condition to pass to the divine? Evidently not, our psychologist, a declared atheist, refers to liberation as regards to a complex. Of course all this borrowed terminology is not adequate for psychoanalysis. Stated once more, by Suzuki himself: "The psychoanalytic unconscious cannot be sufficiently profound as to include the question of nature of the No-Mind". (*The Zen Doctrine of No-Mind*)

I have already said this. For psychosophy, the entire relationship of the external plane with the internal ultimately constitutes a vicious circle that keeps man in Ignorance. *Liberation consists of the transcendence of these two planes*. The unification of the Mind is not the union of the conscious with the unconscious, but the *union of the spirit with the Spirit* or, if one prefers, of the individual mind with the Universal Mind.

But let us descend again. The answer to Fromm's question lies in the facts. Have any of the patients who experienced this sensation of freedom and well-being after de-repressing certain contents of the unconscious followed a religious life? Have they felt the need to express this experience vehemently, with the surety of one who knows? Have they interpreted the sacred classic texts or written religious books? Have they begun a life of retirement to devote themselves to contemplation? No; however, this is what is invariably done by those who have gone through what in religion is called enlightenment. Why? Because this experience removes all man's premises, it transcends all his ideas; it exceeds all his expectations and radically *transforms* him. After this he cannot continue leading a normal life like other mortals, for the simple reason that he has ceased to be "normal"; and forever. Enlightenment is not a psychological experience but a religious experience. It does not produce a temporary feeling of freedom and happiness, but the absolute certainty of knowing oneself to be liberated forever, and the immeasurable Happiness that only *that* experience can generate.

After the de-repression Fromm says, using a well-known Zen expression: "A new realism dawns in which 'the mountains are mountains again' ". Too soon our author wants to see the mountains as they are, quickly forgetting that first one has to go through the experience when the mountains cease to be mountains and, with mountains all of reality. And yet this Zen expression is not entirely correct, for the mountains, as well as all beings after *satori*, will never again be the same. The essential perspective, in fact, confers another vision of the world; reality is *submerged* in its Essence that in this way gives it its Being. This is why, after this experience, and not before, *things are as they are.* But the prior condition is to have experienced the *samadhi of Emptiness*, as it is called by some Mahayana masters, and this is nothing but the *total unitive experience,* in which only *pure Consciousness* exists (see my schema of the mind). "Where all things are wiped away, even a state of imagelessness ceases to exist for the Yogins; in the sameness of existence and non-existence, the fruit (of wisdom) is born to the wise." (*Lankavatara Sutra*) It is then and only then that the mountains become mountains again. It is only then that "True nature moves with perfect freedom, discriminating all forms in the objective world, and inwardly unmoved in the first principle" (Hui-Neng, *The Plataform Sutra*). This relationship has been graphically demonstrated when we saw the correspondence between the *unified conscience* and the *mediate unitive conscience*.

I believe that what has been said is sufficient, at least for the attentive reader, to be clear about the radical difference that exists between Zen Buddhism and psychoanalysis, as well as the insuperable distance between what is essential in religions and in psychology.

Fromm, as we have seen, was on the right track, only he should have continued with the detachment that he proposed. After having overcome the ties of family and race, those of the species remained, on which his humanism is based, and all misunderstood humanisms; this is a knot that is impossible to untie without the change of perspective that psychosophy offers. Without it, the demands and even the existence of the rest of living beings depend on the reasons that we generate according to our whims.

Beyond the species and sentient beings, the vegetable and the entire mineral kingdom are still there, the concrete world, *and it is after (or before) the world where the transcendent is found.*

The three authors we have commented on lacked the same thing: knowing that the individual horizon can be overcome; that man can transcend his biological limitations and thus reach the *Transcendent*. Ignoring the existence of the Transcendent, they did not search for a method that would lead them to it, nor were they worried about leaving their habitual point of reference: the self. Of this, in spite of all the inconveniences that it presents for self-knowledge, of the misunderstanding that we have with our kin and of all the barbarities that our species commits because of it, they had no doubts. Not only do our psychologists have no doubts, but neither does man in general, who seeks by all manner of means to improve the knowledge and situation of the self; which is an increasingly fearsome double-edged sword.

Art, morality and religion could not find a satisfactory explanation through the Freudian theory of the unconscious. I believe that they have found their home in the *central consciousness*, seat of the Creative; not in a dark unconscious, but in a luminous and elevated consciousness.[(2)] Nor could the healthy and adult man be explained in terms of his relationship with his parents and his sexual attributes (even when these terms are used figuratively); it was necessary to cut the umbilical cord with Freud, in order to bring him out of the embryonic state and restore his universal dimension.

Coming out in defence of Zen Buddhism is a way of expressing my gratitude to its great Masters. It is only natural, they helped me, not so much on my long way there, which could have been shortened if I had known them better, but on my way back, when incorporating all the misery and suffering of this world in a spirit that had no desire to return. In other words, they taught me to love you, reader.

Notes

(1) The general outline is laid out in *The Evolution of the Spirit.* (Har-Anand Publishers, Delhi)

(2) For a philosophy of art I will refer the reader to *The Roots of Art.* (Ebook)

CHAPTER TWENTY

Knowledge and Action of the Unitive Man

The body of knowledge that we have been acquiring makes up the *unitive man*. I will try to give an idea of the sense of his action.

We all know in some way (rather latently), why religions declare themselves against bodily pleasures, but everything seems to indicate that very few are fully and permanently aware of the implications. The theories that pit corporeal against spiritual life far from explain, much less resolve, the situation because opposition implies struggle, and where there is struggle there can be no peace, and without peace the subject is altered (this is useful for Jung). Let us see how our discipline faces this problem.

When our spirit is *centred*, it is at rest and maintains a contemplative attitude. When the stimulus of pleasure appears, if the subject does not manage to maintain this attitude, a displacement of the spirit is produced, which goes astray during this lapse of his nature. For he who is rooted in his Centre, this loss will be nothing but a harmless distraction, as on seeing the individual spirit take its first steps, it will be called to unify itself again. This is not the case of the common man who's horse rider is already liable to identify with the horse, and instead of remaining indifferent to the stimulus and thus keeping the animal calm, tries to subdue it with reasons, which usually leads to exciting it even more. When the rider is agitated, it is because he has ceased to be such; we are now dealing with a centaur on the run that can only be stopped by a Hercules (his unitive spirit).

The prohibition of pleasure itself tends to direct our gaze outwards, towards the external plane where we have our ethical code which we try to adapt to circumstances through reasons; but this elaboration prevents us from understanding the direct message of our moral conscience, when this is the light that illuminates the entire panorama. We all have in our hearts the sword with which we can quickly cut the Gordian knot of pleasure when it arises. Once externalised, we untie with one hand and tie with the other, and we are inclined to forget what on the one hand displeases us and remember our achievements on the other, merits that we constantly hang on the chest of our self-as-image.

To act correctly, the first thing is to eliminate all spiritual disturbances in the most efficient way possible. The proper instrument for this objective is a *living morality* which is what the alert spirit, the unitive man possesses, he knows that *the path that leads to psychic equilibrium is no different from the moral path*. We are talking here of a total equilibrium, not that of the "common" man, whose equilibrium is conditioned and circumstantial. Conditioned by his great baggage of beliefs including the weighty image of his ego, determined by multiple motivations that he ignores; circumstantial, because common man simply is moral until he ceases to be. Create some propitious circumstances for him, with the stimuli and approval of "his own" (those who fall within the radar of his ego's projection) and you will see in him an evil doer; send a thousand men to take a population of "enemies", and you will be able to count on one hand those who repress their savage instincts.

Looking in the mirror of moral conscience, man sees a sharp image of himself; without it, the reason on duty (of the moment) will be enough. We cannot speak of a stable morality in the "common" man who decorates his image in keeping with the circumstances, and not even of morality when it is subjective-objective, that is, subjective with indeterminate amendments of "personal" reasons.

Discernment inevitably tends to externalise the original impulse, distorting it, as the virtue of purity and spontaneity is tainted by the slightest calculation, and this often appears in the very act of discernment. It happens in the way that the rapture caused by the beauty of a precious stone disappears by calculating its price: as soon as we calculate it we are no longer in the precious stone of our unitive conscience.

The psychic order (total, not for this or that, even criminals have ingenuity), is inseparable from the moral order and this is nothing less than a manifestation of Harmony, or if one prefers (from an individual perspective) it depends on the relative perception of Harmony.

What we call morality is an expression of the moral conscience, which is nothing but an outburst of Harmony. Morality is not, as some who are externalised believe and see utility even in the lilies of the field, a need for this or that. It is a cosmic need for harmony that comes in an indiscernible fashion, like an instinctive desire that takes shape when it is discerned. This form will be harmonious to the extent that Harmony is perceived and distorted to the extent that it is ignored. The interpretation will vary according to the individuals and the times, it will depend on the degree of the human being's integration, that is, his unification with his psyche and his environment.

We do not have the luxury of simply being amoral like the other animals and to live free of our obligations, because we do not live within the natural order like they do. Man must assume himself to be a moral Being, much before being a rational being, and take charge of the great responsibility that falls to him. As a separate and rational being, man has placed himself in the most convenient perspective to see only the advantages and not the obligations. This perspective which is that of the "common" man is simply immoral. *More than anything else man needs to moralise himself.* This does not necessarily mean accepting external norms but *integrating, harmonising to become a human Being*. But to become such, to really act as a moral Being, he must diametrically change his perspective, perceive, think and work from his unitive (moral) conscience from which, and only from which, he can be objective with the external world and with himself.

For a long time the union of the object and the subject has been intended and announced, but the experience that makes this union possible transcends all intellectual conception. If this is not understood, this aspiration will only become reality in a world of ideas. The truth is that for there to be knowledge, as those who propose such a union understand it, there always has to be an object and a subject. Even the directly observing and experiencing mutable spirit, who observes and experiences and which we propose as a means of self-knowledge, is a subject, in a certain sense, albeit distinct from the self because it has no *part* or identification with the *subject*. Now, when this spirit recognises it's *true Nature*, this *spectator* realises that he is nothing more than such, that he is nothing more than conscience, that actually he had always been the *universal Conscience*[1] who was seeing through his *unitive conscience*. This means that for the disappearance of the subject-object duality, the elimination of the first is a condition; and this implies having followed a rigorous path of moral purification, and of having reached a transcendent Reality that is the domain of the *sacred*.

It is when conscience becomes Conscience that everything becomes Immutable and from here it is observed how it flows over the World, like a lake that seems imperturbable but from which pure water ceaselessly flows, thus extending the *sacred* over all things. It is in this way that true knowledge, wisdom, is achieved; the ultimate objective of psychosophy.

From this perspective the unitive man perceives how the perfect Order, the universal Spirit, by pouring itself over individual spirits incites them to perfection and to the establishment of this Order in their spatio-temporal circumstances. Hence how the harmonious relationship that the Spirit generates between things has a *religious, moral and aesthetic projection*, which although it is the same manifestation, man divides in this order for its better comprehension and application. When he perceives correctly, however, he can appreciate the relationship: a stunted old tree; a young nobleman slain in battle; a beautiful woman driven by poverty to sell herself, for example, express a moral and aesthetic disorder; we imagine heroes and heroines to be beautiful and semi-divine in our unconscious desire to integrate them into the same Order.

The unitive man expresses, even with all his human limitations, the same *primary manifestations* as the universal Spirit. He himself knows to be a manifestation of it. For this reason, he loves all beings and wants to establish a Harmony between them, and for this he preaches Good.

At no time, and this should be clear, does psychosophy pretend to dispense with morality. In effect, he who can act independently of all established morals is the unitive man because he is rooted in his moral conscience, and this allows him to manifest it *spontaneously*. To reach this state he has had to leave his selfishness, through altruism and thanks to his love for his fellow man and his dedication to Divinity. *Unitive man is the fully morally mature human*.

To reach this maturity the renunciation of the self is not strictly enough, it is also necessary to renounce all subtle identifications of the self, although they might apparently present themselves as contrary to it, such as the most elevated ideas and the most virtuous actions. One must transcend even love; only then is there Liberation. But, understand well, this is achieved through love and moral order, and whoever reaches this state the first thing he does is express Love and moral Order. Thus for the unitive man it is only natural to express these. For him his inspiration is the expiration of the universal Spirit and his aspiration is the inspiration of the Same. He experiences it approximately like this.

Man has never failed to recognise the faculty of being objective with oneself as a superior attribute. Those endowed with it, to the point of transcending their interests, tastes, or personal inclinations, that is, those who have been able to apply it in the moral order, have been admired as wise. This recognition reveals the intervention of the unitive conscience, or what is the same, the (latent) innate wisdom of man. For all these reasons we can say that *morality is the obedience to our unitive conscience* that we put before our individual conscience. It is to lean towards unitive tendencies before the egocentric ones. Moral conscience is a conscience common to all, there is no egocentric moral conscience. We are not talking of a collective morality in an external sense. Morals are a matter of conscience; but this is not the individual but our common Nature that manifests itself individually. When we say obedience, it should not be interpreted as a self that objectively discriminates the call of "his" conscience, as the moral conscience is already objective and does not need arrangements, but rather the clear perception of the spirit. Only being exteriorised requires the effort to be objective with one's own conscience. The centred spirit perceives the unitive and egocentric forces directly on its own plane. Then it lets itself go, it leans out of natural attraction, out of Love, towards its Nature.

He who knows his Nature will no longer be able to commit evil intentionally, since it would be going against himself. It is only through ignorance that evil is committed. The unified spirit is *moralised* as it is One with its moral conscience. The unitive Man knows that his morality does not depend on an individual and rational decision nor on his will, as these faculties are only tools to actualise what was already determined on more profound levels. *This spontaneous and natural submission to the unitive forces derives inevitably from the recognition or, rather, the Knowledge of his true Nature.*

The Spectator that we are observes the World in an absolutely objective manner. It is this lack of differentiation that allows us to see things as they are: the Reality. The Spectator who sees, feels and hears through or by means of the particular individual is none other than the human Being. Strictly speaking, he sees, feels and hears through all individuals, but as long as they are alienated from themselves, they will continue to see and hear from their very narrow perspective. There is nothing here of "the other world". We are speaking of the One we really are. We are simply speaking about mental health, integrity, *vital plenitude*, of the human Being.

The consequences of this end of this century are nefarious, never has so much human blood been shed. Crimes without hesitation or remorse, increasingly committed by minors, psychopaths, or perverts, are yet more eloquent indications of the state of mind in which our civilisation finds itself. Everything seems to indicate that violence and madness are increasing; from which follows the need for awareness before falling prey to it. This violence, for now hidden and contained within the majority, again awaits for the moment to manifest itself. This madness does not happen "just because", it is directly related to the dissatisfaction of contemporary man. Let us understand once and for all, *we can never fully satisfy the self for the simple reason that it is not real.* Happiness is beyond it.

From an egocentric perspective it is only natural that each and every one wants "to have his own way", and when reasons are not enough for this, force is resorted to; which is what other animals do. In this respect discernment has been used to transform the cudgel into a canon and the latter into a nuclear weapon, and thus to make the jungle progressively sophisticated and dangerous. It is a priority of psychosophy to get us out of this jungle, to lead us to overcome man's primitive stage, but for this we have to prove that there is something more than shadows, to see some ray of light.

Psychosophy is certainly born of what I have called a *total unitive experience*. But the author does not intend that his authority be accepted only in the name of the said experience, but rather that the reader put his theories and practices and the method proposed here to the test so that he himself can try and verify the truths that are exposed. Moreover, psychosophy has been structured for this purpose. The author did not need it for himself and he could well have limited himself to describing his vision, and perhaps comparing it with some religious texts of renowned authority to gain the recognition of the reader; but the author is not interested in this. He does not want to tell others what they have to do, he wants others to *know* what they have to do. Psychosophy, thus, has a social function, it aspires to a change in society. But its author, to whom his curiosity for history has taught some lessons, is not satisfied with offering a new ideology. Nor with promoting external changes, such as those that keep modern man so occupied, that the adverse winds of history soon sweep away. He is interested in generating an intrinsic change in man himself. Then history can follow its natural course.

For this awareness it is not necessary to cover the entire path that we have been following. Psychosophy is a path towards transcendence, it is true, but this does not mean that there is nothing before the end because on this path life, the epic story of each man, and the history of all humanity unfolds. Our species has a long way to go to cover it all, and unfortunately, as it stands today, it seems quite possible that man will destroy himself before it is finished. As we have seen, there are different stages, but it is enough to complete the first in order to recognise the correct path. On a second journey, a little further, we find our moral conscience, and this is all we need to live in peace. A significant number of unitive men would be enough to stop this mad race with no fixed objective and would divert history towards its correct Destiny. It all depends on you, dear reader.

Notes

(1) For an extensive explanation of this concept, see my work *The Search for Universal Consciousness* (Motilal Banarsidass, Publishers, Delhi).

EPILOGUE

Maxims and Paradoxes

He who wants to extract knowledge from a philosophy book should measure his own ideas with that of the author instead of judging the ideas of the author.

Although we speak the same language, we speak different languages given the motivations that inspire us. For this reason, although I have been saying it for 2600 years, I am still not understood.

In his indisputable need to be loved, the human being manifests his need to live in Harmony.

In times of decadence virtue is the most poorly paid.

How many evils would be avoided if we knew to what extent our external ambition is determined by our internal dissatisfaction!

Superior men (and more so women), serve as scapegoats on whom inferior men unload the hatred that they have been accumulating in their failed attempts at integrity.

The stricter we are in judging others, the more virtuous we feel. This is moral pride and thus an ethical aberration that can be blamed on a lack of wisdom.

While men retain their egocentric perspective, it is inevitable that they continue to identify more with Barabbas than with Jesus. (I am referring to the inferior and the superior man that we carry within, not to the historical characters, who, being dead and gone can be judged without risk according to conventional ethics).

A permanent obstacle encountered by all those who aspire to wisdom is created by oneself. Indeed, by wanting to know from one and for one,

one generates a vicious circle that keeps one in ignorance, because true knowledge consists, fundamentally, in the art of shaking off *the one* who wants to know, that is, in ceasing to be what one is in order to *Be*.

With our 'self' on our backs we carry too great a burden to enter the narrow path of knowledge; for this reason so many are left out.

What is most valuable is acquired in the act of letting go; in general, when we think we win, we lose.

Morality to survive, aesthetics to live, religion to be; without these three pillars there is no civilisation that can sustain itself.

Only he who recognises his ignorance is prepared to transcend himself.

Where are you going in such a hurry? Raise your head and you will see that faced with infinity there is all the time in the world.

The struggle against time, which is man's eternal struggle, is not won by going faster, but when time stands still.

He who has not been able to stop the mind can only have ideas of Reality.

The infinite is there to remind us that we have to transcend ourselves beyond what we can imagine. (Message heard during a unitive dream).

To think that we cannot know the Whole, is to presuppose that we have been born without the faculties that we need in order to live in this reality; which is much to believe, or too much to assume.

Whoever is alienated from the Whole, is alienated from Himself, and vice versa.

We want more and more, we want more because we are All; when we know this our ambition ends.

We do not have to look for Love here and there as it is everywhere. We are Love, but since we ignore this, we come to blows for a handful of personal love.

The Present is like a fond memory, because in it we rediscover ourselves.

There is no more secure refuge than the Void, because in it we have nowhere to tie the 'self'.

A small spirit cannot harbour a great love, and without this there is no way out.

The need for material wealth is proportional to the poverty of the spirit.

Dogmas sclerotize the spirit, they bind knowledge.

True self-knowledge does not consist in the series of ideas that we have of ourselves, however correct they might be, but in the perception of the empty paper on which we write them.

Harmony is the relationship that exists between all sounds and silence.

Postponing the present means postponing life and making of it a nightmare. Modern man lives in this dream without peace.

There are few who lift their heads out of the human anthill to contemplate the infinite; although we all live within it.

If when you are old you lose peace because you want to live longer, it is because you have wasted the time that you now want to recover.

Life itself is a paradox. There is a time to live and a time to learn but there is not a time for both. And he who lives without having educated himself, as well as he who has educated himself without living, invariably shows a shortcoming.

Another great paradox of life, closely linked to the earlier one is that man must inevitably prepare for death, and this learning takes a lifetime.

And from this one deduces that if there is one thing that one should not do in life, it is to waste time, and yet this is what the vast majority of people do.

"After me the deluge", the egoist exclaims. "After me, Order", thinks the altruist.